HISTORY OF THE JEWS

PAUL GOODMAN

HISTORY
OF THE JEWS

Revised and Enlarged by
ISRAEL COHEN

With An Introduction by
DR. ABBA HILLEL SILVER

EST. 1852

E. P. DUTTON & COMPANY, INC.
New York, 1953

Library of Congress Catalog Card Number: 51-6128

INTRODUCTION

By DR. ABBA HILLEL SILVER

Rabbi of The Temple, Cleveland, Ohio

Students of Jewish history will welcome the appearance
of an American edition of Paul Goodman's HISTORY OF
THE JEWS. This concise, authoritative and very readable
volume has passed through eight editions since it first appeared in 1911, the most recent of which, was revised and
enlarged by Israel Cohen, in 1951. It is fitting that an American edition should now be issued, and made more readily
available to the largest Jewish community in the world.

It is of utmost importance for the preservation both of
the Jewish people and of its faith that the Jews of the United
States should become better acquainted with the past experiences of their people, with the problems which they faced
and the manner in which they confronted them, with the
techniques for survival which they evolved as well as with
their contributions to the progress of mankind. For the
major responsibility for carrying on the burden of their people's proud heritage in the Diaspora will from now on, because of their numerical strength and favorable situation,
be theirs.

The American Jewish community is one of the more recent among the Jewish communities of history, albeit the
largest and by far the most prosperous. It has many distinctive features. It is set in a distinctive environment. Nevertheless, its experiences are not entirely unique. Its organizational
structure has precedents, and its problems of survival are

not without parallel in Jewish history. It would, therefore, be wise on the part of American Jews to take into account the experiences of other Jewish communities in the long past, and to consider well the years of many generations.

In the past, centers of Jewish life shifted from one part of the world to another. At times, several important centers existed simultaneously. In our day we saw the oldest and noblest centers of Jewish life in Europe practically destroyed. Providentially, two other centers are rising today and are growing in strength and significance—the national center in Israel, and the Diaspora center in the United States.

The American Jewish community owes it to itself and to history to mobilize its spiritual resources for carrying on the historic work of Judaism. It will have to find these resources in the future largely within itself. It will no longer be able to live on borrowing. It can no longer expect its spiritual and cultural provisions to come to it from the Old World. Old World Jewry no longer exists as a provisioning center. American Jewry will have to prepare its own victuals. Fortunately, it seems to be a law of Jewish existence that the "turning down of one lamp always reveals another burning."

American Jewry is not altogether unprepared or unequipped for this task. American Jewry is organized, perhaps over-organized. It possesses if not a sufficient, at least not a meager quota of synagogues, schools, libraries, Rabbinic seminaries, and social agencies. More are in the process of building. American Jews have also demonstrated a fine sense of solidarity and loyalty, particularly in the recent desperate years when unprecedented disasters swept over their fellow Jews in Europe and when the historic challenge reached them to assist in the restoration of the State of Israel. Their reactions were those of a sound and healthy organism. A great hour did not find them a small people. All this is good building material for the future, and encourages the hope that these fine qualities will be utilized for the spiritual and cultural tasks of tomorrow which will insure a worthy and fruitful career for this, the largest Jewish community in history.

The most recent chapters of our history are among the darkest and the brightest recorded. They tell of appalling disaster as well as of miraculous resurgence. The tragic story of the ravage and devastation of the European Jewish communities and the isolation and nigh-total eclipse of Russian Jewry stand in almost parallel columns alongside of the glorious story of the rebirth of the State of Israel, the Hebraic renaissance, the remarkable growth of the Jewish communities in the Western Hemisphere, and the strong recoil from weakness to strength anywhere. The most powerful forces converged to destroy the Jewish people in recent years, and they took a frightful toll, but the Jewish people has again emerged from the deep shadows and has resumed its march through history. Much of the story of that march of destiny will in the indeterminate future be recorded by the Jewish community of the United States.

There is ground for confidence, not only because of its present inner soundness, but also because of the American democratic milieu in which it will continue to move and have its being. It is a friendly and stimulating environment. There is a strong concordance between the spiritual and ethical traditions of the two peoples. The Founding Fathers of the American Republic, and many before them who established colonies on the shores of the New World were greatly influenced by the heroic ideals of human freedom and human equality of the Hebrew Scriptures. Their "self-evident truths," their dogma of inalienable human rights, the doctrine that "resistance to tyrants is obedience to God" are key ideas of the Bible, and it was the Bible that gave political sanction to their political revolution. These ideas have never been wanting in American life from its inception to this day. They have constituted the classic elements which have given uniqueness and distinction to the American way of life. They have passed through many crises, including the world-wide crises of Fascism, Nazism and Communism, and have survived.

The Jewish community finds itself in the midst of a people which for a hundred and seventy-five years has maintained a government, built on the foundations of human rights and on consent, not constraint. The American genius strives to achieve the best possible way of life for the largest possible number of citizens through their own voluntary enterprises, through free experimentation, and step by step through the evolutionary processes of trial and error. It rejects all proffers of ready-made millenniums at the spearpoint of revolution and dictatorship, and it has succeeded in avoiding the horrors of purges and liquidations, of terrorism and expropriation, of espionage and slavery, from which the Jewish minority has suffered so catastrophically in recent years.

American life possesses the grace of tolerance. The American people is a composite people. Many races shared in the discovery, exploration, colonization and development of this great country. It is a nation made up from its very inception almost entirely of immigrants. American life is a mosaic in which many peoples of varying backgrounds have found cohesion in a unified pattern. Despite occasional and, at times, serious lapses, there has prevailed a wholesome attitude of good will, tolerance and coöperation among the American people.

It is in the midst of such a people, dowered with such kindred and accordant traditions and institutions, that the Jewish community will live, grow and develop in the future. The Jews of the United States are not unaware of their favorable position, nor are they unmindful of the challenge to worthy and loyal participation inherent in it. They have already made significant and substantial contributions to the social and cultural progress of America, to its economic development, and its military defense.

The five million Jews of the United States have also given clear indication that they are wanting neither in loyalty to Judaism and world Jewry, nor in generous support of the re-established State of Israel. There is, of course, much that needs to be done by them to achieve a full and creative Jewish life and to insure survival, but "they may rest in trust because there is hope."

PREFACE TO THE EIGHTH EDITION

Since the publication of the last edition of this book in 1939 there have been so many momentous events in the history of the Jewish people, that its author was naturally anxious to revise it and bring it up to date. But unfortunately Mr. Paul Goodman was in poor health for some time before his death, which occurred on August 13, 1949, and was thus prevented from realizing his intention. I was therefore more than ordinarily pleased when, at the suggestion of his family, the publishers invited me to undertake the task, as we had been linked for the greater part of our lives by ties of intimate friendship, and I felt that I would be paying a personal tribute to his memory by continuing where he had left off. I have therefore revised and enlarged this book in harmony, I trust, with the spirit in which he had conceived it.

During the past decade two epoch-making events have taken place that are far more important than any in the previous nineteen hundred years of Jewish history and that have wrought fundamental changes in the Jewish scene. The first is the extermination of one-third of the Jewish people by Hitler's butcheries and gas chambers; the other is the re-establishment of Jewish national independence by the creation of the State of Israel. These two events, as well as the active part played by Jews in the Second World War, are described in the three additional chapters that I have written to bring this history up to date. The catastrophe that overtook the Jews in Europe and the establishment of the Jewish State in Palestine present such a multiplicity of varied aspects and have had such far-reaching effects that it was impossible, within the proportions permitted by the plan of this work, to attempt anything more than an outline. But I believe that I have given a sufficiently adequate account of all the salient facts relating to those events as well as to the other outstanding developments of the period to enable the reader to understand the main problems of the present Jewish situation.

ISRAEL COHEN.

PREFACE TO THE FIRST EDITION

The history of the Jews presents the struggles for light and life of a people small in numbers and negligible in political power but great in achievement and unparalleled in endurance. This people, whom the historians and geographers of ancient Hellas hardly deigned to notice as a strange Syrian tribe, had already then produced one of the most remarkable literatures of all time as well as a body of men who were later on acclaimed as the ethical and religious teachers of mankind. While in their most flourishing political state the Israelites formed only a petty Asiatic kingdom, the descendants of those who served the Pharaohs and whose national existence was wiped out by Nebuchadnezzar the Babylonian about two thousand five hundred years ago still represent one of the most active and progressive human groups of to-day.

What the Jews as a *Kulturvolk* mean to the world, not merely as an ancient factor but as one of the living forces of modern times, may be gauged by a comparison of the contributions which the Jews have made during the last century to all aspects of civilization with the almost inappreciable activities during the same period of the historically and politically favored Greeks.

If we take away the Jews from the realms of thought and life—if we imagine that there had not existed those who gave birth to the spiritual, ethical, and dogmatic forces of Christianity; that Mohammedanism, the Arabian replica of a militant Judaism, had never seen the world; that we knew nothing of those and other Hebraic influences which, in name, substance, and action, have repeatedly changed the course of history—then both Eastern and Western civilization would appear to us beyond recognition.

The Jews are one of the very rare races with a definite mission in the development of mankind—a mission of which the actors are conscious, if, at times, unwilling agents, destined to play the part of historic advocates for the freedom of the human conscience, in contravention of their own jealous and uncompromising adherence to ethical Monotheism and to the moral purpose of human life—the imperishable Jewish contributions to the foundations of civilization.

The Jews have, however, not only given birth to prophets of the mission of Israel, but, strangest of all, they have also produced the greatest adversaries of their own claims and corporate existence. Paul, the apostle of the Gentiles, who boasted of being a Hebrew of the Hebrews, was the dogmatic founder of the world-conquering religion of which Jesus the Messiah (Christ) was the spiritual and ethical inspiration; Spinoza, the most dissolving philosopher of the modern age, broke the trammels of supernaturalism; Karl Marx, the scientific creator of the Socialist movement, became the cosmopolitan prophet of the disinherited of the whole human race.

In spite of the extraordinary kaleidoscopic changes in Jewish history—from the conquest of the now extinct and forgotten Canaanites to the combat with the widespread and powerful forces of modern anti-Semitism—an extensive survey of it presents a cycle of manifestations and problems that continually repeats itself. In substance, Jewish history is concentrated on the never-ending struggle between the universalistic and particularistic tendencies of Jewish thought and life, and, from the conflicts between Prophecy and Priesthood to those of Nationalism and Assimilation, we discern the same heroic effort to save the Jewish life by losing it. Never has such solidarity been exhibited between the scattered atoms of a race that frequently even lack molecular attraction, yet never has a people risen to such sublime heights, with entire oblivion of itself. It is because throughout the Jewish struggle for life there appears one underlying, fundamental purpose—the fulfilment of law and prophecy in their workings in history.

Jewish history has shared the fate of the Jews in that it has been treated either from an offensive or defensive, and too frequently, from the double-edged didactic, point of view. In the following pages, the course of Jewish history has been traced without reference to the question whether the Jews have the right to exist. The subject of Judaism as a world-religion has been dealt with by me in *The Synagogue and the Church* (Routledge, 1908), but, irrespective of the justification or condemnation of Judaism, our interest is surely due to the history of a people which, according to the natural law of the survival of the fittest, has justified itself by its very existence.

P. G.

London, November 14, 1909.

CONTENTS

PAGE

Introduction by Dr. Abba Hillel Silver 7

CHAPTER I. THE ANCIENT ISRAELITES

The Historical Records—The Patriarchs—Israel in
Egypt — Moses — The Exodus — The Torah of
Moses—The Conquest of the Land—The Judges—
The United Monarchy—The Kingdom of Israel—
The Kingdom of Judah—The Prophets 23

CHAPTER II. THE SECOND TEMPLE

The Babylonian Captivity — The Restoration — The
Samaritans—Ezra and Nehemiah—A Silent Evolu-
tion—The Conflict with Hellenism—The Macca-
bean Revolt — The Hasmonean Dynasty — The
Herodian Dynasty—Pharisees, Sadducees, and Es-
senes—The Rise of Rabbinical Schools—Hellenistic
Judaism—The Rise of Christianity—The Spread of
Judaism—The Shadows of the Roman War—The
War with Rome—The Fall of Judea—The Last
Struggle for Independence 34

CHAPTER III. THE TALMUDIC AGE

The Dispersion—The Rally—Judaism in Babylonia—
The Talmud — Under the Cross — Under Neo-

PAGE

Persian Dominion—Under the Crescent—In Western Europe—Social and Economic Conditions . . 62

CHAPTER IV. THE GOLDEN AGE OF JUDAISM

The Geonim—Karaism—The Chazars—The Spanish Epoch—Hispano-Jewish Culture—Moses Maimonides—The Franco-German Schools 83

CHAPTER V. THE DARK AGES

The General State — Sufferings and Trials — The Forces of Resistance—The Crusades—In Medieval England—In Central Europe—Spain and the Inquisition—Reaction Within—The Cabbalah—Pseudo-Messiahs—Italy—Turkey—Poland—The Cossack Rising—The Hassidim—The Rise of Tolerance—Spinoza—In the Middle of the Eighteenth Century 100

CHAPTER VI. THE ERA OF EMANCIPATION

The Modern Epoch—Moses Mendelssohn—The Enlightenment and Neo-Hebrew Literature—Yiddish —The New Learning—The Reform of Judaism— The Struggle for Emancipation—Emancipation in England—Russia—The United States of America —Cultural Progress — Self-Emancipation — Anti-Semitism—Zionism 150

CHAPTER VII. REACTION

The First World War—The Aftermath—Jewish Minority Rights—In Soviet Russia—In Nazi Germany—In Fascist Italy 185

CHAPTER VIII. THE JEWISH NATIONAL HOME

The Foundations — Zionist Leaders — The Balfour Declaration—The British Mandate—Culture and Economics—Prelude to a Commonwealth . . . 199

CHAPTER IX. A RECORD MARTYRDOM

An Unparalleled Catastrophe—Pre-War Sufferings in 'Greater Reich,' Italy, and Hungary—Repression in Poland and Rumania—Persecution in Poland—Massacres in Russia—Fate of Balkan Jewry—Concentration Camps in Western Europe—Campaign of Extermination—Rescue Measures—Extent of Losses—Displaced Persons—Emigration from Europe 211

CHAPTER X. WAR SERVICES AND PEACE TREATIES

Services in all Allied Nations—Jews in British Defence Forces—In Dominion Defence Forces—In American Defence Forces—In the Soviet Forces—Services of Polish, French, and Greek Jews—Services of Palestinian Jewry—Total Jewish Contribution—The Peace Treaties—Reparations 226

CHAPTER XI. THE JEWISH STATE

The Need for Independence—Labor Government's Changed Policy—United Nations' Historic Decision

PAGE

—Role of American Jewry—End of Palestine Man-
date—Birth of Israel—Arabs' War against Israel—
Bernadotte Proposals Rejected—Israel's Victory—
Progress and Prospect 235

INDEX 247

CHAPTER I

THE ANCIENT ISRAELITES

§ 1. *The Historical Records*. The history of the Jews reaches back to a primeval age of human civilization, to those archaic times when gods walked the earth and held intercourse with the children of men. But whereas the descent of other nations of remote antiquity is lost in the dim mists of mythology, the collection of literature known as the Bible has preserved a remarkably simple, and yet vivid, account of the origins and early history of the people called the Hebrews, Israelites, or Jews.

§ 2. *The Patriarchs*. Abraham, the Hebrew (i.e. from the other side of the river [Euphrates]), the first of the patriarchs from whom the Jews trace their descent, came of so-called Semitic stock from Ur, in Chaldea, which was then, more than two thousand years B.C.E., an important center of civilization. Tradition has it that a divine call came to him to leave his home and country and proceed southward to the land of Canaan (Phoenicia), or Palestine (the land of the Philistines), while he received the promise that his descendants should live there as a great nation and play a unique part in the history of the human race. In the national records, his son Isaac and grandson Jacob (or Israel) are described as pastoral chieftains, who moved about with their flocks in the then thinly inhabited land of Canaan. In the course of their migrations the family eventually settled in the rich pasture-lands of neighboring Egypt.

§ 3. *Israel in Egypt*. It was in Egypt, in the course of centuries, that, from a small clan, the Children of Israel (B'né

Israel) rose to be a people considerable in numbers. Living on a frontier exposed to the inroads of numerous marauding enemies attracted by the wealth and culture of Egypt, the Israelites incurred the suspicion that they would prove dangerous to the country, to the inhabitants of which they were indeed entirely foreign in race, religion, and occupation. To prevent such a probable contingency, the Israelites were turned into Pharaonic serfs, and set to labor at those gigantic works and monuments which have remained the wonder of posterity. The barbaric cruelties enacted by their Egyptian taskmasters broke the spirit of this shepherd-people.

§ 4. *Moses.* At such a critical time there appeared on the scene one, who, by the stupendous and enduring character of his work and the transcendent effect of his world-mission, not only stands as the most luminous figure of antiquity, but as a mighty conqueror of the human soul, whose influence has been pulsating throughout the ages with ever-increasing vitality. Moses, who was to become the leader and teacher of the Children of Israel, appears to have been brought up as an Egyptian and to have taken no interest or share in the servitude of his people. It was by an accident that he became alive to the slavery which crushed his kith and kin. On seeing one day an Egyptian taskmaster beating one of the Israelites, the generous indignation and racial consciousness of Moses were roused, and he killed the Egyptian. To escape Egyptian vengeance for his daring act, he left the country. But the enslavement and wrongs of his people pursued him to the wilderness of the Sinaitic peninsula to which he betook himself. While engaged there in the peaceful pursuit of a shepherd, his musings brought before him a vision of the deliverance of his brethren, and he obeyed the voice which, recalling to him the purpose of the Eternal in His promise to the patriarchs of old, bade him lead the people of Israel out of Egypt.

§ 5. *The Exodus.* The enfranchisement of a nation of

slaves trodden under the heel of a mighty military power—such was the task which presented itself to Moses, who was by nature a man halting in speech and of humble disposition. But when the appeal came to the Israelites to free themselves from the Egyptian yoke, "they hearkened not unto Moses for anguish of spirit and for cruel bondage." The extraordinary self-assertion and confidence which Moses, in conjunction with his brother Aaron, inspired in the downtrodden Israelites, their deliverance from the crushing tyranny of the Egyptian, as well as the cohesion and discipline maintained among such a vast horde of rebel slaves, are more eloquent testimony than all the recorded supernatural signs and wonders to the inscrutable spiritual force which then brought the religion of Israel into being.

§ 6. *The Torah of Moses.* The exodus of the Israelites from Egypt (about 1220 B.C.E.) became the most far-reaching event, and has always been considered as the central incident, in the political and religious history of the Jews. With the liberation of the Israelites from Egyptian bondage, there began their life as a free people, destined to take possession of that land of Canaan to which their steps were now directed. The invasion and conquest of that country might have been accomplished with more or less success if a daring and skilled warrior had led the Israelites, while their rough patriarchal and tribal organizations and rudimentary monotheistic traditions would have furnished them with the necessary political and religious bonds of a national life. The Israelites were, however, not merely to supplant the inhabitants of Canaan, but, as a people providentially selected for a high purpose in the education of the human race, were to form an ideal polity, where individual and public righteousness should be the guiding and binding principles of law and order; where the authority and worship of the one God of Israel was to hold undivided sway—so that the existence of the people of Israel should be assured for ever.

The cornerstone of the Torah (Instruction, or Law) of Moses was provided by the Ten Words (the Decalogue), which solemnly proclaimed the absolute and undivided unity and incorporeality of God, and gave a concise epitome of the moral law which was to govern the lives of the Israelites.

In order to keep them effectively separated as a people dedicated to a high service, the Torah ord ined rites and observances which were intended to strengthen the national consciousness and the moral fiber of the Israelite by guiding and educating him in the fear and love of God, and it also contained laws and regulations for good government, both of the whole community and of its component parts. Apart from its unswerving insistence on the monotheistic conception and worship of God, the outstanding features of the Torah of Moses—speaking from a broad and comprehensive standpoint—were the sacredness and moral purpose of human life and the equality of all without distinction, including the foreigner and the slave, before the law. In this the Israelites were to form a striking contrast to the natives of Canaan, against whom and their seductive immoral polytheism the Torah of Moses pronounced itself with ruthless severity. With the claim of authority from on high, and an appeal to the divine in man, the Torah demanded personal holiness as well as justice and righteousness in social relations. The tender mercy to be shown to the weak and the needy, and an exceptionally high sense of consideration for the unprotected foreigner, are remarkable traits in the Torah of Moses, which were later on summarized in the love of God with all one's heart, soul, and belongings, and the love of the fellow-man, even though a stranger, as oneself.

§ 7. *The Conquest of the Land.* It was about 1160 B.C.E. that the Israelites invaded Canaan by crossing the River Jordan under the leadership of Joshua, the successor of Moses.

Of the tribes into which the people of Israel was divided, some had contented themselves by staying behind and settling on the eastern bank of the Jordan, for the invaders met with fierce resistance on the part of the natives. The holy war which had been proclaimed against them was for centuries carried on with only partial success, and although the Israelites were able to overrun the country, and to gain a firm footing there, they had often to submit to serious reverses and to the humiliating yoke of their enemies. In these sanguinary struggles for the possession of the land, the Israelites developed a martial disposition, which marks that epoch as the heroic period of their history. The rugged wildness of Israelitish life in those times stands out in striking contrast to the regulating and restraining influences which made themselves felt in later ages.

§ 8. *The Judges.* The frequent disasters that overtook the Israelites, and which were largely due to their divisions and tribal jealousies, produced a new kind of leader, known by the title of Judges (Shophetim, cf. the Carthaginian Suffetes). They were men who by some act of public valor or sagacity had proved their fitness to lead the people against oppressors or rebels. Certain of these Judges, like Samson, distinguished themselves by personal feats of prowess, but usually they were successful commanders whom their grateful tribesmen or adherents invested with the authority of a military and civil dictator. There appear to have been women also who were accepted as Judges, and one of them, Deborah, exercised considerable influence. The last and greatest of the Judges was Samuel, who was recognized by the whole people. But the old age of Samuel and the pressing danger of the Canaanite enemies, convinced the divided and democratically disposed tribes of Israel, even against the urgent advice of Samuel, that they required a common ruler who would lead them to war and judge them in times of peace.

§ 9. *The United Monarchy.* The first one selected for the

dignity of king was Saul, a man of commanding presence and proved military ability. His many successful campaigns, especially against the Philistines, who still threatened the security and independence of the Iraelites, as well as the partially re-established political unity of the people, justified both the office and the selection. But private troubles, brought about by differences with his former patron, Samuel, and by jealousy of the remarkable martial exploits of his armor-bearer David, made the end of Saul's reign an unhappy one, and in a disastrous battle he put an end to his life.

With David, Saul's successor on the throne, there begins a period of great prestige and prosperity for the Israelites. David, who was justly described as "cunning in playing, a mighty man of valor, a man of war and prudent in speech," raised them to an important military power, and established a short-lived stability and unity of his people. He conquered Jerusalem, and made this, the Eternal City of the Jews, the political and religious capital of his kingdom. The extraordinary magnetic influence exercised by David on the Israelites and the halo with which they surrounded his reign. he bequeathed to his family, which became recognized as the legitimate dynasty of Jewish rulers. Endowed with a poetic genius of a high order, he laid the foundations of that collection of Hebrew devotional literature, the *Psalms,* which has stirred the hearts of men of countless generations, of all races and all climes.

In the dispute which arose concerning the succession to David's throne, he himself selected his son Solomon, who developed his father's achievements by raising the kingdom to a still higher state of strength and magnificence. Solomon, who was the most important king of his day between the Euphrates and the border of Egypt, endeared himself to his subjects by building a national temple of remarkable splendor on Mount Moriah in Jerusalem (937), and by the prestige which now distinguished the Israelites among the conquered and surrounding nations. Solomon's friendship with Hiram, King of Tyre, was turned into a commercial alliance between the powerful Israelite and the enterprising Phoenician. The joint maritime expeditions which were sent out by them from the port of Ezion-Geber (near Akaba), on the Red Sea, as well as the skilled Tyrian workmen lent to Solomon, brought to the agricultural Israelites a vast measure of wealth and artistic productions. His reputation for wisdom, for the composition of gnomic sayings and riddles, gave him an added luster in the memory of the Israelites.

Solomon was the *Grand Monarque* of the Israelites and, like the French Louis XIV, the glories of his reign involved the ultimate ruin of the country. His matrimonial alliances with the King of Egypt and other foreign sovereigns, as well at the creation of a large Oriental harem, established in Jerusalem the authorized worship of various idolatries which aroused the ire of those zealous for the exclusive worship of the God of Israel, while the extravagance of his rule and the accompanying introduction of new, burdensome taxation and forced labor brought disaffection among his subjects and the disruption of the kingdom after his death.

§ 10. *The Kingdom of Israel.* The division of the Hebrew monarchy into two parts, Judah and Israel, was the most momentous national event since the invasion of Canaan. The smoldering disaffection and the jealousies of the northern tribes broke out into an open flame on the accession of Solomon's son, Rehoboam. The revolt was headed by Jeroboam, formerly an officer in Solomon's service, who, owing to a conspiracy, had been forced to escape to Egypt. Jeroboam returned to his native land with the favor of the King of Egypt, whose interest it was to weaken the formidable power of the Hebrew kingdom. A deputation, headed by the former rebel Jeroboam, was sent to Rehoboam to demand guarantees for the rights of the northern tribes which had been violated by Solomon, but the new king imperiously refused to redress any grievances. In the successful revolution which ensued, Jeroboam was elected to reign over the so-called Ten Tribes, under the title of King of Israel.

The kingdom of Israel, which existed for about two centuries, was troubled by frequent dynastic disturbances, palace revolutions, conspiracies, and assassinations. Jeroboam, the first King of Israel, set himself to widen the breach between the two Hebrew States, and, to prevent the religious fusion between both political sections of the people, established separate shrines with semi-idolatrous worship to supersede the central sanctuary in Jerusalem. Later on, forced by the threatening power of the Empire of Damascus, the Israelites re-established friendly relations with their kinsmen of Judah. The northern kingdom, however, had too little stability to maintain its independence. In spite of repeated gallant attempts, and even some signal successes, against the encroachments and attacks of Damascus, the kingdom of Israel fell a prey to the mighty conquering power of Assyria. Under the reign of the Israelite King Pekah, the Assyrian Emperor Tiglathpileser III carried away a large number of Israelites captive. His successor, Shalmaneser IV, again invaded the country, took Hoshea, the last King of Israel, prisoner, and, in 721 B.C.E., after a siege of three years, the Assyrians, under Sargon, captured Samaria, the capital, and, by carrying the people away into exile, put an end to the kingdom of Israel. The captives practically disappeared amidst their foreign surroundings, and, as a separate entity, Jewish history knows them no more.

§ 11. *The Kingdom of Judah.* Different in very important respects from the inglorious end of the northern kingdom was the fate of the sister-State of Judah, or Judea. Though it could also not escape the cataclysms which were brought about by the rise and fall of the neighboring empires, it survived all of them. The reasons for this resistance are first of all to be found in the allegiance which the people continued to pay to the royal house of David, and in the religious cohesion effected by the renowned national sanctuary in Jerusalem. While the kingdom of Judah was at the beginning more or less protected from northern invasion by the intervening kingdom of Israel, it was Egypt which proved a dangerous neighbor. Under the reign of Rehoboam, the first of the kings of Judah, Shishak, of Egypt, swept over the land, and carried away from Jerusalem the gold and other treasures of the Temple and royal palace. Indeed, the apparently inexhaustible wealth of the Temple and the precious metals used in its construction and appointments, proved attractive objects for the cupidity of foreign invaders. The kings of Damascus, Israel, and Assyria, who raided the land of Judah, plundered those treasures themselves or were bought off with them. Of far more serious consequences, however, proved the conflicts between the rival powers of Egypt and Babylonia, between which Judah served as a buffer-state, so that it was placed in the inextricable difficulty of having repeatedly to take sides with one power against the other.

Grave trouble broke out when Necho II, of Egypt, marched northward to come to grips with the Babylonians, and King Josiah, of Judah, considered it necessary to oppose the passage of the Egyptian army through his territory. At the battle of Megiddo, the well-meaning Josiah was defeated with great slaughter and lost his life (608). Confusion and disaster followed on this event. Necho interfered with the election to the throne, on which he placed his own nominee, Jehoiakim, Josiah's eldest son, and put the country under tribute to Egypt. Judah, however, soon passed under the ruthless yoke of the Babylonian Nebuchadnezzar. Jehoiachin, the son and successor of Jehoiakim, together with many of the aristocracy, was carried away captive to Babylon, and his uncle Zedekiah, the youngest son of Josiah, the twentieth and last King of Judah, was placed on the throne. Instigated

by Egypt, Zedekiah rebelled against Babylonia; Nebuchadnezzar invested Jerusalem, and, after a siege of a year and a
half, stormed the city and razed it to the ground (9th Ab,
586 B.C.E.). The King, Zedekiah, was blinded and taken in
chains to Babylon, where he died in a dungeon; the most
important and useful parts of the population were carried
away into exile to that country, and the once fair and flourishing kingdom of Judah became a howling wilderness. In
language of moving pathos and power, the Lamentations of
Jeremiah depict the heart-rending ruin which had overwhelmed the Judean nation.

§ 12. *The Prophets.* Amidst the disruptive influences of
events which brought about the downfall of the kingdoms of
Israel and Judah, amidst all the gloom and terror which
preceded and followed those great and crushing disasters,
there stood out a class of men known as Prophets (Nebiim).
At first regarded as mere visionaries, who, in their ecstatic
trances, could foretell the future, the prophets became the
mouthpieces of the God of Israel in their zeal for Him and
their warning admonitions against the moral transgressions
of His people. Instead of saying smooth things to flatter the
national vanity, the prophets denounced their own countrymen with pitiless severity, and threatened them with the
doom of Heaven for their sins. In times of distress and
calamity, the prophets, however, generally guided the people,
and, in language of poetic tenderness, inspired it with trust
in God and confidence in His ultimate merciful dealings with
those, who, in spite of all, were to remain true to the Covenant which He had made with their fathers.

The prophets whose utterances and writings have been
preserved to us show an extraordinary variety of types of
the highest moral grandeur. We have Samuel, who had unselfishly led the people during a long and eventful life; Elijah,
the fierce champion of the Lord God of Israel, who could
only recognize Him in the "still, small voice"; Nathan, who

crushed to the dust the guilty warrior-king David, by the words, "Thou art the man!"; Amos, the herdman of Tekoa, whose only partiality for his own people was his threat that their greater moral consciousness would bring a severer punishment for their sins; Micah, with his appeal, "What doth the Lord require of thee but to do justly, love mercy, and to walk humbly with thy God?"; Isaiah, the far-seeing statesman, with his burning anger against the prevailing luxury and licentiousness and his consuming zeal for righteousness; Jeremiah, the noble-minded patriot, who warned and threatened, and then bewailed and shared, the sad fate of his stricken people; Ezekiel, a captive in a strange land, proclaiming the dignity and responsibility of every human soul and the moral government of the world; the illustrious seer of the Restoration, the so-called second Isaiah, who announced the ultimate realization of the universal hopes of Israel. It is difficult to know what to admire most in these teachers and tribunes of humanity—whether their truly matchless eloquence, which would have been enough to invest their utterances with immortal fame; their unsurpassed conception of ethical Monotheism, which has become the distinguishing mark of the religion of Israel throughout the ages; their lofty ideal of the mission of their people in history; their passion for social righteousness, or their dauntless courage in enforcing it. Certain it is, that they have indelibly stamped their glory on the people of Israel, and have decisively shaped the spiritual and moral evolution of mankind.

CHAPTER II

THE SECOND TEMPLE

§ 1. *The Babylonian Captivity.*

By the rivers of Babylon,
There we sat down, yea, we wept,
When we remembered Zion.
Upon the willows in the midst thereof
We hanged up our harps.
For there they that led us captive required of us words of
    song,
And our tormentors required of us mirth, saying,
Sing us one of the songs of Zion.
How shall we sing the Lord's song in a strange land?
If I forget thee, O Jerusalem,
Let my right hand forget her cunning.
Let my tongue cleave to the roof of my mouth,
If I remember thee not:
If I prefer not Jerusalem above my chief joy.

Such were the sentiments which animated the Judeans, or Jews, who were in exile far away from their own native country. These feelings became, however, subdued by the healing process of time, and were gradually replaced by an entirely different outlook on the course of events. If the hallowed Temple, where God had dwelt in His glory, was destroyed; if Jerusalem, the pride of the nation, was in ruins; if the whole land was lying waste—yet the God of Israel, to whom the Temple had been dedicated, still lived, and His people, to whom the land of Canaan belonged by ancient promise, still had its being.

"Seek ye the peace of the city whither I have caused you to be carried away captive, and pray unto the Lord for it," was the remarkable advice which the prophet Jeremiah addressed to his distressed compatriots, and they followed his counsel. In a short space of time the Jews of Babylonia grew into a flourishing community; some of its members, like Daniel, even rose to high rank at the imperial court, while King Jehoiachin, the last but one of the kings of Judah, had a seat of honor at the royal table of Evil Merodach, the son of Nebuchadnezzar. But of infinitely greater importance than their material prosperity was the development which their spiritual outlook assumed. From a cult national in scope, the religion of Israel became universal in effect. Deprived of the centralizing Temple with its animal sacrifices, the exiles in the various places of their dispersion established houses of prayer where God was indeed worshiped in spirit and in truth, and here the reading and exposition of the Torah of Moses gradually became a fixed institution. The idolatrous tendencies which prophets and priests had been unable to eradicate, vanished with the catastrophe that shook Israel to its foundations, so that, amidst all vicissitudes, the Jews remained the faithful bodyguard of that pure and ethical Monotheism which was so loftily proclaimed by one of the Jewish master-minds of that period: "Thus saith the Lord, The heaven is my throne, and the earth is my footstool: what manner of house will ye build unto me, and what place shall be my rest? For all these things hath mine hand made, and so all these things came to be, saith the Lord; but to this man will I look, even to him that is poor and of a contrite spirit, and that trembleth at my word."

§ 2. *The Restoration.*

When the Lord turned again the captivity of Zion,
We were like unto them that dream.
Then was our mouth filled with laughter,

And our tongue with singing:
Then said they among the nations,
The Lord hath done great things for them.
The Lord hath done great things for us;
Therefore we are glad.
Turn again our captivity, O Lord,
As the streams in the South.
They that sow in tears shall reap in joy.
Though he goeth on his way weeping, bearing forth the seed,
He shall come again with joy, bringing his sheaves with him.

It was not long after the destruction of the Jewish commonwealth that there occurred an event which convulsed the
great Babylonian Empire, and brought it to a dramatic fall.
The new star which had arisen in the person of Cyrus, the
ruler of conquering Persia, also changed the fortunes of the
Jewish people. In the year 539, within half a century of the
captivity, Cyrus issued an edict permitting the return of the
exiled Jews to their native land and the rebuilding of the
Temple in Jerusalem. It was a decree of incalculably far-
reaching consequences, worthy to inspire that wonderful
psalm which sang of the resurrection of a people. Yet, in
spite of the intense enthusiasm and high hopes it evoked,
the response was very meager on the part of the bulk of the
people, who had evidently found a permanent home in Babylonia. Only a comparatively small number of Jews, led by
Sheshbazzar, a prince of the house of David, returned to
Jerusalem. They proceeded to rebuild the Temple, but the
opposition they encountered from various quarters forced
them to discontinue the work. It was only under Darius
Hystaspes that Zerubbabel, also a member of the royal line
of David, who had returned with another group of colonists,
was able, together with the High Priest Joshua, supported
by the prophets Haggai and Zechariah, to complete the interrupted work of the rebuilding of the Temple (516). Great
indeed was the jubilation of those who were privileged to

witness the re-establishment of the sacred edifice, but the old men who had seen the former Temple "wept with a loud voice."

§ 3. *The Samaritans.* The opposition to the reconstruction of the Temple and capital of the former Jewish State had come from a strange quarter. The Samaritans, a mixture of foreign colonists introduced by the Assyrian Shalmaneser on the destruction of the kingdom of Israel and of the dregs of the original population that were then left behind, had adopted the religion of the land, and on hearing of the proposed rebuilding of the Temple, they offered to participate in the establishment of the new sanctuary. The small band of Jews who had come back to their country with the zeal and enthusiasm of patriots and reformers were, however, determined not to share the glory, nor to expose themselves to the dangers which a religious amalgamation with the semi-idolatrous Samaritans would have entailed. The refusal by the Jews of the Samaritan offer led to an intense hatred between the two nations. The Samaritans, adhering to a peculiar text of the Torah of Moses, built a rival Temple on Mount Gerizim, which was eventually destroyed with the city of Samaria by the Jewish High Priest, John Hyrcanus, in the year 109 B.C.E. During the course of Jewish history we meet the Samaritans as now and again they rise into meteoric prominence. They joined the Jews in their last struggle for independence, and, after a formidable insurrection under the Emperor Justinian (530 C.E), were reduced to insignificance. Surviving many vicissitudes, the Samaritans have dwindled to an interesting remnant of about 160 souls, who still inhabit Shechem (Nablus), the ancient center of their history.

§ 4. *Ezra and Nehemiah.* The rebuilding of the Temple in Jerusalem would have availed little to the future of the new Judean settlement, and still less to the future of Judaism, the religious polity of the Jews, if there had not appeared

Ezra the Scribe, who, with the moral earnestness and zeal of a religious reformer, gave an entirely new tendency to Jewish history. The Jews became first and foremost a religious community, in which the study of the Sacred Writings and the observance of their institutions were to be the great purpose of Jewish life. This regenerator of Judaism, of whom it was afterwards said that he restored the Torah which had been forgotten, came from Babylonia with a body of colonists, bringing with him a decree of King Artaxerxes Longimanus which gave full authority for the carrying out of the object they had in view. One of his first acts for the purification and preservation of the community was to take energetic steps to put a stop to the widely prevailing marriages with foreign women, and even to insist on their dismissal in the case of those who had contracted such mixed unions. Of epoch-making importance was his establishment of the Torah of Moses as the basis of Jewish life and thought —a measure which more than anything else ensured the continuance and vitality of Judaism.

In his strenuous work of reform, Ezra was effectively associated with, and supported by, Nehemiah, a cupbearer to Artaxerxes. He came to Jerusalem in the capacity of governor, and armed with powers to rebuild the walls of Jerusalem. This most necessary and important work was carried out by him with great energy, especially as the workmen had to go about armed in fear of being attacked by Samaritan and other enemies. This Jewish patriot, however, not only interested himself in the strengthening and good government of the city, but also took a leading part in the religious revival of the community. After a stay of twelve years, he returned to Babylonia, but subsequently paid another visit to Jerusalem in order to amplify and enforce the reforms and enactments introduced by Ezra and himself.

§ 5. *A Silent Evolution.* For the next two centuries few incidents of stirring historic importance have been preserved to us, and yet it was a period of immense consequence to the future of Judaism and religion generally. During this period, a silent evolution, unheeded by the people concerned and entirely unknown to the outside world, went on in the growing Judean community. This people, practically undisturbed by the contests for world power which were then raging, or regarded as of no account by the mighty conquerors and armies who swept past and over it, was yet undergoing a process of fermentation which was ultimately to effect a revolution in the whole all-embracing domain of religion and morals. The varied writings contained in the Hebrew Bible, undoubtedly the most remarkable and most influential collection of literature known to man, were then sifted and settled by the Jewish scribes and religious authorities with a conscientiousness which should have earned for them the gratitude of posterity. The reforms of Ezra and Nehemiah bore abundant fruit in the orderly development of Jewish religious tradition and life. The Great Synod, a body of somewhat uncertain composition and duration, applied itself to the solution of the new spiritual problems which arose with the ever-changing needs of the Jewish people. But in economic and political directions also the Jews made vast progress under the sheltering care of comparative peace and obscurity. The great struggles with Greek civilization and Roman militarism which lay before the Jewish people proved repeatedly the inexhaustible spiritual strength and the high qualities of patriotic courage and devotion which animated and sustained it.

§ 6. *The Conflict with Hellenism.* The seclusion of Judaism was broken by the appearance at Jerusalem of Alexander the Great (332), whose conquests were not only to inaugurate a new chapter in Universal History, but also to bring Judaism on the world-stage, and to throw it into a deadly conflict with Hellenic thought and civilization. It was truly a dramatic moment when the High Priest Jaddua met Alexander to offer him the submission of the Jewish people. The Greeks had no conception of the forces which were hidden in the mind and life of this apparently strange and insignificant nation of barbarians, but, with an instinctive insight, Alexander took kindly to them. After his death Palestine passed under the rule of the Egyptian Ptolemies, who proved well disposed towards the Jews. They accorded them many marks of favor, and several Jews even rose to the command of the Egyptian army. The Jews of Alexandria, which probably had Jewish settlers from its foundation, began to play a very important part in this great commercial emporium and center of Hellenic philosophy. The Alexandrian Jews, who possessed the full rights of citizenship and were placed under the authority of their own head, with the title of ethnarch, prospered materially and intellectually, and were to exercise a far-reaching influence on the development of Judaism. Unfortunately, the Jews in Palestine became an object of contention between the rival dynasties of the Ptolemies of Egypt and the Seleucidae of Syria. This contest between the two powers was entered upon by the Seleucid Antiochus III, the Great, when Palestine fell into the hands of Syria (203).

The Hellenizing process, which had made rapid progress among the Egyptian Jews, reached their co-religionists in Judea, and particularly among the upper classes it became a general tendency to adopt Grecian names and manners and to affect a corresponding disregard of Jewish custom and sentiment—an attitude which many of the necessarily separatist Jewish people have at all times of intellectual expansion been prone to adopt. Such a course was, however, bound to lead to an enfeeblement of the Jewish power of resistance against the pressing attractions of Grecian life, and to a gradual dissolution of the religious and moral bonds of Judaism. It was under Antiochus IV, surnamed Epiphanes (the Illustrious), and nicknamed Epimanes (the Madman), that the struggle between the Hellenic and Hebraic influences on the Judean people came to a head.

§ 7. *The Maccabean Revolt.* The Jewish settlement in Judea had gradually acquired the privileges of self-government, and both the Seleucidae and the Ptolemies not only left the Jews to manage their internal affairs, but also recognized the High Priest as their natural ruler. The hereditary office of High Priest, which had descended from father to son, now became a matter of dispute and of venal competition, to decide which the intervention of Antiochus Epiphanes was called in. Antiochus, whose greed had been whetted by the tempting offers of the rival candidates, entered Jerusalem and plundered the treasures of the Temple. The resentment which this sacrilege aroused among all sections of the Jews led to an outburst of savage fury on the part of Antiochus against them. He sent an armed force to Judea with orders to spare nobody nor anything there. The Syrians behaved as in a rebellious country, and the people were plundered and butchered without mercy. Not satisfied with this, Antiochus issued an edict forbidding the practice of Judaism under the penalty of death, and, as a finishing touch, the Jews were compelled to worship the idols which were specially erected, one of them even at the Temple of Jerusalem.

These latter measures directed against the Jews came as a new experience to them. Amidst all their manifold misfortunes, they had never yet been subjected to religious persecution, and Antiochus Epiphanes was the first in the long line of the persecutors of the Jews for conscience' sake. The inroads which the Syro-Hellenic manners had made among the upper classes, even among the priests, in Judea, found Judaism ill prepared to withstand this unexpected and fierce onslaught. In spite of the passive resistance which the Syrian officers and executioners encountered, and the martyrdom of many faithful Jews, the struggle was an unequal one, and was likely to end in the dissolution of Judaism in its native home.

A sudden blow struck against this tyranny by an aged priest was to change the whole course of events. Mattathias the Hasmonean, in the town of Modin, near Jerusalem, raised the flag of revolt, and roused his countrymen from their sense of paralyzed helplessness (167). The five sons of Mattathias, surnamed the Maccabees, led the revolt which was to win the independence of the Jewish people.

§ 8. *The Hasmonean Dynasty.* After the death of Mattathias (166), his son Judas became the leader of the Jewish insurrection. Judas Maccabeus was a true hero—very probably a magnetic personality, beyond doubt a devoted patriot and brilliant leader. His valor and resourcefulness were prodigious, and his genuine piety was tempered by common sense. Judas was successful beyond possible expectation. He defeated the disciplined Syrian army with his small band of untrained warriors; he entered Jerusalem and rededicated the Temple to the service of the God of Israel. The feast of Hanucah still commemorates this signal event in Jewish history. The struggle with the Syrian power nevertheless still continued, and Judas died fighting bravely against overwhelming odds (160). In order to ensure the advantages gained by the Jews, Judas had entered into a treaty of alliance with Rome—the growing power with which the Jews were later on to enter into a life-and-death struggle. Judas's brother, Jonathan (161-143), carried on the fight with ability, though with varying success, and he was succeeded by Simon, the last surviving son of Mattathias. It was Simon who finally obtained from Syria a recognition of the political independence of Judea, and he was solemnly invested by the people with the hereditary dignity of High Priest as well as of the civil and military leadership of the Jews.

John Hyrcanus I, son of Simon (135-104), was a successful ruler, who enlarged the frontiers of Judea and raised it to a high degree of prosperity. He waged successful wars with the Samaritans, whose temple on Mount Gerizim he destroyed, and with the Edomites, whom he forcibly compelled to adopt the Jewish religion. Towards the end of his reign, however, he became entangled with the religious parties of the Pharisees and Sadducees, who then entered into that turbulent political rivalry which was to bring such sore tribulation on their common nation. John Hyrcanus, after a reign of thirty years, was succeeded by his eldest son Aristobulus, whose brief reign of about a year was marked by the murder of his mother and favorite brother Antigonus. Alexander Jannaeus, another son of John Hyrcanus, was a strong ruler who engaged in a number of foreign enterprises, and extended the boundaries of Judea. Under Alexander's wife, Alexander Salome, the only post-exilic Jewish queen regnant, who succeeded him, the people enjoyed nine years of peace, but the fight for the crown which broke out after her death between her sons Hyrcanus II, the High Priest, and Aristobulus II, brought ruin to the country, and led to the ultimate extinction of the Hasmonean dynasty and house.

§ 9. *The Herodian Dynasty.* The fall of the Hasmoneans was brought about by the calamitous intervention of Rome, and accelerated by the rise of a family of foreign descent which was to rule the Jews in the last days of their independence. In a fatal moment, both the contending brothers, Hyrcanus II and Aristobulus II, decided to invoke the assistance of all-powerful Rome. Their representatives appeared before Pompey in Damascus, and pleaded the respective merits of the aspirants for the throne, while the long-suffering people, too, had taken care to send a deputation to Pompey, asking him to relieve them of both unwelcome rulers. As the result, Pompey marched on Jerusalem, and took the defended and fortified Temple by storm (63). On entering the Holy of Holies, where the High Priest only appeared once a year (on the Day of Atonement), Pompey was struck with wonder and awe at the entire absence of any visible representation of the Deity in that mysterious sanctuary. Strangely enough, he left the vast treasures of the Temple untouched, and reinstated Hyrcanus in the dignity of High Priest and ruler of Judea.

Hyrcanus, who was to be burdened with the priesthood for a long and stormy period of forty years (79-40), was a weak and easy-going man, altogether unfitted for the exposed parts he was called upon to play. Throughout he was instigated and supported by a crafty, self-seeking Edomite, Antipater, who held the reins of government while his nominal master was made to serve his deeply-laid schemes. These efforts culminated by Hyrcanus being put out of the way, and in the ultimate election by the Roman Senate of Antipater's son, Herod, as King of Judea.

The reign of Herod, called the Great (37-4 B.C.E.), constitutes a long series of murders and outrages. He killed a number of the Sanhedrin, the chief religious and judicial tribunal of the Jews, as well as several of his ten wives, among them the beautiful Mariamne the Hasmonean, and a number of his own children. As Augustus once put it, it was better to be such a man's swine than his son. Swayed by unscrupulous ambition and fierce jealousy, he shrank from no crime which would further his aim or satisfy his suspicion. In order to ingratiate himself with his Roman masters, he built a number of Grecian cities in honor of the emperors, and introduced un-Jewish customs, such as Greek games and combats with wild beasts, into Judea. To flatter his vanity, he rebuilt the Temple in Jerusalem on a magnificent scale, and otherwise comported himself with regal pomp. As he had lived, so he died. During his last days he planned to throw the whole nation into mourning on his death by slaying their most prominent representatives.

Herod was succeeded by his son, Archelaus, but, as the result of an appeal to Rome, Augustus divided Herod's kingdom and apportioned Judea proper, Idumea, and Samaria to Archelaus, who only received the title of ethnarch. While the Herodian family was contending for the sovereignty, the Jewish people experienced a time of great tribulation. The country was in a state of anarchy, subjected to massacre and pillage by Jewish friend and Roman foe. While the so-called Zealots were patriots who considered fair all means that went to rid the country of the hateful foreigner, they became mixed up with doubtful and dangerous elements, like the Sicarii (daggermen), who used patriotism as a cloak for all manner of crime and outrage. Archelaus' reign of nine years was full of misery. He was ultimately summoned to Rome and banished to Gaul, and, with his departure, Judea sank into a Roman province, administered by a procurator resident in Caesarea, and subject to the authority of the prefect of Syria.

§ 10. *Pharisees, Sadducees, and Essenes.* The eventful times through which the Jews had passed since the Maccabean revolt against the tyranny of Antiochus Epiphanes, and the stand which was then made by the bulk of the people against the subversive influences of Hellenism, had brought about a division of the Jews into religious parties, which were likewise colored and guided by political sympathies and tendencies. Mattathias the Hasmonean had turned to those who were "zealous for the Law," and these faithful adherents of the Mosaic institutions, distinguished as Assideans (Hassidim, Pietists, Saints), then became the dominant party in the Jewish commonwealth. The ultimate victory of the Maccabean arms still brought, however, no final reconciliation between the various sections of the Jewish people. Hence, there grew up two opposing parties—Pharisees and Sadducees—who represented differing interpretations of Judaism which long survived the existence of those sections.

The Pharisees (those who "separated" themselves) suc-

ceeded the Assideans in the conscientious observance of the
Torah of Moses and of its traditional development among
the people of Israel. It is unfortunate that the religious
earnestness and patriotic zeal of these Jewish Puritans should
have been largely transmitted to us by unfriendly critics and
rivals. To the primitive Christians, the religious-minded
Pharisees were the immediate and most exasperating opponents, and the violence of the disputes between them is
reflected in the diatribes and denunciations against the Pharisees in the New Testament, but it is hardly fair to the
Pharisees to judge them through the coloring of inherited
religious prejudice. The democratic Pharisees undoubtedly
rendered lasting service to Judaism by curbing the priestly
and aristocratic pretensions of the Sadducees, whose frequently pronounced Hellenistic proclivities constituted a
veritable danger to the religious individuality and political
independence of the Jewish nation. The Pharisees made the
Sacred Writings the common property, indeed the obligatory
possession, of every Jew, by raising their study to a duty
most pleasing to God; and, by the institution of certain
ceremonial observances, transferred the center of gravity of
the religious life from the Temple, with its sacrifices and
priesthood, to the synagogue and the home. A body which
thus placed the knowledge and the ministrations of religion
into the hands of the people, cannot have been that self-seeking and obscurantist sect which traditional ignorance represents the Pharisees to have been. As it was, they assisted in
an evolution of Judaism which survived without any spiritual
strain or shock the destruction of the Temple, and maintained the intellectual vitality of the Jews amidst all the darkness that subsequently surrounded them.

Another Jewish sect, the Essenes, grew out of a certain
number of Pharisees, more strict than their fellows, or of a
more contemplative turn of mind, who, tired of the political
troubles that agitated their people, withdrew into secluded

spots, particularly to the wilderness bordering on the Dead Sea. There they settled in communistic colonies, whose wants were few, and became famed for their charitableness and austerity of morals. But in direct opposition to the basic idea of Pharisaism, that all the acts of life should be hallowed by being placed at the service of God, the Essene recluses became imbued with the Oriental theosophy which regarded matter and spirit as irreconcilable principles. The other-world ideas of the Essenes, largely alien to Judaism, found comparatively few adherents, of whom John the Baptist is the best known, but proved later on of great influence in the rise of Christianity.

§ 11. *The Rise of Rabbinical Schools.* In considering the various sections of Judaism, it ought to be borne in mind that all of them agreed in its fundamental principles, and that the Temple was always recognized as the House of God of all Israel. The spirituality and unity of God were axioms above and beyond discussion, and the inviolability of the Torah of Moses undisputed. At that time, the Jewish religion under Palestinian auspices had not yet elaborated a speculative philosophy, and it was much later that it was formulated into dogmatic principles. The Mosaic institutions and ordinances being universally accepted as the rule of both public and private life, it became necessary to amplify the provisions which the Torah had made for the governance of Israel. There can be no doubt that the religious, civil, and criminal laws and regulations set out in the Torah of Moses had to be interpreted in their practical application, and that they had to be accommodated to changing circumstances; nor can it be denied that, on the one hand, the germ of many enactments found in the Torah called for development, and that, on the other, new rules had to be devised to meet the fresh contingencies arising in the stress of life. It is, therefore, in the nature of things that those who administered the Mosaic Code developed a chain of tradition which included precedents and principles essential to all well-ordered legislation. It was due to the sense of continuity which governed this development of the Torah, and to the vivid consciousness of the divine sway over Israel, that led the Jewish doctors, the Rabbis, to assume authoritative tradition as a concurrent, if unwritten, part of the recorded Law of Moses.

The scribes and members of the Great Synod, who revised and fixed the canon of the Jewish Bible, carried out a highly delicate and important function of tradition. The scribes, however, not only attended to the extremely careful transcription of the Scriptures, but translated the Hebrew original into the Aramaic vernacular and explained it to the people. Out of this grew the Midrash and Haggas dah, the homiletical and general exposition of Scripture, and the Halachah, the legal decisions deduced from Mosaic and other enactments. The members of the Great Synod, which existed roughly from Ezra the Scribe till the invasion of Alexander the Great, considered themselves the immediate successors of the last of the prophets, Haggai, Zechariah, and Malachi, and the oral traditions accumulated by them were further developed by the Elders, and then by the Tannaim (Teachers), who flourished from 10 to 220 C.E.

Of fundamental importance to the systematic development of tradition were Hillel and Shammai, and the schools called after their names. Jewish learning had already been flourishing in Palestine before their appearance, since Hillel came from Babylonia to Jerusalem for the purpose of extending his studies. He found in Shemaiah and Abtalion (Sameas and Pollion) teachers of eminence, and ultimately became head of their college. Hillel, whose public activity in the schools and the Sanhedrin extended from about 30 B.C.E. to 10 C.E., is not only one of the most illustrious, but also one of the most *sympathique,* figures of Jewish history —a master distinguished by nobility of character, greatness of erudition, and breadth of view. The gentleness and humility of his disposition and his love of peace became proverbial. Of notable interest is his reply to a scoffing would-be proselyte who demanded to know the essence of Judaism: "What thou wouldest not that thy neighbor should do unto thee, do not unto him: this is the whole Law, the rest is only a commentary." It was in this broad spirit that Hillel and his disciples were opposed to Shammai and his school, which was distinguished by the rigidity of its interpretations and views. Hillel, whose authority as a teacher was added to his high dignity of President of the Sanhedrin, was the ancestor of a line of Jewish spiritual leaders who held sway until the fifth century. His most eminent disciple was Johanan ben Zaccai, a fine type of that admirable race of Jewish scholars who, amidst all the clash of arms and the turmoil of warring factions, silently labored in their colleges at that mighty fabric of Judaism which was to brave and withstand the storms and ravages of future ages.

§ 12. *Hellenistic Judaism*. Concurrently with the growth of Judaism in Judea and its fruitful branch in Babylonia, another development of Judaism had taken place in the wide Greek-speaking world, of which Alexandria was the Jewish center. The Jews living amidst Greek surroundings became imbued with Hellenic influences, which showed themselves not only in their Greek speech and names, but also in the intellectual and spiritual life. Although retaining a deep attachment to the Jewish motherland and an affectionate veneration for the great Sanctuary on Mount Zion, the Jews of Egypt established as a rival to it the Temple of Onias at Leontopolis, which was the only other Jewish fane in the world where sacrifices were offered up. The Hellenistic Jews lost the knowledge of the Hebrew language, so that the Sacred Writings had to be translated into the Greek vernacular—a rendering which has come down to us as the Septuagint, the Translation of the Seventy. This Greek Bible was used in the proseuche, or synagogues (both Greek words), and even the prayers in these Jewish places of worship were offered up in the tongue of Hellas. In addition to the Septuagint Bible—then a production of extraordinary kind in its magnificence and rarity, which was to exercise a far-reaching influence on the religious thought of mankind —there grew up a considerable Hellenistic literature which was intended for the instruction and edification of non-Jews as well as Jews. The Jews, thrown into the midst of an alien population with pretensions to fabulous antiquity and immense cultural achievements, endeavored to bring home to those who looked down on them the real greatness of the Jewish people and the superiority of the Jewish faith over the polytheistic religions of their neighbors.

The foremost representative of the Hellenistic Jews was Philo Judaeus, of Alexandria (born about 20 B.C.E.; died after 40 C. E.), a man of profound religious feeling and noble character. The life of Philo possesses a special interest and charm, as he was the forerunner of a type of Jew whom we must regard with particular sympathy. Of high social standing (his brother was alabarch, or chief, of the Jews of Alexandria) and imbued with the best foreign culture of the time, he was nevertheless warmly attached to the faith of Israel, and took a zealous interest in the welfare of his coreligionists. He wrote a number of works in Greek, setting out the sublimity of the teachings of Judaism, and defended it with much ability and dignity against the malicious attacks of its opponents. When serious trouble arose in Alexandria through the endeavor of the hostile populace to force the Jews to place an image of the Emperor Caligula in their synagogues, he formed part of the Jewish deputation which went to Rome to put the case before that mad ruler of the world empire. As a philosopher, Philo holds a permanent position among the notable thinkers of antiquity. Adapting his ideas on the Jewish religion to the philosophy of Plato, he introduced into Judaism a speculative element which was to exert a far-reaching influence. The allegorical method of interpretation in which Philo excelled, though not received permanently into the Jewish system, entered largely into the creation and composition of the future theology of Christianity.

§ 13. *The Rise of Christianity.* Amidst the fermentation, political and religious, which disturbed the Jewish people as it struggled under the yoke of Rome, there occurred an event which was to shake the foundations of the ancient world and to change the course of human history. The galling oppression of the stranger, and the bitter sense of helplessness under the crushing power of the Roman legions, bred in the Jews a wild despair which made them look forward more eagerly than ever to the appearance of someone with extraordinary powers, who, as the Messiah (Anointed), would, in accordance with ancient oracles, free them, and, with them, the world, from the prevailing material and moral bondage.

Among the various claimants to that office of danger and honor who arose in the last days of Jewish independence, and who were ultimately crushed as political rebels by the Roman power, was Jesus of Nazareth. In the Jewish history of his time Jesus played no prominent part. At the age of thirty, coming into contact with the Essene John the Baptist, he took up his cry that the generally expected end of the world and the subsequent "kingdom of Heaven" were at hand, and he announced that he had come to save "the lost sheep of the house of Israel." In thus turning to the forlorn outcasts of society, he added an exquisitely tender note to the spiritual harmony of man. If his message was clothed in the words and ideas of the prophets and sages of his people, his personality has shed its rays over a large portion of the human race. But the time of his appearance was out of joint, and the very following he secured proved his undoing. He fell a victim to the anarchy and turbulence which were to bring untold misery on the Jewish nation, and to the suspicious jealousy of the Roman authorities, who were glad of a pretext to do away with any popular leaders who might give rise to disturbance. Life, whether it was that of a mere thief or of a religious genius of the first order, was then held in light esteem, and crucifixion, the favorite mode of Roman capital punishment, was as much the order of the day as the guillotine during the French Revolution. Jesus was arrested and crucified with two others, and, with an allusion to the charge against Jesus and bitter mockery of the Jews in their own capital, the Roman executioners placed over his cross a board with the words: "Jesus of Nazareth, King of the Jews."

The profound impression which "the Nazarene," who in his struggles had shared the fate of all reformers in all times, had created on his disciples was infinitely increased by the bitter pangs caused by his unexpected and shameful death. After their first bewilderment, the little community that had looked upon him as their lord and as the expected deliverer of his people, discovered in the sacred writings which were their daily spiritual food that the Messiah was to suffer ignominy and death before his assured triumph. It was only this faith, this certain hope that Jesus would soon return to earth to carry his mission to an end, which distinguished the adherents of Jesus from the mass of their countrymen. But the influx of Hellenistic Jews, with speculative ideas and antinomistic tendencies, changed the course of things. Led by Saul, afterwards named Paul, of Tarsus, a man of intense emotion, high-strung temperament, and boundless energy, the Hellenists declared for the abolition of the Mosaic institutions and the consequent dissolution of Judaism. The struggle between the original apostles and disciples of Jesus, who remained zealously attached to Judaism, and the growing number of his Gentile followers (largely semi-proselytes to Judaism), who struck out a path diverging from it, ended in a victory for the latter, and, from a purely Jewish sect, the believers in Jesus the Messiah (Christ) developed into an independent world-religion, Christianity, or the religion of the Messiah. The strictly Judaic Christians were reduced to a Christian heresy, known variously as the Nazarenes or Ebionites, who, on the one hand, were spurned by their Christian co-religionists for denying the virgin birth and divinity of Jesus, while, on the other hand, their unpatriotic refusal to join the Jews in their great struggle for independence led to a deadly enmity, and then to a total separation, between the Jewish Christians and their people.

§ 14. *The Spread of Judaism.* While Judaism was, on the one side, suffering from losses occasioned by the absorption of a number of its members among their pagan neighbors, and, on the other, by the ultimate secession of the adherents of Christianity, large accessions to the ranks were taking place by numerous conversions to the faith of Israel. It is an old, and still current, misconception that Judaism is averse to the incorporation of strangers within its midst. The Jewish theological position, which does not demand a uniformity of dogmatic profession on the part of the outside world, but recognizes the spontaneous moral and religious evolution of mankind, has indeed kept Judaism from developing into a missionary creed, while the medieval legislative rigors and attendant dangers in connection with conversions to Judaism made them unpopular among the Jews themselves. But it is an entirely erroneous idea that the Jews were opposed to proselytism out of sheer tribal exclusiveness. Apart from the assimilation of the aboriginal population of Palestine and the forced conversion of the Edomites, Judaism acquired numerous adherents from among the various nations with which it came into contact from the time of the Babylonian captivity till the rise of the Christian Empire of Rome, when conversion to Judaism came to be treated as a capital crime. Towards the end of the Second Temple we find Jewish proselytes all over the Roman Empire and in neighboring Parthia. In the latter country, the royal house of Adiabene adopted the Jewish faith, and proved its zealous defendants, just as the religion of Israel found adherents even among several members of the Roman imperial family. The outside interest evinced in Judaism and its many proselytes were matters of moment which attracted the attention, and evoked the indignation, of Roman writers, while the Jewish authors of the time and the New Testament records provide ample confirmation of the vast spread of Judaism among the masses. Among the Hellenistic Jews, more in intellectual touch with their alien surroundings, there was a general desire to bring the heathen over to the truth; and, besides their propagandist writings, still extant, there were even men, like the Alexandrian Apollos, afterwards the friend of Paul, who went about proclaiming "the things of the Lord," and who "compassed sea and land" to make proselytes. Before and after Paul appeared on the scene, the question of the circumcision of male proselytes was an open one among the Rabbis, and radical Hellenists debated the advisability of abrogating the Jewish observances in order to further the spread of the spiritual elements of Judaism. It was in the widely scattered synagogues where Paul sought his Gentile, as well as Jewish, converts, and for a considerable time afterwards Judaism was the rival of Christianity in the missionary field.

§ 15. *The Shadows of the Roman War.* While the Jews were thus occupied with their spiritual problems, the days of the Judean commonwealth were drawing to a tragic close under the iron rule of Roman officials. The throes which preceded the political extinction of Judea form a sad period of Jewish history. From the governor down to the meanest legionary, the Romans treated the Jews in their own country with a haughty insolence which was particularly galling to a people so keenly conscious of its achievements. In addition to this, the representatives of Rome came to Palestine with a grasping greed which endeavored to extort from the faraway Asiatic subject-race as much treasure as possible. It is, therefore, not surprising that the Jews shrunk from the Roman census instituted for the purpose of taxation; that now and again they turned against their alien oppressors, and that the usual bloody repression of these revolts left the people more sullen than ever. On some occasions, like the placing of the Roman eagles on the Temple gates, conflagrations broke out which were quenched by torrents of blood.

A stray ray of light appeared unexpectedly by the short re-establishment of the Jewish kingdom under Agrippa I, a grandson of Herod, by Mariamne the Hasmonean. Thanks to the favor of Caligula, Agrippa was invested with the kingly dignity, and he ultimately entered into possession of the whole of Palestine (about 41 C.E.). His brief reign of three years came like a healing balsam to the suffering Jewish people. He not only secured orderly government to the harassed country, but did everything possible to soothe the troubled mind of its people. Of great service to the Jews, both in Judea and in Egypt, was his timely intervention with Caligula, who had ordered his statue to be erected and worshiped in the Temple and other Jewish sanctuaries. His success, however, aroused the displeasure of the Romans, and his suspiciously sudden death left the Jews mourning, while it was riotously celebrated by the foreign population, especially the Roman soldiery, whose brutalities were soon to find ample scope in the final Jewish struggle for independence.

After the death of Agrippa I, Judea became again a Roman province, while his son, Agrippa II, was later on invested with not only the small kingdom of Chalcis and other possessions, but also with the office of supervisor of the Temple and the accompanying right of nominating the High Priest. Agrippa II, who is regarded as the last king of the

Jews, assisted in the subjugation of Judea by the Romans, and, in the enjoyment of their favor, survived its fall for several decades.

The rupture with Rome was at last brought about by the insufferable rapacity and violence of Gesius Florus, the last procurator of Judea (64-66). This Roman governor became the omnipotent protector of bands of robbers who infested the country, and whose plunder was shared by him, and he deliberately goaded the Jews into rebellion so that he might profit thereby. He entered Jerusalem, and, in spite of the purposely peaceful demeanor of the inhabitants, massacred them without mercy. Disappointed at the unexpected want of resistance by the Jews, he called on their leaders, as a proof of their good will, to meet on their way two cohorts of troops who were marching on Jerusalem. Even this was complied with, but the Roman soldiers received the Jewish deputation with such studied contempt, that the affair ended in a general attack on the Jews. The people of Jerusalem rose in their despair, and forced Florus to evacuate the city. But Agrippa, who had all this time been away from Judea, now returned, and successfully prevailed on the insurgents to submit quietly to the inevitable dominion of Rome. So soon, however, as he proposed that the people should recognize the authority of Florus, they broke out into such uncontrollable anger that he was glad to escape from their fury. Some of the bolder spirits thereupon seized the powerful fortress of Masada, near the Dead Sea, while the warlike party in Jerusalem went to the extreme step of refusing to accept any imperial offerings to the Temple, or to have the usual sacrifices for the Emperor there. The moderate leaders, finding their authority unheeded, sent deputations to Florus and Agrippa, begging them to come to their rescue. But it was too late; the suppressed feelings of frantic vengeance excited and nurtured in the Jews, had exploded at last with a terrible violence, and carried everything along with it.

§ 16. *The War with Rome.* It would be futile to inquire whether the fateful insurrection should, or could, have been averted. In the histories of nations, as of individuals, it is success which turns the rebel into a hero, and accounts the revolt of a people against its oppressors among its most glorious events. The Maccabean rising against the powerful Syrians has received universal applause, hopeless though it must be acknowledged to have been at first sight. With the degeneration and profligacy which had generally overtaken the Romans under the emperors; with the callous ferocity and insatiable greed which then marked Roman administration of the subject-races in distant parts of the Empire, the Jews could not for ever escape the fate which had made an end to the other States under the Roman dominion. Continually outraged in their religious susceptibilities by insolent and scheming governors and their subordinates, the Jews of Palestine were also threatened by the foreign settlers there with the same humiliating condition to which the Macedonian conquerors had reduced the native Egyptians in their own country.

At the beginning of their rebellion the Jews were inflamed by the wholesale carnage to which their brethren were subjected by the Syrians and Greeks in the provinces, and they were still further encouraged and entirely committed by the disastrous defeat which they inflicted on Cestius Gallus, the prefect of Syria, who had come to Jerusalem to subdue them —a defeat such as the Romans had not suffered since the destruction of Varus' legions by the Germans. The news of this event created surprise and consternation among the Romans, and the Emperor Nero dispatched Vespasian, the greatest living Roman general, to quell the revolt in Palestine. Vespasian was joined by his son Titus, and, with the pick of the Roman army, they entered on the subjugation of the rebellious Jews with all the accustomed vigor and rigor which had awed the whole Western world into abject submission.

For four long and terrible years this little people in an obscure corner of the Empire withstood the power and skill of the conqueror of the Britons and of the most famous legions of Rome. The war was carried on, on both sides, with implacable ferocity rare in the annals of warfare—the Romans enraged at the obstinate and prolonged resistance of the erstwhile despised Jews; the Jews fighting with all the despair and heroism born in the defence of home and religion against the insolent alien tyrant. It must remain a surprise to the historian, and ought to excite the admiration of posterity, that the feeble Jews, who had dreaded the frown of a Roman procurator, now withstood unflinchingly all the might and majesty of the Roman army. The Jews had become a race of men who knew neither fear nor would hear of surrender. The valor of the rank and file responded to leaders of extraordinary daring and fertile ingenuity—men like John of Gischala, Simon bar Giora, Josephus—the last still more famous as the historian of his people, which, in the time of its direst need, he deserted, and left to its own resources.

§ 17. *The Fall of Judea.* The end, if it had not yet come, was only delayed. The Romans, if not irresistible, still advanced on the Jewish capital and laid it under siege. And to the remorseless carnage of the Romans was added the wild frenzy which had now taken hold of the Jewish people. In the words of the ancient imprecations against them—which seemed to come true with an awful literalness—"without did the sword bereave and in the chambers terror." Something of that delirious violence which in modern times took hold of Paris under the Commune, shook the inhabitants of Jerusalem to their innermost depths. The enemy was at the gates, but the besieged people within, rent in factions, were tearing each other to pieces. The city, filled with a vast population, which had been swelled by the immense number of pilgrims who had come there to celebrate the feast of Passover, underwent all the horrors of civil war while the deadly grasp of the Romans was growing tighter and tighter upon them. Assassination and massacre were general, and even the pavements of the Temple reeked with human blood; then famine made its dreaded appearance, and killed every remaining trace of pity or human feeling.

Vespasian proceeded to Rome to take over the sovereignty of the Empire, and it was left to Titus to bring about the complete subjugation of the Jews. The Jews contested every inch of their territory, of their capital, of the Temple. Their deeds of heroic valor only made the agony of death longer and more bitter. Jerusalem was at last turned into a heap of ruins, and, after a frantic resistance, on the 9th (or 10th) Ab, 70 C.E. (the ominous anniversary of the destruction of the Temple of Solomon by Nebuchadnezzar), the Second Temple became a prey to the flames, and all its magnificence and glory were turned into a mass of smoldering ashes. A cry of horror—the cry of the anguish of death of a whole people—went up to heaven when the miserable remnant saw the destroying flames encircling the noble sanctuary of the God of Israel.

Innumerable were the victims which the war had cost to the Jewish nation, still the end had not yet come. Hundreds of thousands had laid down their lives in the struggle, but the survivors, if not massacred in cold blood, were sold as slaves, sent to work in the mines, or to fight against wild beasts or as gladiators for the amusement of their exulting enemies. Vespasian and Titus celebrated their victory by a triumphal procession in Rome, which was graced by 700 specially selected captives, headed by their dauntless leaders John of Gischala and Simon bar Giora, the latter being finally put to an ignominious death.

§ 18. *The Last Struggle for Independence.* Utterly hopeless was now the outlook of the Jewish struggle for independence, and still, incredible as it may seem, in spite of the complete destruction of Jerusalem and the desolation of the whole country, the Jewish resistance to Rome was by no means over, and was yet to blaze out in a fierce, lurid flame. Several Jewish strongholds still held out, and Masada, the last of them, was only taken by the Romans after the self-inflicted immolation of its defenders. The country was administered with an iron rod, but the calm, where it was not the calm of death, was only an outward one. The land was not only declared as forfeited to the imperial treasury, but all the Jews in the Empire were now forced to pay an annual capitation tax of two drachms to the Temple of Jupiter Capitolinus, in place of the half-shekel which they had hitherto contributed to the Temple in Jerusalem. This special Jewish tax, *fiscus Judaicus,* which was at first collected with great brutality, rigorous care being taken that no one should escape paying it, produced a strong feeling of resentment amongst the Jews.

The war in Palestine had its aftermath in Egypt, the adjoining Cyrenaica, and in Cyprus, where violent collisions between the numerous Jews and their neighbors led to incredible bloodshed between the combatants. Stirred by the inextinguishable hope for the restoration of the kingdom of Israel, and driven to desperation by the contemplated establishment by Hadrian of a pagan city on the site of Jerusalem, even the Jews in Judea began again to prepare for another trial of strength with Rome, which culminated in the year 132, only six decades after the great combat which had proved so disastrous to them. The head of the revolt was Bar Coziba, called Bar Cochba, "Son of the Star" (in allusion to Num. xxiv. 17), of whose deeds of prowess little that is historical is known, but who must be adjudged a leader of extraordinary personal magnetism and a warrior of truly wondrous power and skill. The prayer ascribed to him: "We pray Thee do not give assistance to the enemy; us Thou needst not help," gives perhaps a faithful picture of the man. He was supported by the universally revered Rabbi Akiba, whose unbounded authority over his brethren made the insurrection a national one. The success of the Jews again forced Rome to send its ablest commander, Julius Severus, who came all the way from Britain to break their rebellious spirit. The Jews resisted for a period of over three years, and the war was only concluded with the fall of Bethar, the last Jewish stronghold, and the death of Bar Cochba in its defense (9th Ab—the date of the twofold destruction of Jerusalem—135). The butcheries enacted rivaled those in the war with Titus, over half a million Jews having lost their lives, and the consequences were, if possible, still more disastrous. The religion of the Jews was proscribed, and those found guilty of teaching or preaching it were submitted to the most excruciating tortures which human ingenuity and a devilish lust of blood could devise. Rabbi Akiba was flayed alive and then done to death. Under pain of death, no Jew dared to appear even in the vicinity of Jerusalem, which was now turned into a Roman colony, Aelia Capitolina, and the very name of Jerusalem was henceforth to be obliterated from the mind of man. The Jews, who had been the last of the nations under Roman dominion to fight for what, in all sincerity and with all reverence, we may call the sacred cause of freedom, were at last crushed in the dust, and lay a helpless body, bleeding from innumerable wounds.

CHAPTER III

THE TALMUDIC AGE

§ 1. *The Dispersion.* One of the most far-reaching effects of the Judeo-Roman wars, and of the consequent destruction of the Jewish national center, was the wide dispersion of that people, which has remained to this day one of its most distinguishing features. The Jews who escaped from the sword and fury of the Roman soldiery were met by violent and malevolent Syrians, Greeks, Egyptians, or Roman neighbors, who gloated over the Jewish misfortunes and kept the Jews cowed with threats of still worse results. It is, therefore, not surprising that the Jews, who by their very turbulence appear to have been a high-spirited race, proceeded far away from Palestine to localities where the Jew was a stranger, yet considered as entitled to the protection and respect due to a human being.

The Babylonian captivity had transferred the bulk of the Jews to Mesopotamia, and, in spite of the continuous remigration which took place to Palestine, the Babylonian Jews remained a very numerous community. While living in a compact mass, many of them found their way all over the Parthian and subsequent Neo-Persian empires; they spread Jewish colonies along the shores of the Black Sea, as far as the Crimea, where Jews had already followed in the wake of the Greeks, and cast out branches all over Central Asia, stretching as far as China, where a dwindling community subsisted at Kai-Fung-Foo till recent times. Yet, in however flourishing a material condition they may have been, intellectually the Babylonian Jews were for a long time of no account in Jewish life, but, on the other hand, they remained free from those dissolving influences which threatened the existence of the Jews in the Greco-Roman world, including Palestine. Politically also they were able to offer a safe asylum to their brethren escaping oppression, as well as to resist the Romans in their aggressions on the Parthian territories bordering the Euphrates.

To the Babylonians, as to the Jews of all other parts, Palestine remained the center of the Dispersion. For, in truth, the Torah went out of Zion and the word of God from Jerusalem. The tax of the half-shekel which was sent to the Temple brought in such vast wealth to its treasury that any disturbance of it by the rapacity of sacrilegious invaders affected the price of gold in the markets of the world. The Macedonian conquests and the break-up of the intellectual isolation of the Jews led to a vast and interesting development of the Jewish Dispersion. Under the friendly rule of the Egyptian Ptolemies, who were also masters of Palestine, great numbers of Jews settled in Egypt, where, to judge by the Elephantine papyri that have come to light, Jewish communities of importance had existed from the time of the Babylonian captivity, when Jeremiah and other Jews left for that country. Especially in Alexandria, where they formed an autonomous part of the population, distinguished by their opulence and culture, the Jews rivaled the Greek inhabitants, with whom in later times they repeatedly came into sanguinary collision. While the influential commercial class envied and hated the Jews as their competitors, the lower orders of Alexandria, composed of those mixed and debased elements always to be met with in great Levantine seaports, lent themselves freely to any attack on the wealthy Jews. Thus the malicious attempt to place the statue of the reigning Emperor Caligula in the synagogues, which was stoutly resisted by the Jews, was brought about by the ribaldry and turbulence of the rabble, and the weakness or connivance of the Roman prefect led to the wholesale massacre and degradation of the Jewish citizens of Alexandria. The whole procedure on that occasion had in it all the elements and sequence of events that have become familiar by the modern Russian attacks on the Jews in Odessa, who were placed in a position in certain respects similar to that occupied by their co-religionists in ancient Alexandria. Still the Jews were able to maintain their ground, as their subsequent formidable revolts tend to show. From Egypt, the Jews overflowed into the neighboring Cyrenaica, where they also formed a very populous center.

When the Judean Jews came into official contact with Rome, they had already spread into the Seleucidan territories of Syria, far away in Asia Minor, as well as into the Greek islands, especially Cyprus. In Rome itself the Jewish colony, which arose through the commercial relations with Alexandria and the Maccabean embassy to that city, was largely reinforced by the Jewish captives brought by Pompey from Palestine, and the subsequent troubles helped to fill the place with many more Jewish slaves. The treaty of friendship with Rome, by which it lent its powerful protection to the Jews to the extent of its wide influence, gave a further stimulus to the migration of the Jews, while the unfortunate wars, which made the Jewish slave a glut in the market, distributed them all over the Empire, far away in Greece, Italy, Gaul, and Spain. The broad-minded policy adopted towards the scattered Jewish communities by most of the Emperors, particularly by Julius Caesar, whose friendliness to that people rendered his memory a grateful one among them, was also an effective aid to their dispersion.

§ 2. *The Rally.* The fall of Jerusalem had left the Jews stunned under a catastrophe such as they may have only dreaded, but had been afraid to contemplate. The spirit of the Jews was broken, and they were now even incapable of expressing their unutterable grief in elegies such as com-

memorated the destruction of their capital by Nebuchadnezzar or the bloody persecutions which were still in store for
them a thousand years after. Had the Jews only been a nation like others, they would, like the powerful Carthaginians,
have become extinguished with the end of their State; had
they been a religious community bound to some local sanctuary and with no universal outlook, like that of the kindred
Samaritans, they would have been exterminated, or have
perished for want of a living spirit. But Judaism represented
both a nation with a remarkable past and with a still more
soaring vision of the future, as well as a religion which, in-
contestably the purest and highest of antiquity, embraced
within its range the whole of mankind, and even in its practical workings showed itself adaptable to every clime and
civilization. It may be questioned whether, to attain its goal,
Judaism had done better to divest itself of its nationalistic
embodiments and to have identified itself with the tendencies
assumed by nascent Christianity; but, had this been done,
the Jews would have shared the inglorious fate of the
equally gifted, and much more numerous, powerful and influential Greek people; they would have been overwhelmed
by the flowing tide of Christianity, and, having lost their
heroic consciousness or abdicated their religious mission,
would have ceased to possess any special message, or to make
any additional contribution, to the spiritual and social life
of mankind. Again, if there was any purpose in preserving
intact the ethical Monotheism of the Jews, as distinguished
from Trinitarian and anthropomorphic conceptions of the
Deity, and their social ideal of a kingdom of this world hallowed by justice and righteousness, as opposed to a kingdom
of which heaven is the center of gravity, then Judaism was
fortunate in having at hand men, who, at the most critical
time, had the clear foresight and the determined energy to
save Judaism from the wreckage which threatened to bury it.

Among those who re-established Judaism under the new

conditions, Rabban Johanan ben Zaccai has earned grateful distinction. It was he who, amidst the violence and confusion attending the fall of the Jewish State, recognized that, of all the vast issues involved, the greatest was the preservation of Judaism. Invested with the authority of recognized succession to Hillel, he transferred the nerve-center of Judaism from Jerusalem to Jamnia (Jabneh). He had been in Jerusalem during the siege by Vespasian and, finding that his moderate counsels were of no avail, he escaped the doom of the city by being carried out of it in a coffin on the shoulders of devoted disciples. He appeared before Vespasian, and obtained permission to transfer his activity to Jamnia, which, after the fall of Jerusalem, became the seat of a great Rabbinical academy and of the reconstructed Sanhedrin. Thus the authority of the supreme religious and legislative councils was not only preserved, but the study and development of the Torah (comprising under this comprehensive designation the written canonical Scriptures and their oral interpretations and amplifications) received a fresh impetus. For 150 years after the fall of Jerusalem, a series of men of light and learning, the Tannaim (Teachers), continued their activity as doctors of the Law and as the highest recognized authorities on Jewish life and thought.

Pre-eminent among the Tannaim was Rabbi Akiba ben Joseph, the patriot who suffered martyrdom in connection with the Bar Cochba insurrection (135). Rabbi Akiba finally settled the canon of the Jewish sacred Scriptures, rejecting various books now included in the collection of writings known as the Apocrypha. In order to supersede the faulty and misleading Septuagint translation of the Bible, which was used against the Jews by Christian controversialists, another, more faithful, Greek rendering (now lost with the exception of some fragments) was carried out under his supervision by Aquila, a proselyte to Judaism. Of more enduring service to the orderly progress of Judaism was his systematization of the legalistic aspect of Judaism as developed by continuous tradition. In spite of the profound significance he attached to the letter of Law, he was remarkably free from the shackles of stereotyped interpretation or of a slavish adherence to prejudice, as is shown, for example, in his friendly attitude towards the hated Samaritans. The Mosaic injunction to love the fellow-man as oneself, he declared to be the basic principle of the Torah. Although he was instrumental in introducing the study of the Torah as an all-sufficing object for the exercise of the Jewish mind, he explored the realms of philosophy and mysticism, but, unlike some of his contemporaries, "he entered in peace and went out in peace."

Another factor of great and beneficial influence in the consolidation of the Jewish people was the rise of a new dignity, the holders of which for several centuries figured as the religious heads of the Jewish community. It was Gamaliel II, a descendant of Hillel and grandson of Rabban Gamaliel (mentioned in the New Testament), who succeeded Rabban Johanan ben Zaccai as President of the College, or Sanhedrin, at Jamnia, and who assumed the title of Nasi (prince or patriarch). This office, which remained hereditary in the family of Gamaliel and was officially recognized by the Roman government, was invested with various privileges, and formed not only an effective bond between the scattered Jews, but also raised their standing as a body in the eyes of others. After several changes of residence, the patriarchs, together with their college, settled in Tiberias, on the Lake of Genesareth, where their pontifical court rose to a certain state of splendor. They kept in touch with the faithful by means of legates, who visited the outlying communities, and thereby wielded a unifying authority over the whole Dispersion.

§ 3. *Judaism in Babylonia.* Parallel with the march of events in Palestine after the fall of the Jewish commonwealth, the numerous and compact body of Jews under the rule of Parthia developed certain institutions of their own which were to make Babylonia the home and center of Jewish life and thought. The Jews became united under the authority of a Prince of the Captivity (Resh Galuta), who was also recognized by the Parthian kings as head of their Jewish subjects. The Princes of the Captivity, who claimed descent from the royal house of David, were at first more concerned with administrative functions, and in matters of religion, especially in the fixing of the calendar, had to content themselves to receive the directions of the authorities in the motherland. But the unsettled condition of things in Palestine, particularly the religious persecutions connected with the Bar Cochba insurrection, brought to Babylonia many scholars who gave an impetus to Jewish learning in the populous colony across the Euphrates. In 219 c.e. the return from Palestine of the Babylonian Abba Arica, named Rab (the Master), to his native country, inaugurated for Babylonian Judaism a new era, the effects of which were felt for many centuries to come. Rab, whose utterances and achievements stamp him as a teacher and personality of exceptional power, brought the Babylonians to the front rank of Jewish culture, and the great academies of Nehardea, Sura, Pumbedita, and Mahuza, which gradually superseded the Palestinian colleges, became centers of attraction to vast numbers from all parts willing to acquire or to impart knowledge. With the intellectual advancement of the Babylonian Jews, the office of the Prince of the Captivity also received an added lustre. On the one hand, he was invested with important powers, which gave him the rank and style of a minor sovereign; on the other hand, the Jewish patriarch in Tiberias was harassed and limited in his authority by unfriendly rulers, until the dignity was entirely abolished in the year 415, and the spiritual supremacy wielded from Palestine passed over to Babylonia.

§ 4. *The Talmud.* The accumulated results of the debates, pronouncements, and decisions of the schools in Palestine and Babylonia were ultimately deposited in the Talmud— one of the gigantic monuments of the human intellect. About the year 200 C.E. the Palestinian Rabbi Judah the Patriarch (also called the Holy, on account of the purity of his life, or simply Rabbi) collected and edited the existing materials which had hitherto been handed down in a *viva voce* manner. This compendium, called the Mishnah, comprised in six parts an exposition of Jewish law and custom in all their ramifications, and became the authoritative course-book in the studies of the schools. The compilation of the Mishnah as the code of Jewish private and public life in addition to the Torah of Moses, its foundation, was an event of almost the first order. The Tannaim (the Teachers) of the Mishnah were now succeeded by the Amoraim (the Interpreters) of the academies which flourished simultaneously in Palestine and Babylonia. The discussions and controversies which the dicta and decisions of the Mishnah aroused, the emendations and amplifications which were brought about in the course of time, the questions, answers, and diverging opinions, sublime allegories and profound parables, weighty utterances of eternal import mixed with casual and ephemeral observations, ritualistic minutiae of great length with bold words on things divine, fierce flashes of hatred (too often, alas, justifiable) alongside of the most exalted human sympathies, the folklore together with the wisdom of ages—all these were incorporated in the Gemara, which, together with the Mishnah as its kernel, formed the Talmud. As the Gemara was elaborated more or less independently in the Palestinian and Babylonian colleges, there was formed a "Jerusalem" and "Babylonian" Talmud, but the decay of the colleges in the Holy Land and the greater prestige acquired by the Babylonian schools gained for the Babylonian Talmud a more practical and universal acceptance.

The Talmud, which represents a record of the intellectual and religious life of the Jews for a period of almost a thousand years (from the Babylonian captivity till 500 C.E.), has been so closely identified with the future development of the Jewish people that it has shared their checkered fortunes in all their various manifestations. Internally, the Talmud has formed the battleground of the Jewish mind, and, with all orthodox Jews, its authority as the ultimate court of appeal in matters affecting religious practice is never contested. Whether in the most flourishing periods of Jewish thought, or when all the avenues of learning were closed to the Jews, the Talmud retained its supreme place as a subject of close and unremitting study and research, which in the Jewish theological field it has practically remained to this day. But the closer the connection between Jewish life and the Talmud; the more it proved itself an impenetrable rampart against all the forces of dissolution—the greater became the hatred which it inspired in the Jews' enemies, especially among those who by their religious professions were prevented from attacking the Jewish Bible, the Old Testament. All manner of charges have thus been leveled at the Jews through the Talmud, and apparently substantiated by stray texts torn from their context or by utterances due to the passions and circumstances of the moment. The Talmud, however, deserves this concentrated venom very much less than the excessive reverence as the repository of all wisdom which has long been paid to it in ultra-traditional Jewish quarters. If to the Jew the Talmud is still, next to the Bible, the most important production of the Jewish mind, the non-Jew can only judge it fairly if he approaches it with the understanding which is born of sympathy. The Talmud suffers very greatly by the rugged style of its language, and the loose and unsystematic manner in which it has been collected and edited. The deepest parables (meshalim)—a favorite mode of Jewish teaching that is best known from that semi-Jewish production, the New Testament—are related in a few abrupt sentences, and words of wondrous beauty or of profound moral significance are interspersed between scholastic triflings or naïve tales with which masters and pupils would enliven their discussion on some academic subject. The fact, however, that the Talmud is not a compilation purely religious, but, basing itself on the Pentateuchal legislation, also represents the necessarily extensive code of the civil and criminal law, the *corpus juris* of the Jewish commonwealth —a code which is even still to a certain extent, especially in eastern countries, in active use in Jewish communities of today—must be borne in mind in any consideration of that monumental production.

Two mighty currents flow through the Talmud—the one emanating rather from the brain, the other from the heart— the one prose, the other poetry. The former is styled Halachah (i.e. rule, norm), the other Haggadah (i.e. legend, saga). The Halachah comprises the huge corpus of Rabbinic dialectic, clustering round all questions of law and ritual coming within the purview of Judaism whether as life or as creed. It represents typical ancient Jewish jurisprudence. The Haggadah deals with the lighter side of things and consists of exegesis, allegory, proverb, legend, as well as folklore in its widest sense. The Halachah represents the logical faculties of the Jew at their keenest, his powers of argumentation and investigation. The Haggadah shows forth the Jewish power of soaring aloft on the wings of fancy and imagination, the Jewish genius for painting in language, tender and sublime, all the thousand and one emotions that play upon the human soul. The Halachah, by reason of its difficulty, could appeal only to teachers and professional scholars. The Haggadah, by reason of its winning simplicity, found easy access to all, and has remained to this day a perennial storehouse of edification and delight.

More than 500 years of the closest mental concentration

on the part of the best spirits of the nation went to the making of the Talmud. Once completed, its study became the be-all and the end-all of the Jew's ambition throughout the succeeding ages. In days of direst persecution the Jew could always draw a solace divine, a strength unspeakable from poring over its pages. More still, it kept the intellect of the Jew alive, when many a time the torture, prolonged from age to age, would have sufficed to stupefy and deaden all his higher faculties. No weapon forged against the Jew could prosper so long as he could regale his soul on the spiritual delights of the Talmud. In fine, the Talmud is, alongside of the Bible, the living monument of the characteristic culture of the Jew. More than this, it is the perpetual key to the understanding of Judaism.

§ 5. *Under the Cross.* It was well that the Jews had been setting their religious house in order, for they were about to be subjected to a siege which, in its length and unremitting rigor, stands unique in history. It began with the Christianization of the Roman Empire under Constantine. The Jewish people had naturally chafed under the humiliation which they experienced by the conquest of their land, whose territory, soaked with Jewish blood and hallowed by so many glorious and sad memories, was now parceled out among heathen and Christian settlers, while the imposition of the *fiscus Judaicus* since the destruction of the Temple served further to remind the Jews of the loss of their independence. But, as a whole, they enjoyed under the rule of pagan Rome liberty of conscience and even certain privileges, in so far as their communities were officially recognized and their religious peculiarities taken into cognizance. With the rise of Christianity as the dominant political power, there began, however, a systematic attempt—elaborated by the clergy and enforced by the power of the State—to weaken Judaism by all manner of repressive enactments, and to degrade it into the unholy cult of a cursed people. It is one of the strangest ironies of history that the Christian Church, whose origin is due to Jews, whose spiritual inspiration and highest moral lessons are derived from the lives of Jews, should have been the most implacable foe of the Jewish people and of its religious individuality.

The fortunes of the Jews have not only been very largely influenced by the persecutions and oppressions to which they have been subjected, but these incidents also fill out a large proportion of the canvas of Jewish history. It would, however, not serve the purpose here in view to chronicle at length the recurring attempts to break the spirit of the Jew or to capture his soul. It may be laid down as a rule that those peoples which had not yet been entirely subjected to ecclesiastical control were well disposed towards the peaceful and useful Jews, and it is indicative of their original relations that it used subsequently to be found necessary to forbid the Jews to admit proselytes and to threaten with the penalty of death those who intermarried with their Gentile neighbors. The Church Councils, particularly, devised means to reduce the Jew socially to the state of a pariah and morally to that of a leper. Not only were means taken by the authorities of the Church to prevent any social intercourse between Jews and Christians (one of the first historical references to Jews in England is a characteristic order of Egbert, Archbishop of York [740], forbidding Christians to attend at Jewish feasts), but they spurred the occasionally reluctant, and always more judicial, authority of the secular State into such legislation and administration which took from the Jews the rights of citizenship and even an honorable livelihood. This growing darkness, intensified by the increasingly severe anti-Jewish edicts of succeeding Roman and Byzantine Emperors, was only once lit up by a flash of lightning when Julian, called the Apostate, had ascended the throne. In his desire to subvert the power of Christianity, and to establish a philosophical paganism in its stead, he entered into friendly rela-

tions with the Jews. He abolished the *fiscus Judaicus* and
destroyed the registers in connection with the tax. Perhaps
to win the support of the influential Jews in Parthia, with
which he entered into war, he even issued an order authoriz-
ing the Jews to rebuild the Temple in Jerusalem. This work
was indeed begun, but was interrupted by explosions in the
vast subterranean excavations, and the untimely death of
Julian put an end for ever to any such attempt.

§ 6. *Under Neo-Persian Dominion.* It was fortunate for
the Jews that, free from the power of Rome, either pagan
or Christian, they were able to develop more or less undisturbed in their great settlement in Babylonia. Even when
the rule of the Parthians was superseded by that of the neo-
Persian dynasty of the Sassanids (226 C.E.), the Jews continued to enjoy under their Prince of the Captivity a certain
dignity and security which were absent in their relations with
their Roman conquerors or dominant Christian antagonists.
In the repeated contests between the Byzantine Empire and
the Persians, the Jews, as a border population, played an important part, especially as they could be relied upon to resist
stoutly the yoke of the hated Romans. In the war of King
Chosroes against the Byzantine Emperor Heraclius, when
Syria and Palestine fell into the hands of the successful
Persians, the latter were everywhere welcomed and assisted
by the Jews, who entered Jerusalem with the conquerors and
wreaked vengeance on the inhabitants of this Christianized
city (614). But the Jews were not to enjoy their triumph
long. Fourteen years afterwards, the Persians were deprived
of their conquests, and the Jews were again forbidden to
appear even in the vicinity of their former capital.

Of more lasting consequence was the intellectual activity
of which the Babylonian Jews could boast. Although on the
irruption of the neo-Persians, who brought with them a fanatical zeal for their Zoroastrian, or Fire-worshiping, religion, the Jews suffered at times grievously under the creed

of their new masters, the Rabbinical colleges continued to flourish. It was Rab Ashi, a most famous head of the college of Sura, who, at the beginning of the fifth century, set about to collect the traditions and teachings of the Babylonian academies, and his great work, resulting in the Babylonian Talmud, was continued under his successors and concluded by Rabina II (died 499). With Rabina ended the long line of Amoraim (who, by the Gemara, completed the work of their predecessors, the Tannaim, the sages of the Mishnah), and they were succeeded by the Saboraim, who put the finishing touches to the Babylonian Talmud. It was high time for the Jewish intellectual treasures to have been brought under safe custody, for the Babylonian Jews in the middle of the fifth century experienced severe religious persecutions, in the course of which a Prince of the Captivity was publicly hanged (470). Fifty years after, an attempt by another Prince, Mar Zutra II, to throw off the yoke of Persia, ended with his crucifixion. Nevertheless, the Babylonian Jews maintained considerable intellectual vigor and political importance even under the Arab conquerors of Persia (642), and were yet to give another impetus to the development of the Jewish mind.

§ 7. *Under the Crescent.* While the various Christian Churches were engaged in mutual warfare, there arose on their borders an enemy who swept away some of the most important and extensive tracts of Christendom. Mohammedanism, the greatest opponent by which Christianity has ever been faced, also owes its existence to Judaism. At the time of the appearance of Mohammed, at the beginning of the seventh century, there was a large Jewish population in various parts of Arabia, including the neighborhood of Medina, where a number of independent and powerful Jewish tribes had long ago established themselves. Mohammed, who had come into contact with Judaism and Christianity both in Arabia and in his travels in Syria, was evidently more attracted by the older monotheistic faith. His list of true prophets whom he honored as his predecessors were all Jews; his monotheism was Jewish, in direct opposition to the Trinitarian conception of Christianity, and he only claimed to have restored the religion of Abraham, the father of all the faithful, while many of the ideas and doctrines of Islam, and various institutions and practices he established, were directly borrowed from the Jews. He at first even intended to make Jerusalem the sacred center of the new religion, and Jerusalem is still known among the Moslem as Al Kuds, the Holy. If the irritating opposition he encountered from the Arabian Jews, whose co-operation he was anxious to receive, led Mohammed to attack them until they were driven out from the Peninsula, yet the extraordinary spread of his faith from the Caucasus to the Pyrenees found everywhere Jews anxious to escape from the unbearable yoke of the Christian, and willing not only to submit to any tolerably indulgent master but also to help him in every possible way.

Hence there grew up a certain sympathy between the oldest and the youngest monotheistic religion, so similar in many of their beliefs and observances, and this reacted most favorably on the development of Judaism. The Jews, touched by the *élan* and vivifying spirit which had taken hold of Islam in the first centuries of its growth, underwent a process of rejuvenation in all aspects of life and thought.

§ 8. *In Western Europe.* While the East formed the center of the activities and troubles of the Jews, there grew up in the far west of Europe those communities which were to eclipse the achievements and sufferings of their brethren under Byzantine and Persian rule. The Jews had settled in Rome in the times of the Maccabees, and, by immigration and conversion, new colonies gradually developed in the important centers in Italy, Greece, Gaul, Germany, Spain. On account of their proselytism, the Jews in Rome were not looked upon favorably, and the first religious persecution in the West ensued on that account under Tiberius. Later on,

however, during the invasion of the barbarians in the outlying European portions of the Empire where Jews were
to be found, they enjoyed such protection as their Roman
citizenship (which they had received under the Emperor
Caracalla [212]) and their inoffensiveness and adaptable
usefulness could give them. The Jews, largely as a migratory
element and not belonging to the dominant Christian religion, suffered less than the native population from the fury
of the barbarians, as they swept over the country devastating
everything that came in their way. But the situation of the
Jews changed materially with the spread of Christianity
among the rude invaders. In the Western Roman Empire a
law of Theodosius II (439) deprived the Jews entirely of
the rights they had possessed, and reduced them to the state
of an oppressed and inferior order. The emphatic confirma-
tions and amplifications which this received at the hands of
the Church Councils and influential Christian ecclesiastics
became a fatal legacy which the barbarians inherited with
the civilization and religion of imperial Rome, and proved
the origin of the endless woe which was to overtake the Jews
of Europe for about fifteen long and dreary centuries.

The early history of the Jews in western Europe under
Christian rule is outlined by the discussions and resolutions
of the Church Councils which dictated the policy of the secular Christian rulers. It is noteworthy that the Arians, who
were not swayed by the Catholic Church Councils, treated the
Jews with considerable liberality, perhaps on account of the
monotheistic bonds between both sides. The Arian Theo-
doric, the Gothic king of Italy, proved a powerful protector
of the Jews, and took energetic measures against the highest
Christian authorities, lay and clerical, who had wantonly attacked the Jews in Rome, Milan, and Genoa. The Jews repaid
him by the heroic resistance they offered in the defence of
Naples against the Byzantine general Belisarius (536). The
Jews likewise fared well under the barbarian Franks, even

some time after their adoption of Christianity, but this was changed by the violence of Kings Childebert and Chilperic, and the zeal of the bishops in their eagerness to advance the cause of Christ among the obdurate Jews. The Jews found, however, in Pope Gregory the Great a pontiff who had a higher conception of the dignity and reasonableness of Christianity, and, although most anxious to bring about their conversion, his authority was exercised in favor of the existing, though meager, rights of the Jews. It was in Spain, where Jewish communities were already established at the time of Paul, that they experienced most severely the rigors of Christian legislation. The Visigothic kings of Spain and the Spanish Church Councils seemed, in their frantic efforts for the conversion of the Jews, to have been continually possessed of violent paroxysms which expressed themselves in the most vigorous measures against the Jews, whether baptized or unbaptized. The converted Jews were justly suspected of being false to their enforced Christian professions, and the severest punishments, among which death became a common penalty, were meted out to those discovered to be maintaining in the slightest way their Jewish connections or sympathies. It is characteristic of the manner in which these conversions were being effected and supervised that a number of Jews who had turned Christian begged at least not to be forced to eat pork. The Jews, thus ruthlessly hunted about, encouraged and hailed with joy the invasion of the Moslem conquerors (711), who, on their arrival, found in the Jews valuable allies, into whose hands they placed the captured cities as they proceeded to further conquests. In Germany the condition of the Jews was subjected to the same evolution: while the Jews were at first living in amity with their barbarian neighbors, the increasing influence of the Church was exerted to shut them out from intercourse with the faithful.

A time very favorable to the Jews was the rule of the Carlovingians. Charlemagne employed Jewish merchants in his service, and one of them, named Isaac, was sent by him with an embassy to the caliph Harun al-Rashid (797); he is even said to have interested himself in the intellectual advancement of his Jewish subjects. This enlightened policy was pursued also by Charlemagne's successor, Louis le Débonnaire. The Jews rose to great influence under this monarch, whose confidential adviser was his Jewish physician Zedekiah. From the diatribes directed against them by Agobard, Archbishop of Lyons, it would appear that the Jews had attained a position of importance which might well have aroused the jealousy of a medieval churchman. In his own diocese, the Jews occupied the best quarter of the city of Lyons, just as one of the two mayors of Narbonne was always a Jew. It was not only their wealth, profitable to the king as well as to themselves, which gave them this social standing, but the bishop complained that even the Synagogue fared better than the Church, inasmuch as many Christians went to hear the Jewish preachers, who evidently must have delivered their discourses in the French language. That Agobard's writings and strenuous personal efforts had no immediate effect is in itself an indication of the strength of the Jewish position at the time. But the Jews had good cause to remember the warning of their psalmist not to trust in princes, who are, after all, only sons of men. With other kings and changing times, the dignitaries of the Church had their way at last. The crusades in the eleventh century brought out to the full the artificially stimulated fanaticism of the populace against the first infidels on their way, which was traced by a trail of Jewish blood.

§ 9. *Social and Economic Conditions.* The Babylonian Jews under Parthian and Persian rule, and then under the dominion of the caliphs, lived under normal conditions which permitted them to carry on the occupations of a well-ordered community. The self-governing powers of the Prince of the Captivity, who, in effect, was one of the vassal rulers of the country and maintained a court and retinue of some magnificence, gave him and his Jewish subjects a dignified political standing, while the intellectual activity of the Jews must have raised them far above the level of their neighbors. In Arabia, up to the rise of Islam, the Jews had lived as independent tribes, with the free, martial, and marauding spirit of the other sons of the desert, from whom they were only distinguished by a superiority due to their religious traditions. It was not so under Byzantine and Roman rule, with their spreading influences on the lives and mental outlook of the barbarians. The exclusion of the Jews from the army and the offices of State placed them in a position of civil exclusiveness and inferiority, while the Church branded them as the people rejected by God for the crucifixion of the Savior of mankind. The Jews, torn out by the roots from their ancestral soil, and in other parts of the Empire subjected to the turbulence and fanaticism of people and priests, became unsettled in their mode of life. Wars and insurrections had played havoc with the economic condition of the Jews, and the sale of enormously large numbers of Jewish slaves, who were mostly ransomed by their happier co-religionists, filled the Empire with a Jewish proletariat which was obliged to seek its livelihood in the meanest occupations, among which soothsaying and other charlatanic devices to gull the ever-credulous populace seem to have been of a favorite and lucrative kind. Yet we find the Jews owning and tilling the land in all parts and in considerable numbers. The Church Council of Elvira, Spain (303), found it advisable to prohibit the blessing of the soil by Jews, lest the Christian prayers should prove unavailing. More reasonably, the Church Councils later on continually interfered with the sale of Christian slaves to Jews, and endeavored that no Christian should come under a Jewish master and that Jews should not proselytize among their Christian, or even pagan, slaves. The vast upheavals which were brought about by the invasion of the barbarians, led to wholesale massacres, and, as a more merciful and more profitable measure, to the sale of large parts of the population as slaves. In this traffic the mobile Jews began to take a leading share, and we find them spread far and wide, from England and Bohemia to Persia and north Africa, in order to dispose of the victims of barbarian warfare. In general, however, the Jews occupied themselves with industry and trade; and barter, developed into commerce, became a very important factor and civilizing influence amidst a population which was either attached to the soil as serfs or sought glory and profit in the bloody pursuit of arms. In their commercial undertakings, the Jews were favored by their comparatively high intellectual standard, and by the world-wide connections and community of sentiment and interests which made all Jews members of one family. When Mohammedanism took possession of the East, the Jews acted as the only possible intermediaries between Moslem and Christian lands, and this commercial activity had assumed by the tenth century most extraordinary proportions. All over inhabited Europe, southwestern Asia, and northern Africa, Jewish merchants dealt with the needs and luxuries of civilization. Jewish captains navigated Jewish mercantile vessels which sailed on the waves of the Mediterranean. In the same way, the cosmopolitan Jews became the chief money-changers of the time.

The crusades, however, altered this state of things. By coming into personal touch with the East, the Christians entered into competition with the Jews, and by subsequent legislation were able to restrict the enterprise of their Jewish rivals. The trade guilds, which then began to be formed under ecclesiastical auspices, and from which Jews were naturally excluded, gave the Christian merchant ample scope and security to oust the Jewish competitor. Still it seemed as if the life of the Jews in Christian Europe, made intolerable by religious legislation and persecution, was not to be made entirely impossible by all the avenues to the means of livelihood being closed against them. For, by a strange misinterpretation of the New Testament injunction, "Lend, never despairing" (Luke vi. 35), the Church stringently forbade the lending of money on interest. As such a measure would have paralyzed the ordinary course of life, not to speak of trade and enterprise, and as, furthermore, the salvation of the unbelieving Jews was in any case not considered in the pious enactments intended to protect Christian souls, the Jews received the very valuable, but two-edged, monopoly of money-lending. With this, however, the Jews entered into the darkest misery which awaited them in the Dark Ages, when only a fervent attachment to their faith and an unquenchable hope for happier times saved them from total extinction.

CHAPTER IV

THE GOLDEN AGE OF JUDAISM

§ 1. *The Geonim*. The invasion of Persia by the Arabs, which brought the Jews there under new and more tolerant masters, seems to have been assisted by Bostonai, a Prince of the Captivity, on whom, among other distinctions, the Arab conqueror bestowed as wife a daughter of the Persian King Chosroes II. The dignity of Prince of the Captivity was thus continued, while the principals of the colleges of Sura and Pumbedita rose to new fame under the title of Geonim (singular, Gaon [Illustrious]). Already before the conquest, the Babylonian Talmud had been settled, and had become a subject of devoted and widespread study. The colleges had been repeatedly closed and reopened in the troublous times that marked the end of Persian rule, but the creation of the caliphate with its wide dominion and influence, and the proximity of the Babylonian Jews to the center of the Mohammedan Empire, preserved for the Princes of the Exile and, even more so, for the Geonim, the hegemony so long enjoyed by the Babylonians among the Jews of the Dispersion, who recognized those dignitaries as the highest authorities in Judaism and supported the colleges by liberal contributions. The adoption of the kindred Arabic language as the vernacular of the Jews under Moslem rule, served as a still further bond between the communities which extended and multiplied with the ever widening expansion of Islam in Asia, north Africa, and the Iberian Peninsula.

If the Prince of the Captivity possessed the social distinction of being the recognized chief of his people, among whom he enjoyed the still greater prestige of a scion of the royal house of David, the Geonim were invested with the judicial functions which formerly belonged to the President of the Sanhedrin and with a spiritual authority which was universally acknowledged. From France to India, the Geonim were consulted on questions of religion and law—two cognate subjects—and twice a year, in the months of Adar and Elul (about March and September), there was held a conference, called Kallah, where scholars from all parts discussed a certain specified treatise of the Talmud, as well as the specific points which awaited consideration and decision. But these outward glories of the Jewish people were also to fall victims to the ravages of time. Owing to internal neglect and decay, and the growing fanaticism of the Mohammedans, the Gaonate (which had continued its functions for 450 years), as well as the dignity of Prince of the Captivity (which had existed for about 700 years), expired together in the person of Hezekiah, of Pumbedita, in the year 1040. Towards the end there had appeared one of the most famous of the Geonim, Sherira, to whom we owe our knowledge of Jewish history from the close of the Talmud to his own day, as well as Hai, an independent thinker, but they were far outshone by Saadia (born in Egypt 892, died at Sura 942), truly one of the lights of the exile. Saadia rendered lasting service to Judaism by the creation of a philosophical and scientific basis for the Talmudical conception of the religion. Saadia was the first to present it systematically in accordance with the highest culture of the time. His Arabic translation of the Bible was a work of epoch-making importance to his coreligionists, who thereby also became sharers of the rich and fruitful Mohammedan civilization. A work of much value, and even greater interest, was his *Faith and Dogmas* (*Emunoth Vedeoth*), which for the first time set out the principles and ideas of Talmudical Judaism from a philosophical point of view. Endowed with a penetrating mind and deep religious feeling, a vast capacity for work and a comprehensive grasp of the subjects dealt with by him, Saadia Gaon touched and adorned all aspects of Jewish thought, and laid the seed for its future vitality and development.

§ 2. *Karaism.* The political and intellectual upheavals which ensued on the Moslem conquests, and in which the Babylonian Jews participated either actively or passively, led, among other things, to a certain unsettlement of the mind among them. The traditions embodied in the Talmud which had hitherto held undisputed sway, were now, seriously or frivolously, called into question. The Jews of Arabia, who had been expelled from the Peninsula by the Moslem onslaught and had settled in Syria and Babylonia, were groups almost ignorant of Rabbinical tradition, and, as free sons of the desert, perhaps little amenable to the bookish discipline of the Talmudists. But while such isolated sets of opinion as had been formed could make little headway against the venerable authority of the Geonim and the Princes of the Exile, an effective opposition was offered by one high in scholarly and social standing, and endowed with the necessary energy to unite the diverse anti-traditionist elements.

Such a man was Anan ben David (died about 800). He was the legitimate successor to the office of Prince of the Captivity, which had become vacant in 762, but, whether it was on account of expressed heretical opinions or because of his character, the Jewish authorities passed him over in favor of his younger brother. Anan did not allow this without a determined struggle. He was indeed thrown into prison and was to have been executed by the government, but he succeeded in escaping, and organized a systematic attack on the Gaonate, and on the Talmudical form of Judaism of which it was the highest representative. Discarding the traditions of the Rabbis and their schools, he went back to the original sources of the Bible and formulated his own interpretations and amplifications of the ritualistic and legal laws of the Torah of Moses. It cannot, however, be said that Anan succeeded in his task better than the Talmudists, and personal hatred of them seems to have proved a bad counselor. Nor can Anan be credited with having been either a bold reformer or an original thinker. He kept his eyes close to the Talmudical laws with the object of evading or superseding them by regulations of his own. He thus produced a laborious code which lacked the orderly evolution and the critical deliberation and experience of numerous generations. Hence, instead of lightening the burden of Talmudical legislation or unraveling its complexities, he added to it or made it more involved. With precipitation and without the test of practical consideration, Anan enforced many interpretations of Jewish law which were either so extravagant or so untenable that his immediate followers abolished or changed them without scruple. In certain instances, however, such as his view that the prohibition to kindle a fire on the Sabbath (Exodus xxxv. 3) obliged the Israelite to sit in total darkness during Friday night and to have no warm food during the Sabbath day (which Anan seems to have regarded somewhat like a day of penance, when one was hardly to be allowed to leave the house if situated among Gentiles), Anan's regulations remained valid for all time. If in subsequent ages Christian theologians hailed the followers of Anan as the Protestants of Judaism, the analogy can only be brought out in so far that Anan might be considered as a rebel against the authority of the Talmud, though he was only a reformer of mediocre mind who threw off the historic traditions and the canon law of the Synagogue in order to reconstruct them in accordance with his personal notions.

We must, however, give due credit to the early followers of Anan, who came to be called Karaites (from karah, to read [the written Bible]), that, like all dissenters, they disturbed the intellectual lethargy which had taken possession of the Jews after the close of the Talmud—in the compilation of which they had, so to speak, exhausted themselves—and they also led them back to the invigorating and inspiring study of the Bible, which had become neglected in the absorbing devotion to tradition. The Karaites, who seceded from the so-called Rabbanites, or Talmudical Jews, produced later on a number of men who gave a scientific basis to the tenets of the sect and to its opposition to their Rabbinical brethren. The latter were, however, fortunate in the possession of the Gaon Saadia, who so far overshadowed their Karaite antagonists that they have since then been moving as in a magic circle around the arguments he adduced against them. The progress which Karaism made all over the East, from Constantinople to Spain, was arrested after a few centuries, and thereby afforded a remarkable testimony to the vitality inherent in traditional Judaism. The sense of initiative which had brought the Karaites into being, their early boldness and originality of conception, such as it was, waned with the advance of time. Karaism shrank into a petrified sect, whose adherents, to the number of about 12,000, are now mostly to be found in the Crimea, while several small communities in Lithuania and Galicia, in Turkey and Egypt, still continue their obscure existence.

§ 3. *The Chazars.* The Jewish forces in Babylonia had been fatally weakened by the decay and final extinction of the venerable and universally revered dignities of the Prince of the Captivity and the Gaonate; the Karaites had created the first and only irreparable schism in the body of Israel; the once tolerant and enlightened caliphs had begun to persecute the unbelieving Jews and Christians with equal impartiality; even the Byzantine Emperor Leo the Isaurian, being accused of "execrable" Judaizing tendencies on account of his iconoclastic activities, cleared himself of all suspicion by subjecting the Jews to cruel persecution—yet these were only the labors preceding the birth of one of the greatest and most fruitful epochs of Jewish history. From widely different quarters, at the shores of the Euxine and the Gates of Hercules, on the banks of the Volga and of the Guadalquivir, Judaism received unexpected accessions of strength, while on the Rhine also the old Jewish tree blossomed out with renewed splendor.

If Judaism was hard pressed by Roman, Persian, or Aram, many of its members spread beyond their influence. The international relations of Jewish commerce brought a number of Jews as far as India, and, in the middle of the eighth century, Joseph Rabban obtained a charter from the King of Cochin granting autonomous rights to a Jewish settlement there which has survived to the present day. Of greater consequence was the migration of Jews along the trade routes of the Black Sea and the Volga. In this region lived the Chazars, a people of Tartar race, whose chagan, Bulan, together with his nobles, adopted the Jewish religion (about 740). From the scanty records that have been preserved of this Jewish kingdom of the Chazars, which subsisted for a period of about 250 years, it appears that it had its capital, Atel, near the present Astrakhan, on the Volga, while the Chazarian territory stretched all over the south of Russia. The incursions of the Chazars were so dreaded by the Persians that they built a great wall across the Caucasus to keep them away, while imperial Byzantium had to buy off their hostility by ill-disguised payments, and the Russian dukes of Kiev were forced to recognize the authority of the Jewish chagans of the Chazars by a fixed tribute. The country of the Jewish Chazars was governed in a spirit of exceptional tolerance, so that, for instance, the supreme court of justice was composed of two Jews, two Christians, two Mohammedans, and one pagan to represent the Russians and Bulgars. The chagan Obadiah, the successor of Bulan, invited a number of Jewish teachers into his country, to instruct the people in the tenets of Judaism, and it was only the difficulties of distance and travel which kept this Jewish

State from the general knowledge of the Jews. It was through ambassadors from Byzantium that Hasdai ibn Shaprut, a Jewish statesman at the court of Cordova in the middle of the tenth century, became acquainted with the fact of their existence, and it is to an extant correspondence he initiated with the chagan Joseph that we are indebted for our information regarding the Jewish Chazars. They maintained their power until the year 969, when Sviatoslav, Duke of Kiev, conquered the capital and territory of the Chazars. Many of them withdrew to the Crimea, which also became known as Chazaria, but their political power had gone, and they were lost in the mass of Jews and Karaites who had settled there and in southeastern Europe generally.

§ 4. *The Spanish Epoch.* It is a pregnant indication of the vitality of the Jewish people that, at repeated periods in history, after adverse circumstances seemed to have entirely overwhelmed it, it rose superior to all obstacles, and played again an important part in the affairs of the world. A thousand years after the dissolution of the Jewish national existence, when the Roman world-empire with its mighty Emperors had already become mere faint memories; when Judaism had given birth to a world-conquering religion, the head of which had usurped the throne of the Caesars; when Christianity itself had been expelled from its most ancient and fairest possessions, and the dioceses of Chrysostom, Cyril, and Augustine were peopled and ruled by the circumcised followers of Mohammed, Judaism renewed its youth and led the highest culture of the age. There cannot indeed be any greater tribute to the Jewish mind than the fact that, though very few in numbers, oppressed and despised, they should have surpassed in intellectual eminence all the young and vigorous nations of Europe, who were then occupying with the din of their arms the attention of the world.

The magnificent epoch of Hispano-Jewish history signalized over a thousand years ago the definite entry of the Jews and Judaism into European civilization—not as it was then, but as it was to become in later days. In the darkest period of that civilization the Jews rose to view as the brightest star. If we take into account that, with the exception of a few short glimpses of liberty and honor, the Jews were subjected to massacre, exile, misery, and degradation, their achievements in all fields of human thought can only be regarded with the same admiration as that which we are wont to accord to the people who gave the Bible to the world. W. E. H. Lecky well set out these considerations when, referring to the trials and triumphs of the Jews, he said:

The heroism of the defenders of every other creed fades into insignificance before this martyr people, who, for thirteen centuries, confronted all the evils that the fiercest fanaticism could devise, and the infliction of the most hideous sufferings, rather than abandon their faith. . . . But above all this the genius of that wonderful people rose supreme. While those around them were groveling in the darkness of besotted ignorance; while juggling miracles and lying relics were the themes on which almost all Europe was expatiating; while the intellect of Christendom, enthralled by countless superstitions, had sunk into a deadly torpor, in which all love of inquiry and all search for truth were abandoned, the Jews were still pursuing the path of knowledge, amassing learning and stimulating progress with the same unflinching constancy that they manifested in their faith. They were the most skillful physicians, the ablest financiers, and among the most profound philosophers; while they were only second to the Moors in the cultivation of natural science. They were also the chief interpreters to western Europe of Arabian learning.—. *History of Rationalism,* i, p. 282.

§ 5. *Hispano-Jewish Culture.* The first incident in the course of events which was to lead to the transfer of the center of Judaism from Babylonia to Spain was the arrival in Cordova of a captive, Moses ben Enoch, who had been ransomed by his brethren-in-faith. Moses ben Enoch had set out with three other legates from Sura in order to collect contributions for the college there, but they were all captured by pirates and sold into various quarters of the world, where they became the heads of new Jewish centers of learning. One of them, Shemariah ben Elhanan, settled in Cairo; another, Hushiel, at Kairuan, in Africa; the third, Nathan bar Isaac Hacohen, at Narbonne, and Moses ben Enoch at Cordova. On his release, Moses ben Enoch paid a visit to the local school, and, in his beggarly garb, took a humble place near the door, listening to the exposition of the Talmud by the principal, Rabbi Nathan. Moses ben Enoch, moved by the prevailing ignorance, made an interjection which drew general attention to him, and his explanations so gained the admiration of the assembly that Nathan, with unusual generosity, immediately withdrew from his position in favor of the liberated slave, who was elected by the Jews of Cordova as their spiritual head. The revival of Talmudic studies and Hebrew letters at Cordova was, however, largely due to the influence and munificence of Hasdai ibn Shaprut (910-70), who was invested with various high duties relating to diplomacy, trade, and finance at the court of the liberal-minded caliph Abdul Rahman I. It was Hasdai ibn Shaprut who, in his intercourse with the Byzantine ambassadors to Cordova, had learnt of the existence of the Jewish Chazars, but he evinced even greater interest in the growth and welfare of Judaism at home.

The first distinctions gained by the Spanish Jews were in the fields of Hebrew grammar and poetry, by two protégés of ibn Shaprut, Menahem ben Saruk and Dunash ibn Labrat. Menahem ben Saruk was a pathfinder in Hebrew grammar, in which, however, he was soon excelled by the more scientific Judah Hayuj, and subsequently entirely superseded by Jonah ibn Janah, one of the greatest masters of Hebrew philology (died 1050). Dunash ibn Labrat was the first of a long and glorious line of Hispano-Jewish poets. He developed and beautified the rhythm and meter of neo-Hebrew poetry, which, in imitation of the Arabic muse, had already sprung up in Babylonia, where Eleazar ben Kalir, whose stilted compositions are to be found in the Jewish liturgy for some of the holydays, became the foremost representative of the Payetanim, or liturgical poets.

The break-up of the Spanish caliphate (1013) also involved the Jews of Cordova, who were unfortunate in having espoused the losing side, and were, therefore, expelled from the city. A fugitive from Cordova was Samuel ibn Nagdela (993-1055), who rose to be the vizier of the King of Granada, and was entrusted with the diplomatic affairs of State. Samuel ibn Nagdela, named by the Jews Samuel Hanaghid (the Chief), was not only a generous and discriminating patron of Jewish learning, but himself a scholar and poet of distinction, being both the spiritual and secular head of the community. His son Joseph ibn Nagdela, who succeeded him in his dignities, was, however, not able to maintain himself against the envy and machinations of his enemies, and, on his fall and violent death, the Jews of Granada were given over to wholesale massacre and expulsion. A large number of them went to Saragossa, where Abu al-Fadhl ibn Hasdai was vizier, an office of danger as well as of dignity which a number of Jews occupied in those days at the various Mohammedan courts in Spain. The internecine rivalries and struggles of the Moorish kings and parties brought many ups and downs to the Jews, so that, in spite of all culture and prosperity, they were often forced to flee from one part of the Peninsula to another. Hence, the Jews also came under the rule of Christian rulers in Spain, a number of whom, impressed with the importance of winning over to their side such an influential part of the population as the Jews, sought to do so by tolerant treatment and equitable laws. The Christian kings likewise employed Jews in the financial and diplomatic services, and Alfonso VI, who greatly favored them, had 40,000 Jews in his army. It was on their account that the battle of Zallaca was, by a mutual truce, held over until after the Sabbath. The Jews seem indeed to have taken prominent parts in the wars between the various Iberian States, Christian and Mohammedan, and, as in the case of Judah ibn Ezra, the major-domo of Alfonso VII, Jews were sometimes entrusted with the charge and command of fortified places.

Of universal import are the Jewish philosophers in Spain and those who traced their descent from that country. They include stars of striking brilliance in the philosophical firmament, and their influence on medieval thought was of the highest. It is the peculiar distinction of these Jewish philosophers that, while they were profoundly imbued with the Hebraic spirit, they were at the same time men of remarkably rationalistic thought and bold inquiry, and some of them were poets of the foremost rank. Hebrew poetry, which had been dormant since the times of the Maccabees, to which we owe a number of the most stirring psalms, immortalized with even greater luxuriance, if not with equally sublime simplicity, the happy days and inspired moments which Jews experienced under the sunny skies of Spain. Among the greatest of philosophers and poets who graced that epoch were Solomon ibn Gabirol and Judah Halevi.

Solomon ibn Gabirol (1021-58), who was early in life bereft of his parents and also had to mourn his patron, Jekuthiel ibn Hassan, the Jewish vizier of the King of Saragossa, was of a melancholy disposition, which pervaded his rich and varied poetry. Most of all, ibn Gabirol's renown rests on his philosophical distinction, as the first who introduced Greco-Arabic philosophy into medieval Christian circles. His acquaintance with the Greek and Arabic philosophers he brought into an organized system in his work. *The Fountain of Life* (*Fons Vitae*). This, in a Latin translation from the Arabic and free from any specific theological bias, became later on one of the important sources of Christian scholasticism, which looked upon ibn Gabirol as a Christian philosopher. His best-known poem, *The Crown of Kingdom* (*Kether Malchuth*), which has been incorporated in the liturgy for the eve of the Day of Atonement, is a masterpiece of majestic religious thought and elevated praise of God's glory. Excelling him in depth of emotion and in beauty of expression was Judah Halevi (born about 1086, died about 1140), the greatest Jewish poet since the days when the living source of Hebrew song was dried up by misfortune and neglect. As in those far-away days of old, Zion once more inspired the Jewish muse and raised it to the most exalted heights of divine ecstasy. Judah Halevi possessed the magic wand which made the lyrical waters flow again, and his songs of Zion, depicting the past glory, the unutterable sadness of the present, and the yearnings for the joys of Israel's future, have remained among the most enduring of the spiritual treasures of his people. Like his poetry, his philosophy too was imbued with a passionate love for the people of Israel, which he termed "the heart of mankind." With a lofty spirituality, he set out his conception of the Jewish faith in a work entitled *Hakuzari,* in which he weaves round the story of the conversion to Judaism of Bulan, the king of the Chazars, a philosophical apology of Judaism against the claims of opposing religions. True to his philosophy and his poetry, he turned his steps towards Zion, and, leaving home, family, and friends, he entered on a pilgrimage through Egypt to the Holy City, and died after having, according to legend, reached the goal of his lifelong yearnings.

A philosophical writer, whose warm religious feeling and lucidity of style have placed him among the most popular of Jewish thinkers, was Bahya ibn Pakuda, and his *Duties of the Heart* (*Hoboth Haleba-both*) has maintained its foremost position in the post-biblical devotional literature of the Jews.

A subject of engrossing thought and occupation to the medieval Jew was the interpretation of the Sacred Scriptures, and in this direction also the Spanish Jews took the most prominent part. Some of their biblical commentators were independent, rationalist critics of Holy Writ, when the original text and its criticism were practically unknown to the Christian ecclesiastics of Europe. Abraham ibn Ezra (1092-1167) still retains to the present day a place of honor among expositors of the Bible. Remarkable as an exegetist, he was an adept in grammar, mathematics, astronomy, and astrology (which occupied with alchemy such a large portion of the time of the wise men in the Middle Ages) ; a traveler who, in the twelfth century, knew his way all over the world, from Bagdad to London. If less known to fame, his relative and contemporary, Moses ibn Ezra, was a thinker and poet of many parts and high distinction. Among the travelers of the age was Benjamin of Tudela, an account of whose extensive journeys over Europe, Asia, and Africa has been preserved in his interesting and valuable *Itinerary,* a repeatedly re-edited and re-published book of travel. Of great importance as commentators were the Kimhi family in Spain and Provence, especially David Kimhi (1160-1235), whose *Michlol,* containing a Hebrew grammar and biblical dictionary, and commentaries on the Bible, exerted a far-reaching influence on Christians and Jews alike.

§ 6. *Moses Maimonides.* Whatever distinction must be ascribed to all these poets, philosophers, physicians, astronomers, grammarians, and exegetists, they were excelled and entirely overshadowed by one of the giants of the Jewish people, whose appearance in the twelfth century marks the culminating point of medieval Judaism.

Moses Maimonides (ben Maimon) was born in Cordova in 1135, of a father who was himself a notable scholar. When he was thirteen years of age, Cordova was captured by the fanatical Almohades, who forced all the Jews and

Christians there to adopt Islam. The family of Moses escaped, and, after aimlessly wandering about for some time, went to Fez, where the prevailing persecution forced them outwardly to conform to Mohammedanism, and then, after a short stay in Palestine (1165), they settled permanently at Cairo (Fostat), in Egypt. A physician by profession, Moses Maimonides became famous in the art of medicine; he regularly attended to the court of the renowned Sultan Saladin, and refused a similar position under King Richard the Lion-hearted of England, when he was on his crusading expedition at Ascalon. But in spite of his engrossing occupation, in which he rose to high achievement both as practitioner and author, Moses Maimonides' unlimited energy and capacity overstepped the boundaries of time and the knowledge of his age. A disciple of Aristotle, Maimonides became a master of his philosophy. He wrote on mathematics and astronomy, but, unlike his contemporaries, he declared astrology unworthy of attention. All this was, however, subsidiary to his unrivaled importance as the central figure of Talmudical Judaism. Maimonides, by his monumental work *Mishneh Torah* (also called *Yad Hahazakah, The Strong Hand*), brought the whole unwieldy mass of traditional Jewish law into systematic order, and his statements and views, given with the confidence and authority of a master, became the accepted standard of his own and subsequent generations.

This exhaustive code of Jewish practice was followed by *The Guide of the Perplexed (Moreh Nebuchim)*, a work on the philosophy of Judaism. Lacking the firm and unquestioned basis of the Biblical and Talmudical sources, and conceived in a spirit of bold, if reverent, philosophical inquiry, the *Guide* gave rise afterwards to very bitter disputes among the Jews, so violent that his name was execrated by his opponents, and gave opportunity for the lamentable intervention of the none too friendly Christian authorities. *The*

Guide of the Perplexed was, however, a work which, by its profundity of thought, enlightened spirit, and masterly treatment of the highest spiritual problems, gained the admiration of the best minds of the author's time. Soon afterwards, parts of the *Guide* were translated into Latin, and utilized by the great Christian scholastics, while it was to prove a source of creative thought for the Jews in future ages.

Maimonides may be regarded as first among the rationalists, yet while Jewish thought seemed up to his time without any recognized limits to speculation so long as the Torah and its institutions were respected, it was Maimonides who not only in his *Guide* laid down the lines and limitations of Jewish religious philosophy, but introduced a hitherto unknown definitely dogmatic conception of Judaism, and elaborated thirteen fundamental principles of the Jewish faith which have since remained the accepted basis of traditional, or orthodox, Judaism. There is perhaps nothing which gives so true an indication of the moral strength and spiritual unity of Judaism as the fact that while the Church, with all the pomp and power at its command, could not enforce the solemn decisions of its Councils and recognized ecclesiastical heads, the dogmatic authority of the simple and humble thinker Moses Maimonides was accepted unquestioningly in all the dispersions of Israel.

Maimonides, by his personality, transferred the center of Judaism to Egypt, where he was recognized as the Naghid (Chief) of the Jewish community. He was consulted by Jews from all parts, and his extant replies give an insight into the generous tolerance and nobility of soul of this great son of Talmudical Judaism. He was not only friendly to the Karaites, and took a lenient view of those who, like himself at one time, had been forced to hide under a strange faith, but he also repudiated the narrow view that Mohammedanism should be looked upon as an idolatry on account of the veneration paid to the Kaaba, and regarded Christianity and

Mohammedanism as world-religions with providential purposes in history. Yet a correspondence with a proselyte to Judaism shows that to him it was the faith whose truth ennobles all who place themselves under its allegiance. His death in the year 1204, at the age of seventy, closes a brilliant epoch in Jewish history, and (in allusion to Deut. xxxiv. 10) it was well said of him that "from Moses till Moses (Maimonides) there did not arise one like unto Moses (Maimonides)."

§ 7. *The Franco-German Schools.* A counterpart to the Spanish scholars, though small in comparison, is to be found in the learned men of France and Germany. An impetus to Jewish learning in the south of France which benefited by its proximity to Spain, was given by the arrival in Narbonne of Nathan bar Isaac, one of the four Babylonian legates who had been taken captive on their way. His disciple Judah ben Meir, or Leontin, took up his master's mantle, but it was reserved for Rabbenu (our Master) Gershom ben Judah to establish Talmudical studies in France and Germany on broad and sure foundations. The Franco-German scholars did not attain to the polish and versatility, as well as the philosophical breadth of view, which distinguished their Spanish brethren; but, if the Northerners lacked the touch of genius, they at least possessed in an abundant measure moral earnestness and deep piety. Rabbenu Gershom, who was looked upon by his contemporaries in France, Germany, and Italy as the "light of the captivity," was born in France in 960, and established a school at Mayence, which became for many generations an important center for Talmudical studies. Rabbenu Gershom's activity remained remarkable in Jewish history by his edict forbidding polygamous marriages, and it is astounding that the mere word of a man with no recognized official authority should have been enough to turn this wholesome decree into a law for European Jewry.

The fame of Rabbenu Gershom was even eclipsed by

Solomon bar Isaac, of Troyes, in the province of Champagne (1040-1105), who, under the name of Rashi,[1] became one of the most popular post-biblical writers. This reputation he fully deserved by his commentaries on the Bible and the Talmud, particularly on the Bible, which became the *vade mecum* of Jews of all degrees of learning or ignorance, and helped very much to give them an intelligent meaning of the words of Holy Writ. To the Christian world, too, Rashi became an authority on the interpretation of the Old Testament, especially in bringing out the literal, and not the merely fanciful or allegorical, sense. Luther's translation was largely based on Rashi's exegesis, conveyed to him through Rashi's countryman Nicolas de Lyra, so that it was said: *"Si Lyra non lyrasset, Luther non saltasset."* Rashi, who united a saintly character to vast learning and lucidity of teaching, became the guide to the students of the Talmud in Europe, and his influence, continued by his learned grandsons and sons-in-law, made the Talmud an engrossing object of research among the Jews who were then spreading over the northern parts of the Continent. The most prominent of Rashi's successors was Rabbenu Jacob Tam (1100-71), his youngest grandson, a keen and enlightened mind. Rabbenu Tam was the founder of the Tosaphists, i.e. those who *added* to the Talmud notes and decisions arising out of the studies of the Franco-German schools. Under his spiritual guidance was initiated the institution of Rabbinical conferences to decide on matters of moment which then threatened the very existence of the Jews.

[1] According to a peculiar and favorite Jewish method of naming celebrities by a combination of their initials, e.g. Rabbi Solomon bar Isaac as RaShI, or Rabbi Moses ben Maimon [Maimonides] as RaMBaM.

CHAPTER V

THE DARK AGES

§ 1. *The General State.* Judaism had now produced its ripest fruits in Babylonia and Spain, and the seeds of Jewish learning had even been transplanted into northern Europe. The gloom that had enshrouded the Jews by the growth of the Christian Roman Empire had been pierced by the light which shone on them with the appearance of Mohammedanism as a world power. Under the beneficent sway of Islam when it represented the highest forms of the then existing civilization, the Jews in the Iberian Peninsula had risen to great prosperity, and their intellectual achievements were for centuries to come to grow even in the uncongenial soil of Christian Spain. In Christendom the Jews had, forsooth, enough to suffer from mighty and petty tyrants, from councils and priests of a propagandist Church, intolerant of all opposition within and without. Yet, though treated as obnoxious strangers and unbelievers, at least the Jews in the Carlovingian Empire, and even in England and Christian Spain, found some justice an occasional favor as a useful mercantile class in a state of society in which religion and arms were the only tolerable occupations. If trade was considered less honorable, it was, on the whole, more profitable than either of those professions. Regarded by the rulers as a very valuable source of revenue, even as an indispensable adjunct of the population, and competing with none of them, the Jews not only enjoyed the protection of the authorities, but also largely the passive good will of their neighbors.

But the clouds had been gathering, and the Jews were

overwhelmed by the storm that burst over them. The enlightened caliphs in Bagdad and Cordova were succeeded by oriental despots and wild Moorish chiefs, whose fanaticism swept away the marks of Jewish liberty and dignity. The Prince of the Captivity became a mere memory, and Spain, where the sons of the last occupant of that high office had found an asylum, also soon ceased to be a safe refuge for the harassed Jews. In the decayed Byzantine Empire, now but a shriveled shadow of its former glory, the Jews were torn up root and branch, and the Jewish kingdom of the Chazars had ceased to exist. Meanwhile, at the end of the eleventh century, the crusades finally introduced among the Jews in western Christendom that era of darkness which was to envelop them for over seven centuries, and which was only to be lit up now and again by the indomitable vigor of the Jewish intellect and by the heroic resistance of Jewish faith.

§ 2. *Sufferings and Trials.* It was particularly the crusades which changed the condition of the Jews for the worse in many directions. The wholesale massacre of the Jews, which accompanied the crusades, broke their economic prosperity. The new relations which were now opened up between East and West deprived the Jews of the most reputable and useful part of their business, and drew them entirely into moneylending and petty trading. The outrages against the Jews hung since then like a pall over them, and darkened their friendly intercourse with the outside world; the base and baseless accusations which were leveled against the Jews to condone the violence perpetrated, remained fixed in the ignorant minds of the populace, and proved afterwards inexhaustible causes for murder, plunder, and all manner of persecution. Malice, stupidity, honest bigotry, and zealous piety combined to make the life of the Jew intolerable. It became a current idea that Jews used the blood of Christians, especially of defenceless Christian children, for ritual purposes during the feast of Passover (a charge similar to that leveled against the primitive Christians by their pagan enemies) ; on the occasion of an epidemic, there was a ready belief that the Jews had poisoned the wells; there was a shuddering tradition that the unbelieving Jews insulted and pierced the host as a revenge on Christ. These and other extravagances of a credulous people sent them into frantic outbursts against the Jews, which ended in tragedies the mere recital of which stirs the depths of our emotion. The persecution of the Jews in the Middle Ages presents the saddest tale of human cruelty and suffering, but it would not serve any useful purpose to set out here in detail the long, dreary record of sickening brutalities, the recurring massacres and expulsions, the numerous and elaborate regulations which were intended to degrade and dishonor the Jews, the fanatical determination to brand them as outcasts condemned by God and man.

It is not only that faith was superstitious, that manners were harsh and men cruel in those dark medieval days. It was just this state of things which aggravated the already precarious situation of the Jews. If heretics were hunted down mercilessly, many could escape unnoticed the general proscription; if the Christian serf was treated with less kindness than the beast, he could at least appeal to the self-interest and pity of his superiors. What could the Jew expect, the Jew shut off by religious and racial, by natural and artificial barriers, from the general population? Driven to live in special quarters, which served perhaps as much for his protection as for his abasement, surrounded by oppressive and restrictive proscriptions, which hampered all his movements, the Lateran Church Council in 1215 promulgated its solemn decision that a Jew should wear a distinctive badge on his dress, and Christian authorities set seriously to work to determine the size and shape of the rag which was to be the compulsory mark of Cain on the body of every Jew. Thus degraded, cast out of the pale of humanity by the highest authority on earth, reduced to the most hateful and the meanest callings, the Jews became the butt of the rabble, high and low. Whether it was the spirit of fierce animosity or of coarse ribaldry, such as was known only to the Middle Ages, the life of a Jew was a constant, hopeless martyrdom.

The economic state of the Jews was in every way conducive to the moral degradation to which they were subjected. The exclusion from the soil and every honorable profession or handicraft drove the Jews to money-lending—indeed, a most useful, and even indispensable, function in commercial intercourse, yet one which under abnormal conditions lends itself to extortion and exercises a pernicious effect on both parties to the transaction. The matter became infinitely worse when the Jew was only used by emperor and king, baron and bishop, to draw the substance out of the people, so that it might be more conveniently appropriated by their common lord, for the Jew was only suffered to exist because he was one of the most important sources of revenue to the ruler to whose mercy and caprice he owed his precarious protection. The Jews thereby became the property of their "protectors," who sold, pawned, or bequeathed them at their pleasure. In a moment of generosity, the Emperor would reward some prince or town with the privilege of harboring Jews or would mark his gracious pleasure towards his faithful lieges by canceling their indebtedness to the Jews. It was the appeal for protection, especially during the atrocities of the crusades, which largely brought about this servitude of the Jews. The prince who had protected the Jews from violence, and allowed them further to stay on his land, profited by his clemency, and converted "his" grateful Jews into bondsmen. Attacks on the Jews were thus advantageous from all points, except the Jewish. The German Emperors themselves utilized the fiction that, as successors of the Emperors of Rome, they were the lords of their Jewish captives, and that the Jews were, therefore, the serfs of the imperial chamber. No wonder, that when the Jews found at times their condition so unbearable that they attempted to emigrate, they were stopped on the way. The shortest method of securing all the accumulated wealth of the Jews was to expel them and confiscate their possessions; sometimes, as in the case of Philip Augustus of France, the expulsion of the Jews was soon followed by their readmission.

All this had evil consequences on the character of the Jews who had to submit to this life of wretched misery. Massacre and pillage were not everyday affairs, but in a way worse than these was the degradation which the Jews suffered from the cradle to the grave. The Jew could no longer strike a blow for independence, or even manhood. He had no means to defend himself against overwhelming odds, and he, therefore, sought refuge and security in contempt and obscurity, in calculated cringing and abject submission. It had been made impossible for him to inspire respect, and he gave up the attempt. Only tolerated on account of his wealth, which meant, therefore, life and happiness to him, he had to amass it as well as he could. Surrounded by envious and greedy eyes, he dared not make generous use of his belongings. (As late as the year 1601 the whole estate of Mordecai Meisel, of Prague, the most philanthropic as well as the richest Jew of his time, was, without rhyme or reason, confiscated by order of the Emperor Rudolph II, and the heirs were tortured to reveal any hidden treasure.) The Jewish house of study and prayer, regarded by the outsider as the synagogue of Satan, was situated in some inaccessible spot of the Jewish quarter, away from the ribald gaze of the populace, and out of reach of the hand of fanaticism. Being confined to intimate intercourse amongst themselves, their garb distinguished by a hideous badge, they assumed an air of neglect, and their very speech turned into a mere jargon.

§ 3. *The Forces of Resistance.* The inevitable consequences of this systematic degradation of the Jews were, however, very largely mitigated by the very remarkable Jewish scheme of life. So far from feeling degraded, the medieval Jews certainly considered themselves superior to their surroundings. They were in conscious possession of a faith which excluded all miracle-mongering, relic and image worship, and most other forms of active superstition; they represented a moral standard which eschewed the bloodshed and inhuman cruelties that tainted their neighbors; they upheld a pure and affectionate family life which won over the unwilling admiration of their enemies; they formed a voluntary brotherhood which knew of no serf or slave; they represented a culture of acknowledged grandeur which reached back a thousand years before their adversaries were heard of; in an age when many of the highest dignitaries, and even princes, could hardly write their names, the Jews employed a system of universal education; at a time when faith was raised into the highest principle, they produced their keenest thinkers. Added to all these considerations, religious emotion of the purest and most exalted type quickened the self-consciousness of the Jews, steeled their patient endurance, and stirred them into heroic resolves, such as, in their intensity and duration, stand unparalleled in the experience of mankind.

Thus, to the medal of the dull, drab wretchedness that surrounded Jewish life, there was an obverse, which was hardly observed by the outside world. If, in spite of all degradation, the Jews maintained an intellectual superiority over their more favored neighbors; if, after all their vicissitudes, they showed themselves on their emancipation ready and anxious to enjoy the rights so long withheld from them, and if they were able so soon to divest themselves of the servitude of immemorial ages, we must ascribe this miracle to the inner life of the Jews, to the religious and social institutions of Judaism. The strength of resistance and cohesion was furnished by the high idealism, which, in spite of all outward sordidness, necessarily pervaded the thoughts of the Jew who suffered for his faith; by the wondrously mapped-out life of healthy physical habits, intellectual exercise, and family affection. The Jew was a sober, industrious, and sexually moral man in his daily affairs. In times of epidemic it was remarked, and it was a dangerous accusation, that Jews suffered least. The regulations of personal cleanliness enjoined by the Jewish religion, the extreme care devoted to the selection and preparation of food, were more than enough to overcome the disadvantages presented by the naturally cramped and pestilent conditions prevailing in the Jews' quarters. What if cleanliness, by being invested with the sanctity of religious ordinances, had thereby become to the Jew a part of godliness? In the Middle Ages, when cleanliness was a rare virtue even among the upper classes, the Jewish laws of purification must have exerted an enormous influence on well-being. The bath may indeed have been taken and the person adorned in honor of the divinely instituted Sabbath; the hands washed preparatory to the meal as a religious injunction; the flesh-meat scrupulously investigated by the force of ritual ordinances; spring cleaning of a most conscientious kind disguised under the obligatory preparations for the feast of unleavened bread (Passover); yet the blessings of health, and of the light and air that the ghetto (Jews' quarter) would admit, were all the same vouchsafed to the Jew, when all other circumstances combined to reduce the standard of life to the lowest level.

Of even greater value and consequence than the care bestowed on the body was the cultivation of the mind. In the darkest ignorance of the Dark Ages, study was regarded by the Jews as a religious duty second to none. If this study was at the worst periods restricted to Jewish sacred lore, it maintained and hallowed intellectual pursuits from which not even the meanest Jew was considered exempt. To the Jew of the Middle Ages, the highest ambition and ideal was —not to be rich, but to be counted among the learned in the community. Ignorance was a disgrace, for it was only the scholar who commanded true respect. So much was study part of the ordinary day's work that the function of a Rabbi was an unpaid honor, and the Jew's meeting house, the synagogue, was termed the school (the shool [from the German *Schule*], as English Jews call it). This attitude reached back to the early Talmudic age (as in eastern lands it still continues partly to the present day), when every Jew was also exhorted to earn his living in such a way as not to turn his obligatory knowledge of the Torah into "a spade to dig with." When the medieval Jews were thrown back upon themselves, this devotion to scholarship was intensified, and made the Jews a nation of literati. The sharpening of the mind by the dialectics and arguments in which the Talmud, the chief object of Jewish study, abounds, produced a zest for knowledge, that quick capacity which the Jews were able to show when, after many centuries of stunted growth, they were afforded some fair measure of opportunity.

Last, but not least, the medieval Jews were distinguished by a wide and generous benevolence by which no son of the Covenant was considered an outcast. There was no circumstance in life which was not provided for by an all-embracing charity. Great care was taken to render this charity (euphemistically termed *zedakah,* righteousness) free from the taint of humiliation, and even the Jewish beggar, especially if he presumed on some learning, assumed a demeanor which made it clear to the donor that his was the privilege to give what may justly be demanded of him. Everywhere the fugitive Jew found a welcome at the table of a somewhat more favorably situated co-religionist, a welcome not as a poor stranger, but as a guest (*oreah*) ; the Jew sold as a slave could rely on being ransomed by his brethren-in-faith. Like every good deed, personal service to the community was considered a divine commandment (*mitzvah*), whereby benevolence assumed that touch of tender solicitude which could only be due to the experience of the uncertain and fitful fortunes of a medieval Jew.

The social conditions which shut the Jews out from familiar intercourse with their neighbors made the Jews only at home amongst themselves, and their common interests formed a bond of union which their adversaries neither rightly understood nor justly forgave. Debarred from public activity, the Jew concentrated his attention on his own circle. The family became an object of intense devotion, and home life the center of all-absorbing thought. The Sabbath and the holydays, in which riotous living was unknown, did as much for the fostering of the ties of family and kinship as of religion. Loyalty to the community was invested with a sanctity which made apostasy an unexpiable sacrilege. The false and slanderous accusations against their former co-religionists, to which many Jewish converts to the dominant faith lent themselves, made them particularly odious to those who, in spite of all, had remained true to the House of Israel.

§ 4. *The Crusades.* The crusades called forth the first systematic onslaught on the Jews in Central Europe. Not that Jewish blood had not already been shed there without anger or provocation. The first persecution of the Jews in Germany had occurred at the beginning of the eleventh century, when, probably owing to the conversion to Judaism of a priest, Wecelinus, the Emperor Henry II expelled the Jews from Mayence and other places, and many Jews, including a son of Rabbenu Gershom, were forced to turn Christian. Large sums of money stayed the persecution, and the new converts were even allowed to return to Judaism. This outbreak against the Jews was, however, as nothing compared to the terrible visitation that overtook them in the upheaval caused by the crusades. While the advance guard of the crusaders had passed, leaving the Jews more or less undisturbed, there gathered in northern France a vast undisciplined host of about 200,000 crusading marauders who spread terror wherever they made their dreaded appearance. Preceded by a goose and a goat, which they expected to lead them to Jerusalem, their aimless fanaticism was fired by the suggestion that here at hand were infidels like the far-away Saracens, to wit, Jews who had killed Christ, and that it would be an eminently Christian act to convert or exterminate them. Rapacity spurred the wild zeal, and the crusaders threw themselves on the Jewish communities on their route; all over the districts bordering on the Rhine and the Danube, death was the fate of the unconverted Jews who fell into the hands of the crusaders, and utter ruin of those who escaped. Twelve thousand Jews in the Rhenish cities are reckoned to have thus given their lives for their faith. In Worms 800 Jewish bodies were buried after the crusaders had done their work; over 1,300 were done to death at Mayence. Very few accepted Christianity even for appearance' sake, while a large number, especially women and girls, took their own lives and those near and dear to them. The crusaders continued their bloody work all along their way as far as Hungary, but the miserable fate that overtook them there was regarded by Christian and Jew alike as a just visitation of God. The spirit in which even the best of the crusaders carried out their holy task may be judged by the fact that when they at last entered Jerusalem, under Godfrey de Bouillon, they drove all the Jews there into a synagogue and burnt them alive (1099). It must, however, be added that the calamities which had overtaken the Jews were largely due to the rabble, and, with few exceptions, were not countenanced by the bishops, some of whom even protected them with energy and kindness. The German Emperor, Henry IV, who had been away in Italy, was full of indignation at the dark deeds that had been perpetrated in his absence, and he even allowed the Jews who had been forcibly converted to Christianity to return to their ancestral faith.

In the second crusade (1146), the bull issued by Pope

Eugenius III, according to which all those in debt to the Jews were absolved from paying interest on joining the crusade, was a bad incentive given by the head of the Church to those who had a score to pay off against the Jews. It is small wonder, then, that the idea of taking away the possessions of the Jews found favor even with the authorities, and was countenanced by Louis VII of France. In Germany, the Jews along the Rhine were threatened with the fate that had befallen them during the first crusade, and it required the energetic intervention and all the authority of the saintly Bernard of Clairvaux to avert the entire annihilation of the Jewish population. The Emperor Conrad III also took the part of the Jews, both from sheer humanity and to avoid the devastations which resulted from the anti-Jewish outbreaks. The Jews obtained the privilege to settle in a number of towns where they were able to defend themselves. But even the best protection they were able to secure for love or money did not save them entirely from massacre and pillage or enforced baptism. A number of Jews had taken refuge in the palace of the Archbishop of Mayence, who was also the chancellor and prime minister of the Emperor, but they were murdered by the mob in his very presence. We find that even Rabbenu Tam, the most renowned Jew in Europe, was set upon by the rabble, and, having been dragged into a field and nearly done to death, only escaped martyrdom by the timely intervention of a friendly knight, who saved him on the promise of receiving a horse as reward. This incident is typical of what a Jew could expect in those dark days.

With the third crusade, which was promoted by Pope Innocent III, who had declared the Jews as doomed to perpetual servitude for having killed Christ, their degradation by official authority of the Church reached the culminating point (1215).

§ 5. *In Medieval England.* The very precarious position which the Jews held everywhere is exemplified by the history of the Jews in England. Already in Saxon times there were, no doubt, Jewish merchants and slave-dealers in England, but they came over permanently in larger numbers with William the Conqueror (1070), and settled in London (in Old Jewry, off Cheapside), Oxford (where Moses Hall and Jacob Hall give evidence of their residence), and other parts of the country. These Jews of French origin and speech enjoyed a large measure of freedom and prosperity. Their peace was, however, disturbed in the reign of Stephen by an accusation that in Norwich the Jews had killed a Christian boy for their Passover (1144), and this boy was turned into a saint—St. William of Norwich—while the Jewish objects of this infamous charge paid for his canonization with their lives, and their co-religionists were made to suffer heavily in their goods. This blood accusation was the first raised against the Jews anywhere, and was shortly followed in England by two similar charges. The case of one of these, St. Hugh of Lincoln, was commemorated by Chaucer in his *Canterbury Tales* ("The Prioress's Tale"), and gives some indication of the savage hatred with which the "cursed" Jews came to be regarded in medieval England. Nevertheless the Jews continued to prosper under Henry II, and rose to great wealth and prominence in the country. A most serious set-back occurred, however, on the accession of King Richard the Lionhearted in 1189. A deputation of leading Jews appeared at his coronation at Westminster, but, on being refused admission there, they were attacked by the mob. Meanwhile the report was spread in London that the king had ordered the Jews to be killed, and the populace turned to the Jewish quarter, and began their work of murder and plunder. The Jews defended themselves in their stores and houses, but during the night the houses were set on fire, and the Jews who attempted to escape were put to death. King Richard was powerless to stop the outbreak, and after his departure for the crusade similar attacks on the Jews occurred at Lynn,

Stamford, Bury St. Edmunds, Norwich, and elsewhere. The tragedies that were enacted in those places assumed a dramatic grandeur in York, where the Jews had taken refuge in one of the towers of the king's castle. Fearing treachery by the governor, however, they afterwards shut themselves up and refused to admit him. The Jews were thereupon besieged by the authorities as well as by the mob lusting for their wealth and blood. A monk celebrated mass every morning before the citadel, and, robed in his white surplice, called on the people to destroy the enemies of Christ. When in his imprudent zeal this fiery ecclesiastic was crushed to death by a stone hurled at him, the fury of the besiegers knew no bounds, and the Jews, to the number of about 500, seeing that the end had come, decided to die by their own hands. Joce, their head, slew first his wife and children, and the great self-immolation was concluded by the death of Joce himself at the hand of Rabbi Yom-Tob, of Joigny, who, having led his brethren in their heroic resolution, finally killed himself. The gates were opened by a few Jews, who had hoped for mercy, but, in spite of their supplications for baptism, they were slain, and the victors, disappointed at not finding the bonds held by the Jews in the castle, repaired to their keeping place in the cathedral and there burned them. It was for this crime against the King's Exchequer, and not for the outrage on the Jews, that some attempt was subsequently made to bring the culprits to justice.

The belated, scanty, and ineffective protection afforded to the Jews put them more than ever in the grasp of needy and greedy kings. Elaborate precautions were now taken to record and check the usurious transactions of the Jews on which the king levied heavy imposts for his own personal gain. For this reason, King John favored them; but presumably finding the regular revenue too small for his wants, he imprisoned all the Jews, and extorted by the most violent means the wealth possessed by them. The vast sums thus extracted from the coffers of the Jews were too tempting for the same profitable measures not to be repeated by both barons and kings. It even came to this, that there was convened a so-called Jewish Parliament to which were summoned the richest representatives of the Jewish communities; they were then informed that his most gracious Majesty required 20,000 marks, which they were to collect as well and as fast as they could. The enormous exactions drained even the wealth of the rich Jews, and the competition of the privileged Caorsini, the Papal tax-gatherers and usurers, reduced the Jews to sore straits. Then an Act of Parliament (Statute of Judaism, 1275) attempted to reform the Jews; it forbade money-lending and directed the Jews to engage in other occupations, which for practical purposes were then closed to them. Many Jews took to debasing and clipping the coin of the realm, but on one day (1278) all the Jews were arrested, and 293 of them were executed in London and a large number also in the provinces. The coin and their goods went to the king, and the people took their share in plundering the Jews on their own account. The measure of tribulation of the Jews in England was now full to overflowing. What was wanting in rapacity or in honest objection to the usurious practices of the Jews was supplied by fanaticism. Even one of the most enlightened ecclesiastics (Robert Grosseteste), who had no desire to rob them of their lives, used this singular argument in favor of the Jews: "As murderers of the Lord, as still blaspheming Christ and mocking His Passion, they were to be in captivity to the princes of the earth. As they have the brand of Cain, and are condemned to wander over the face of the earth, so were they to have the privilege of Cain that no one was to kill them." What must have been the words and thoughts of those who were clamoring for the lives and souls of the Jews? Those people certainly had their way, for a decree was issued banishing absolutely and irrevocably all the Jews in the realm and confiscating their belongings. Any Jew found in the country after the time-limit of the expulsion was to be executed by hanging. By October 1290 about 16,000 Jews, preferring the bitterness of exile to the shame of apostasy, had quitted the inhospitable soil of England to face new dangers in strange lands.

§ 6. *In Central Europe*. While England was spared all further persecution of the Jews for the simple reason that no professing Jew openly settled in the island kingdom until the middle of the seventeenth century, when Christians had become alive to higher conceptions of holiness and humanity than those prevailing in the Middle Ages, the whole of Europe was during that interval a witches' kettle of rapine, murder, and expulsion. In France, Philip Augustus had all the Jews in his kingdom arrested, their immovable property confiscated, and about 100,000 were driven into exile (1182). Yet such was the temper and greed of this monarch, and, more important still, such was the unhappy and insecure position of the Jews, that shortly afterwards negotiations were entered into between the king and the Jews for their readmission into France and the continuance of their former traffic (1198). The Jews were again to amass wealth for the benefit of the king, to be expelled when the king suffered a twinge of his Christian conscience or an extraordinary desire for money. Louis IX treated the Jews like the pious robber-knight he was, and their expulsion by Charles VI in 1394 closed for a long time the history of the Jews in France. Attempts subsequently made by Jews, especially from Spain and Portugal, to enter the country, led to an order of Louis XIII (1615) forbidding Christians under pain of death and confiscation to shelter Jews or even to converse with them.

In the wide tracts of land under Germanic influence, the Jews lived on numerous volcanoes, represented by the caprice or helplessness of the many great and small princes. The Jews had to pay for all the troubles that befell the German people. The Jews were accused of having been in treasonable correspondence with the Mongolian invaders; the Black Death (1348-51) gave rise to the charge that the Jews had poisoned the wells. On such occasions, the Jewish communities of whole regions were swept away by fire and sword, and the fugitives subjected to the most revolting atrocities. The Jews were still suffered only because they represented a certain value which could be used in raising revenue. Of course, in the religious disturbances the defenceless Jews were placed between hammer and anvil. Thus they sank into a despised class, and, until well into the eighteenth century, they remained out of touch with the general world, and without that dignity and influence which learning and wealth might have bestowed on them.

Meanwhile the harassed Jews in the German countries had found a refuge in the neighboring kingdom of Poland, where they escaped the political convulsions and religious fanaticism that tore central Europe into innumerable bleeding fragments. Jews from southern Russia had, no doubt, settled in Poland even before the introduction of Christianity there, but it was the German Jews who, driven in all directions by the frantic violence of the crusaders and during the horrors of the Black Death, came to Poland in large numbers, and even imposed their German language (which, with Slavic and Hebrew admixtures, developed into Yiddish) on the Jews of eastern Europe. In Poland the Jews not only enjoyed peace, but many privileges of a trading class. In an agricultural population composed only of nobles and serfs, the presence of the Jews was of essential advantage to the country—a fact which was long recognized among the rulers of Poland. In a charter granted to the Jews by Boleslav Pobozny, King of Great Poland (1264), they were accorded important privileges which served as the basis of later legislation. In spite of the efforts of the Church to place the Jews under a ban of social degradation, the Polish Jews continued to prosper, and Casimir III, the Great (1309-70), who was much attached to his beautiful Jewish mistress Estherka, issued another charter incorporating the Jews among the integral elements of the Polish population. Poland became an asylum for the hunted Jews, the only oasis in the great barren desert of intolerance, and the Polish Jews, therefore, rapidly grew in numbers and became of great importance in the religious and economic development of Jewish life.

§ 7. *Spain and the Inquisition.* A country at the other end of Europe, where the Jews had risen to unparalleled power and achievement, was feverishly endeavoring to get rid of them. Christian Spain bore from the very beginning of its history an unenviable distinction in religious bigotry, and this expressed itself most emphatically in the case of the Jews. The influence of the Jews was evidently of such important consequence in the Iberian Peninsula that in the Christian reconquests of the country the Jews did not by any means fare so badly as might have been expected. They rose to high rank in the various States, and the later history of the Spanish Jews presents a record of brilliant contributions to civilization as well as of sublime heroism in the selfless attachment to their faith. The Sephardim, as the Jews of Spain and Portugal are called,[1] stand in a category by themselves in the relentless persecution that was waged against the Jews in the Middle Ages. Unlike their co-religionists in other parts, the Spanish and Portuguese Jews were not strangers in a strange land, degraded or protected

[1] The Spanish and Portuguese Jews and their descendants all over southern Europe and the East belong by their origin, distinctive religious ritual, and pronunciation of Hebrew, to the smaller section of the Jewish people known as Sephardim (from Sepharad [Obadiah 20], the traditional Hebrew name of Spain), while the Jews of northern and eastern Europe and their American emigrants are comprised under the name of Ashkenazim (from Ashkenaz [Gen. x. 3], the Hebrew appellation of Germany).

by their ruler for his own benefit, but Spaniards in speech and thought, with all the refinement and graces of a high civilization, combining the chivalry and dignity of Spanish gentlemen with Jewish humanity and enlightenment. Among them were men well versed in affairs of state, and, as diplomatists and financiers, their services were as much requisitioned by the Christian princes as they had been by their Mohammedan predecessors. Instead of Arabic, the Jewish Spaniards now employed Castilian as their mother-tongue, which became so engrained in their being that even today this language is still spoken and written (in Hebrew characters) by many descendants of those Sephardi Jews who, over four centuries ago, left their native country for the hospitable soil of Mohammedan Turkey. Jewish men of talent and genius continued the work of their forbears, and, as the chief translators and mediators between the ancient classical and Moorish cultures and the thought of the nascent European civilization, these medieval Jews rendered a service of unique value to the development of the human mind. The natural sciences were enriched by important contributions, and the era of discoveries, which were to prove the glory and downfall of the Spanish and Portuguese nations, was advanced by them both scientifically and financially. They stood foremost as physicians, and their fame led even persecuting Popes to employ them. Rodrigo Lopez, the physician who was executed on a charge of attempted poisoning of Queen Elizabeth, and who in Jewless England is supposed to have suggested to Shakespeare the character of Shylock, was one of those ubiquitous Jewish doctors, who, in Christian or Jewish garb, were prized at the courts of the most Christian princes. The deeper the Jews of Spain became imbedded in the nation, the more painful was the wrench which tore them out with their very roots.

The Church which had enforced its canons and views all over Europe, at last turned to the anomalous position occupied by the Jews in Spain. Lashed into violent zeal by the rise of obstinate Christian heresies in southern France, the Catholic authorities were not inclined to tolerate the hateful Jewish influence in neighboring Spain. Fiercely in earnest, the friars and other agents of the Church went about the country inveighing against the Jews, their ill-gotten wealth, their avarice, their deadly unbelief, and these charges found the more ready credence among the ignorant and exploited populace as the prosperous condition of the Jews had long been an eyesore to them. Towards the end of the fourteenth century, the Jews were attacked in one city after another, and suffered all the horrors which the zest for plunder could add to the lust for infidel blood. The immunity and profit with which these wholesale massacres were perpetrated under the encouragement and protection of the all-powerful clergy, led to numerous repetitions of savage outbursts by the brutalized Spanish mob. Over all these excesses was spread the comforting veil of Christian zeal, and, in the midst of the most frightful and merciless outrages, the Church would always be open to receive the submission of the obdurate Jewish souls. Before and after these scenes of carnage, the eternal salvation of Jewish souls was the dominating issue. Among the most conspicuous of the agents of the militant Church was the Dominican Vicente Ferrer, whose efforts alone resulted in the conversion of 35,000 Jews.

Not contented with the successes of the Church, the converted Jew Joshua Lorqui, or Geronimo de Santa Fé, physician to Pope Benedict XIII, induced his Holiness to order a public disputation on the respective merits of Judaism and Christianity, or rather on the falsehood of Judaism, so that the Jews might be effectively convinced by Joshua Lorqui out of the mouths of their leading Rabbis. This disputation, which took place at Tortosa, and continued from February 1413 to November 1414, was opened by the Pope personally in the presence of a brilliant assembly. It is needless to add that the disputation did not have the hoped-for result on the Jews and only tended to aggravate their lot.

Such, with variations, were the misfortunes of the Jews in Spain, but they were to rise into even a more poignant tragedy under the pious Ferdinand and Isabella, at the end of the fifteenth century. The successful efforts of the Church had filled the country with many converted Jews, who, by their intelligence and wealth, had penetrated all ranks of society, and had even risen high in the Catholic hierarchy. The ecclesiastical authorities suspected, however, and with good reason, that, while outwardly Christian, most of these converts retained their former Jewish ideas, and even harbored a secret attachment to their ancestral faith and practices. The most drastic steps were taken to eradicate this danger from the very heart of Catholic Spain. The Inquisition, that monstrous ecclesiastical institution which stands condemned at the bar of history as the vilest organization ever devised for the enslavement of the human mind, was in the year 1480 let loose on those new Christians, and the dungeon, the rack, and the stake dealt unsparingly with those on whom even the breath of Judaizing suspicion had fallen. The imprisonment and torture of men and women were carried out with relentless energy, and thousands paid the last penalty at the stake. In the country where gory bullfights are still popular amusements, the burning of lapsed Jews and heretics became a favorite entertainment and a great occasion where the court and fashion met in becoming festive mood to celebrate an auto-da-fé (act of faith). In 1483 the matter was taken in hand by the Grand Inquisitor, Thomas Torquemada, of unenviable memory, who spared none, since even the priesthood and the very Inquisition were honeycombed with faithless neo-Christians. Figures can give no conception of the demoniacal terror exercised by the Inquisition, of the excruciating cruelties enacted by the torture of the suspected, of the infamous means utilized to discover possible culprits.

Yet all was in vain. The numerous Jews whom frenzied fear had driven to seek refuge in the Church were in their calmer moments overtaken by remorse. Contemptuously known as Marranos (a term of doubtful derivation) by Jews and Christians, they could not hide their identity from their more steadfast brethren who shamed their inconstancy, nor from their Christian neighbors whom by the waters of baptism they had cheated of the excuse of robbery and hatred. Excuses to attack and rob were, however, often invented, and the Marranos, like their former co-religionists, were overtaken by the fury of a pious savagery.

Baffled by the persistent perverseness of its Jewish converts, the Church resolved on the extreme measure of expelling all the unbaptized Jews from the Spanish domains. A supreme attempt was made by the Jews to ward off the deadly blow, and their chief spokesman, the polished courtier and gifted scholar Don Isaac Abravanel, who had held the office of royal treasurer, with honor to himself and benefit to the Crown, offered to the king as a last resort a ransom of 30,000 ducats to avert the dreaded edict. At this critical jucture, Torquemada is said to have interposed, crucifix in hand, with the dramatic appeal to the king and queen: "Behold Him, whom Judas sold for thirty pieces of silver. Sell ye Him now for a higher price and render an account of your bargain before God." The doom of the Spanish Jews was sealed, and by the last appointed day, the 9th Ab (the ever-memorable anniversary of the twofold destruction of Jerusalem) in the year 1492, about 200,000 Spanish Jews had left their homes, the graves of their forefathers, for ever. Within the whole range of history, of all the sublime manifestations of the grandeur of the human soul in its self-sacrificing attachment to pure idealism and truth, there is no parallel to the heroic, unflinching resolve of these Jewish exiles from Spain. A word, and they might have remained in full possession of peace, honor, and wealth, but astonishingly few spoke that word. It had been their country for centuries, the country to which their forefathers had added dazzling splendor and to which they themselves were attached with all the fibers of their being. The exiles saw nothing before them but the dark hostility that would greet them everywhere, the utter degradation to which their brethren had been reduced in other lands. Nevertheless, all this was braved for the sake of the Lord God of Israel, for the sake also of the freedom of the human conscience to which civilized men of all opinions now pay sincere homage.

The exiles were pursued by all the hardships and dangers which hunted strangers suspected of hidden treasures could expect in those days of heartless intolerence and widespread robbery on sea and land. It would be too harrowing to set out at length the manifold and intense tribulations of these devoted refugees. Many of those who had escaped to neighboring Portugal, where they were admitted at so much per head, were soon afterwards exposed to still greater horrors than those from which they had just fled. Whatever fiendish cruelties had yet been left undone in Spain were now carried out in Portugal with all manner of cowardice and perfidy. By order of King Manuel, suddenly organized raids were made on Jewish children, who were torn from their parents, to be brought up as Christians; traps were laid for those endeavoring to escape, if only with their bare lives, and they were coerced into baptism or sold as slaves. Yet these fiendish persecutors, with tragic irony, had ever the name of God on their lips. Fortunate were those exiles who escaped from Portugal and turned to southern France and Italy. To the latter country went the eminent family of Don Isaac Abravanel (1437-1508). More fortunate still were the numerous fugitives who found a warm welcome in Mohammedan Turkey, whose sultan, Bayazid II, expressed his surprise that Ferdinand and Isabella had impoverished their country and enriched his by such useful subjects.

In spite of all, the Marranos still carried on their secret practice of Judaism, and, for centuries afterwards, numbers of them continually left for other parts where they could openly profess the religion of their forefathers. Meanwhile, the Inquisition in Spain and Portugal pursued uninterruptedly its unholy work, and extended it with the same zeal to the regions of the New World that came under their sway. Well into the eighteenth century, burning stakes with holocausts of Jewish victims lit up the ever-increasing decay and decomposition of the once flourishing and mighty Spanish and Portugese nations.

The race of Marranos in Spain is now entirely merged and indistinguishable in the general population. But so tenacious has been the Jewish consciousness among the Marranos who had found a refuge in northern Portugal at the end of the fifteenth century that even in these days approximately 15,000 of those crypto-Jews, with peculiar prayers and ritual observances of their own, still exist in more or less cohesive groups in over thirty towns and villages in that part of the country—a living witness to the vitality of Judaism unique even in Jewish annals.[1]

§ 8. *Reaction Within.* The gathering clouds at the end of the eleventh century, the persecutions under Christian and Mohammedan rule, also affected the tone and temper of the inner life of the Jews. With Moses Maimonides Jewish thought and progress had reached their zenith. For a time,

[1] Arthur Carlos de Barros Basto, the first Marrano in Portugal to return openly to traditional Judaism within the last century and a half, has brought about a Jewish revival among many of his fellow-Marranos; he has been aided by the Portuguese Marranos Committee in London, with which, since its establishment in 1926 for the promotion of this *"Obra do Resgate"* (Work of Redemption), Paul Goodman was associated in the capacity of honorary secretary. A synagogue, mainly for the use of the neo-Jews in northern Portugal, was erected in Oporto in 1938 by the family of Sir Elly Kadoorie, of Shanghai—440 years after the last synagogue in Oporto, subsequently converted into a church, closed its doors to Jewish worship.

Jewish learning flourished in Provence, and, apart from the Kimhi family already mentioned as notable commentators of the Bible, special reference must be made to the remarkable family of Ibn Tibbon, translators, who rendered a large number of Arabic works, Jewish and non-Jewish, into Hebrew, the universal language of the Jews. Among these translations was also Maimonides' *Guide,* which, originally written in Arabic, was now made available for the whole Dispersion. The bold philosophical utterances and speculations of the Jewish sage were not, however, to pass unchallenged by the enlarged circle of his readers, and a violent polemic ensued between the supporters and opponents of Maimonides. In the year 1233, a law was issued against those who studied the *Guide* or other similar philosophical works, to which dread sentence the supporters of Maimonides replied with a counter-excommunication. Things came to such a pass that the opponnets of Maimonides, headed by Solomon of Montpellier and Jonah Gerondi, appealed in their zeal to the tribunal of the Catholic Inquisition, which was then concerned with the heretical Albigenses. This court readily lent its powerful aid, and condemned Maimonides' writings to be burned. Such a fatal sequel aroused the indignation of all Jews against the Rabbinical zealots who had dared to invoke the assistance of the hateful Inquisition in matters of Jewish faith. R. Jonah himself was so stricken with remorse that he vowed to undertake a pilgrimage to Palestine, in order to beg at the grave of Moses Maimonides for the forgiveness of the master. But the matter did not end here, for the Church now felt itself called upon also to sit in judgment on the morals of the literary productions of the Jews. A converted Jew, Nicholas Donin, submitted to Pope Gregory IX a number of charges of immorality and blasphemy against the Talmud, and, by order of Louis IX of France, a disputation took place in which Rabbi Jehiel, of Paris, was the leading Jewish spokesman against Donin; but, whatever the argument, the Catholic court of inquiry ordered the Talmud to be burned. Under the threat of death, the Jews had to hand over their copies of the Talmud to the authorities, and twenty-four cartloads filled with those treasured books were publicly burned in Paris (1244), on the same spot where the writings of Maimonides had been burned some time before.

Another public disputation between a converted Jew and a prominent Rabbi leads us to Moses Nahmanides (1194-1270), one of the great figures of the thirteenth century. In spite of his clear mind, the troubles of the times left their impress on his voluminous writings, and he heralded the age of mysticism. Late in life he was called upon to enter into a public disputation on the truth of Judaism with Pablo Christiani, one of the most virulent of Jewish converts to Christianity, who made it the purpose of his life to persecute and slander his former co-religionists. The disputation was held in Barcelona in the year 1263, in the presence of King James of Aragon and his court, and lasted four days. Contrary to general expectations, Nahmanides maintained the Jewish cause with such fearlessness and dignity that the king presented him with a sum of money to signify his esteem of the Jewish champion. But when the Dominican judges spread the rumor that Nahmanides had been worsted in argument, he published the disputation for the benefit of those concerned. By this he incurred the displeasure of the king, who, forced by the Dominicans and the Pope, exiled Nahmanides from the country. At the age of seventy, Nahmanides left all behind him, and proceeded to the Holy Land. He became the center of a new Jewish life in the desolate Land of Israel, where he passed his remaining years.

Meir of Rothenburg (1220-93), the most eminent German Rabbi of the time, who also undertook a pilgrimage to Palestine, was not so fortunate in this respect as Nahmanides. Under Rudolph of Hapsburg, the German Jews were so sorely oppressed that many of their wealthy people in the

Rhineland made up their minds to emigrate *en masse*. Meir of Rothenburg headed them, but on the way he was recognized by a baptized Jew, who denounced him to the authorities. Meir was handed over to the Emperor, and, to put a stop to an emigration which would have deprived him of considerable revenue, he had the far-famed Rabbi imprisoned in the tower of Ensisheim, Alsace (1286). If Rudolph expected that he would extort much money from the Jews as a ransom for their spiritual leader, he was disappointed, for, to prevent any repetition of such a stratagem, Meir ordered his brethren not to obtain his release by any payment of money. He passed seven years in confinement, and after his death his body remained there unburied for another fourteen years, until it was allowed to be removed for a large sum of money by a pious admirer of the deceased Rabbi.

That the Jewish mind had now arrived at a decadent stage was evidenced by the withdrawal of Jewish scholars from the spirit of free inquiry, which had produced its ripest fruit in Moses Maimonides. A thinker of genius of a different type was Solomon ben Adret, of Barcelona (1235-1310), a pupil of Moses Nahmanides, who became the leading authority in the Jewry of his day. Ben Adret concentrated his attention on the Talmud, and his view of the dangers of extraneous studies was marked by the anathema which he, together with others, pronounced against those who occupied themselves with natural or metaphysical sciences before their thirtieth year. That the Jewish intellect was nevertheless slow to succumb to obscurantism, was shown by the lives and writings of Judah Alharizi, the author of *Tahkemoni,* one of the most remarkable productions of medieval belles-lettres, and Jedaiah Bedersi (died about 1340), who wrote against Solomon ben Adret a defence of philosophy and science, and achieved lasting fame by his *Examination of the World* (*Behinath Haolam*), which has been translated into various languages, including English. Still more renowned was Levi ben Gerson (Gersonides), or Leon de Bagnols (1288-1344). He was a biblical commentator and astronomer of distinction. His Hebrew description of an astronomical instrument invented by him was translated into Latin by order of Pope Clement VI. His fame rests, however, on his philosophical work, *The Wars of the Lord (Milhamoth Adonai)*, which deals with the most thorny problems in a spirit of lofty independence and originality. Another philosopher of note was Hasdai Crescas (1340-1410), whose *Light of the Lord (Or Adonai)* represents an important contribution to the philosophy of Judaism, as does also the more popular *Fundamentals (Ikkarim)* of his pupil Joseph Albo (d. 1444). All these, however, were the after-glow of the setting sun of Jewish thought, which now came to be dominated by men like Asher ben Jehiel (1250-1327; a pupil of Meir of Rothenburg), and his sons, who settled in Toledo, and introduced among Spanish Jews that spirit of German exclusiveness which found its whole intellectual activity in the intensive study of the Talmud. In this they were followed by Isaac ben Sheshet and his successor Simon ben Zemah Duran (d. 1444), who flourished in Algiers at the end of the fourteenth, and the beginning of the fifteenth, century. The last is reputed to have been the first Rabbi who, owing to needy circumstances, was in receipt of a regular stipend.

§ 9. *The Cabbalah.* The darker the world grew for the Jews the more they took refuge in the intricacies of the Talmud or lost themselves in the maze of mysticism. The Jews were staggering under the blows that fell on them in remorseless repetition. There were the great expulsions from France in 1306 and 1394, which reduced the French Jews to beggary, and spread them with their misery far and wide; a hare-brained crusade by a wild rabble of the so-called Shepherds, which began in 1320, some time after a readmission of the Jews into France, involved the Jews there and in Spain in untold bloodshed and ruin; the Black Death and the frantic excesses of the Flagellants, which in their turn produced paroxysms that wiped out of existence hundreds of Jewish communities and pursued the escaped fugitives with a bestial ferocity which should have shamed even the Middle Ages. The massacres in Spain and the final great expulsions from the Iberian Peninsula were to fill the bitter cup to overflowing again and again. No wonder that the innate optimism of the Jews and the naturally joyous character of Judaism deepened into an unwonted gloom, and produced an un-Jewish asceticism which looked upon this world in very truth as a vale of tears—a state of things which could only have been made worse by the barbarization which later on engulfed the Jews of Germany and Poland.

The mystic lore of the Jews, known under the name of Cabbalah (Tradition), could claim ancient lineage, since the Essenes, at the time of the Second Temple, indulged in esoteric speculations which were presumed to have been handed down from days of old and were only known to the initiated. The work of creation related in Genesis and the Divine Throne described by the prophet Ezekiel were the great themes that exercised the ingenuity of mystic minds, which lost themselves in fancies ranging over the vast unexplored regions of theosophy, cosmogony, angelology, etc. Eastern wisdom and Greek philosophy were called into requisition; many Talmudic masters, as well as Philo and Paul, were deeply infected by these ideas, which, under the form of Gnosticism, were to prove a very serious menace to the orthodox development of Christianity. To this was added a miscellaneous collection of theurgic and magic notions, incantations, etc., which represented, so to speak, the practical part of mysticism or Cabbalah.

This medley of Jewish religious philosophy and spiritual quackery received its most important literary embodiment in the *Zohar (Splendor)*, which, ascribed to the famous Rabbi Simon ben Johai (of the 2nd century C.E.), owes its composition to Moses de Leon, who flourished in Spain at the end of the thirteenth century. The Cabbalists multiplied, and the *Zohar* became the Bible of their mystic doctrines. In their speculations, in which God was conceived as the Infinite (*En Soph*) with ten Emanations (*Sephiroth*), there were riotous fancies on the essence of the Deity and the riddle of life, and they altogether represented an unsuccessful attempt to grasp the dim, floating shadows of the eternal. It proved, nevertheless, a welcome diversion for troubled souls which the merely intellectual studies of the Talmud and of rationalistic philosophy were not able to appease. Especially in the East, Cabbalism found many adepts, among whom Isaac Luria, an ascetic saint living in Safed, Palestine, in the middle of the sixteenth century, was the most remarkable. It must be admitted that the Cabbalah raised Judaism at times into the highest regions of the most sublime spirituality and supplied that mystic element not always so pronounced in Judaism. Unfortunately the Cabbalah came to be mixed up with religious charlatanry and degraded into a grossly sensuous attempt to lay hold of the unfathomable for other than purely spiritual objects. The efforts to press the Cabbalah into the service of magic and necromancy debased it still further. The fantastic nature of the Cabbalah also attracted a number of Christian thinkers (notably Pico della Mirandola and Reuchlin), some of whom thought that they could discern the dogmas of Christianity in the theories of Jewish mysticism.

§ 10. *Pseudo-Messiahs*. Among the first notable results of this devotion to occult speculation was a strange development of the Messianic idea. The darkness of Jewish life was illumined by the hope that the Messiah would appear in his promised glory, and the vision of faith soon found tangible proofs of the wish for redemption from the ills of the world. More serious than the spurious enthusiasm was the consequent melancholy disappointment which followed it. Among the earliest of these cabbalistic pseudo-Messiahs who played upon the credulity of the people, or were perhaps carried away by their own hallucinations, was the Spaniard Abraham Abulafia in the thirteenth, and the German Asher Lemmlein at the beginning of the sixteenth, century, whose appearance, however, only evoked local excitement. Much more interesting were the careers of David Reubeni and Solomon Molcho, whose bold claims made a considerable stir in the world at large. David Reubeni entered on the scene as the brother and ambassador of a Jewish king of Chaibar, in Arabia, and endeavored to interest Pope Clement VII and King John III of Portugal in his scheme, which was for them to support him with arms and ammunition in the conquest of the Holy Land from the hands of the Mohammedans. Reubeni must have made an extraordinary impression everywhere, not least on the Marranos in Portugal, who witnessed his princely reception in that country into which no professing Jew was allowed to enter. One of these Marranos, Diogo Pires, returned formally to Judaism, assuming the name of Solomon Molcho. Molcho proclaimed the advent of the Messianic age in the year 1540, in which Reubeni was to play the leading part. After various bold adventures, both of them appeared with their pretensions, or plans, before the Emperor Charles V. This, however, proved their undoing. Solomon Molcho was burned at the stake as a lapsed neo-Christian (though even at the last moment his life was vainly offered to him for his recantation of Judaism), while David Reubeni was taken to Portugal, where he was done away with by the Inquisition.

Extravagantly strange as were the lives of these two adventurers, still more remarkable and of much greater influence was the Messianic enthusiast and impostor Sabbethai Zebi, in the seventeenth century. Born at Smyrna, Turkey, in 1626, Sabbethai Zebi became addicted to cabbalistic ideas and to those ascetic habits which were then held in high esteem. The advent of the year 1666, which many Christians as well as Jews considered to be the Messianic era when the Jews would be restored to their ancient land, quickened his imagination and led him publicly to assume the role of the expected Messiah (1665). The support which he found among his deluded countrymen spread all over the Jewish Dispersion, and gained everywhere numerous and enthusiastic adherents. He was regarded as the Messiah, and prayers of a florid style were offered up for him in the synagogues. Distance and rumor lent unlimited charm and force to Sabbethai Zebi's extraordinary personality, and the delirium took hold even of people of sober judgment and high culture, such as were to be found among the Spanish and Portuguese Jews in Amsterdam and Hamburg. Among those who dared to oppose the dominant Sabbethaians was Jacob Sasportas, the first Haham (or Rabbi) of the newly established congregation of Spanish and Portuguese Jews in London (1665). Sabbethai Zebi, emboldened by his success, even went so far as to order the change of the Jewish fast days into days of rejoicing to mark the arrival of the Messianic times. The decisive moment came when he left Smyrna for Constantinople, where he was arrested by the Turkish authorities on landing. Even now his followers crowded around him, and were able to maintain him in his imprisonment with much luxury. He was, however, denounced at Turkish headquarters by Nehemiah Cohen, a Polish rival to the Messiahship, and Sabbethai Zebi was brought before the sultan, Mohammed IV, whose throne Sabbethai Zebi's devotees probably expected him to occupy as the king of kings. At the critical juncture the great drama was turned into low comedy, for, to save his life, the Messiah donned the Turkish turban as a sign of his conversion to Islam. Sabbethai Zebi was rewarded by being appointed the sultan's doorkeeper. In spite of his inglorious end, he had such a fascination over his adherents that a considerable number of them went over with him to Mohammedanism, many, no doubt, suspecting in the apostasy of their master some hidden meaning beyond their comprehension. Numerous disciples of Sabbethai Zebi evidently still upheld his evasive claim to the Messiahship, but his double character was, after all, to end fatally for him. He was banished to Dulcigno, in Albania, away from all Jewish companionship, and there he died in 1676. The evil he wrought, however, lived after him. It was with difficulty that the disappointment and shame of the believers in Sabbethai Zebi were obliterated and that peace was restored to the faction-swept Jewish communities. In Turkey, the Sabbethaians who adopted Mohammedanism maintained themselves as a separate body, neither completely Jewish nor Moslem, and excluded by both on account of their double religious life. Until recent times, the Sabbethaians, called the Dönmeh (Apostates), numbering about 15,000, were to be found mostly in Salonica as a Judeo-Mohammedan sect, but were dispersed over Turkey with the re-conquest of Salonica by the Greeks and the subsequent Graeco-Turkish exchange of population.

The last of the notable race of Messianic adventurers, who are of great psychological as well as historical interest, was Jacob Frank (born in Podolia about 1726; died at Offenbach, Germany, 1791). He availed himself of the still extant traces of the Sabbethaian mystification to create a Messianic movement in his own favor. The religious charlatanry and gross licentiousness of these new sectarians moved the Rabbis to justified opposition, and the so-called Frankists were excommunicated and denounced to the authorities. The Frankists, finding themselves persecuted and forsaken, pretended to Catholic beliefs, and thereby gained the goodwill of the Church. This patronage, however, imposed on the Frankists the necessity of entering the Catholic Church as a body, and though at first they attempted to lead a double life as a separate sect, they gradually merged entirely in Christianity.

Frank nevertheless kept up his impudent pretensions, which brought him great wealth from his adherents, to the end of his life.

§ 11. *Italy.* In three countries of unequal states of culture —Italy, Turkey, and Poland—the Jews enjoyed a tolerable measure of tranquillity, and even a certain prosperity. In Italy, especially under the eyes of the Pope, the Jews fared not badly, comparatively speaking. As a rule, the Popes were more indulgent towards the obscure Hebrew communities (shall we say, more truly Christian towards them?) than the prelates and minor officers of the Church in other parts, nor were the rich Popes subjected to the same temptations as the impecunious kings and nobles who used the Jews as financial milch cows. A number of Popes entrusted even their sacred persons to the care of Jewish physicians, and some of the pontiffs gave a generous refuge in their realms to the Jewish victims of Christian persecutors. The prosperity and enterprise of the Italian towns not only bred a more enlightened people, but also a large and opulent class of merchants, and even the Christian money-lenders, under the names of Lombards and Caorsini, had little cause to envy the wealth of the handicapped Jews. An incident which brought the Jews of Rome into general prominence was the conversion to Christianity of one of their number, Petrus Leonis, whose family rose to great distinction in the eleventh century, and in the third generation produced an anti-Pope, Heraclius II. The odium of his Jewish descent was the strongest objection against him, and even Bernard of Clairvaux, who had so nobly defended the Jews during the massacres of the second crusade, considered that the blood which had flowed in the veins of Christ and His apostles was an unexpiable offense in the temporal head of the Christian Church. Among the Jews who benefited by the enlightenment which reigned in Italy more than elsewhere in Christendom may briefly be mentioned Nathan ben Jehiel (died 1106), of Rome, the author of the *Aruch,* an important Talmudical lexicon, while Immanuel, of Rome, a friend of Dante, wrote *Mehabberoth,* on the lines of the *Divina Commedia* of the illustrious Florentine. Obadiah Sforno and the German Elias Levita were among the most important of the Hebrew teachers of Christian scholars, who, in the sixteenth century, turned to Hebrew as one of the sources of inspiration. Of the numerous Jewish men of letters who participated in the New Learning were Elias del Medigo and Judah Leon of Modena, philosophers; the Frenchman Joseph Hacohen, a pathfinder in Jewish history, whose work *The Vale of Tears* (*Emek Habacha*) is a valuable record of Jewish sufferings during the Middle Ages; Azariah dei Rossi, who in his *Enlightenment of the Eyes* (*Meor Enaim*) displays an original and refreshing acumen in Jewish literary criticism. Of the sons of Don Isaac Abravanel, who had headed the great exile from Spain, and whose diplomatic abilities found considerable scope in Naples and Venice, Leo Hebraeus achieved fame with his *Dialoghi di Amore,* while the youngest son, Samuel Abravanel, who occupied an influential position at the court in Naples, was a Maecenas and the center of a large circle of Jewish scholars. The Catholic Counter-Reformation, which darkened the intellectual life of Italy, extinguished also the Jewish light that had shone in that country.

§ 12. *Turkey.* The conquest of the crumbling Byzantine Empire by the Turks proved of inestimable benefit to the Jews, who found in the Turk a tolerant master, able to appreciate the business capacities, if not the scholarly achievements, of the Jews. To the Jews under oppressive Christian dominion, especially to the refugees from Spain, Turkey became a haven of refuge, and Palestine was resettled with several communities to which men of renown, most of whom had come there from abroad, gave again a position of some importance. The greatest of these Rabbis were

Isaac Luria, the master of the Cabbalah already referred to, and Joseph Caro (1488-1575), whose *Shulhan Aruch* (*Prepared Table*) has remained to this day the authoritative code of Jewish law and practice. A less enduring, if more dazzling, career was that of Don Joseph Nasi, Duke of Naxos (d. 1579). Born in Portugal and brought up as a Marrano, he left his native country after various adventurous peregrinations, and settled in Constantinople together with his aunt, Gracia Mendesia (d. 1569), who, by her vast wealth and its enlightened application in many good causes, as well as by her personal charm and culture, was the most engaging Jewish woman in the Middle Ages. Don Joseph married her daughter Reyna, and by his riches and address rose to high favor at the court of Sultan Sulaiman II. This influence was even increased under his successor Selim. Joseph Nasi was invested with the dignity of Duke of Naxos and with the possession of that and surrounding islands, as well as of a large tract of land in Palestine whereon he rebuilt the town of Tiberias and otherwise promoted Jewish colonization there. He acted as the recognized foreign adviser of the powerful sultan, and treated with the ambassadors of the Powers represented in Constantinople. His authority can be gauged by the fact that he arrested a number of French ships in Alexandria for non-payment of certain sums owing to his aunt by the French Government, and this high-handed action was supported by the sultan against the protests of France. Don Joseph was also instrumental in inducing the sultan to engage in a war with Venice, and it was only the opposition of his rivals at the Turkish court that prevented his being raised to the dignity of King of Cyprus. Under Selim's successor, Joseph lost the power he had exercised in affairs of State, but he continued to the end the active and generous interest he had always displayed in the fortunes and endeavors of his brethren.

A rival of Joseph Nasi was Solomon Ashkenazi (1520-

1602), who likewise wielded great influence. He opposed Don Joseph in the war with Venice, and was selected by the sultan as the representative of Turkey in the peace negotiations. The senate of the Venetian Republic (to which city we owe the word "ghetto" as the name of the Jewish quarter of a town) was very reluctant to treat with a Jewish ambassador, but he was eventually received with all the pomp and ceremony attaching to the dignity and the importance of the occasion. At the same time he was instrumental in having revoked an edict of expulsion with which the Jews in Venice were then threatened. Solomon Ashkenazi also took part in the diplomatic negotiations which resulted in the election of Henry of Anjou as King of Poland, and, after Henry's return to France, he engaged in the Turkish support of Stephen Bathori to the vacant Polish throne.

§ 13. *Poland.* Poland, including the grand duchy of Lithuania, was for a long time a country in which the Jews found a ready welcome, and, as practically forming the middle class, they came to be recognized as a necessary adjunct to the autochthonous population. The Polish Jews were invested with internal self-government, and, since the middle of the sixteenth century, for about 200 years, they possessed a central organization, the Council of the Four Lands (or parts of Poland), which, like a diet, met half-yearly and transacted civil and religious affairs relating to the Jews of Poland. Yet the backward state of the country, in which only the nobles and priesthood enjoyed a certain amount of culture and well-being, had its depressing influence on the Polish Jews, who, in want of some contact with a native civilization, eschewed all scientific pursuits and concentrated their whole attention on the Talmud. This was not, however, with that wide philosophic outlook with which the Talmud was treated by the Spanish masters, or with the scientific interest which has been devoted to it as a great document of Judaism in the investigations of the nineteenth century, but largely as an end in itself. The Jewish idea of the high merit of study was exclusively applied to the Talmud, and all the fruitfulness of the Jewish mind was spent in creating a labyrinth of commentaries and an endless number of super-commentaries, while ingenuity displayed itself in finding various ways out of the self-created maze. Whatever intellectual or even religious value this might have possessed was largely counterbalanced by the obscurantism which the one-sided devotion to the Talmud engendered. Hence the vast energy and keenness of mind evidenced by the great Polish Talmudists did not produce any original idea in Jewish thought or any quickening influence on Jewish life. On the contrary, the Polish Jews, in spreading over western Europe, proved a retarding influence on their co-religionists in other lands, especially as the considerable Jewish knowledge they undoubtedly possessed placed the ecclesiastical offices and the religious education of the young in their hands. This was particularly the case in Germanic lands, which, for Jewish purposes, extended from Hungary to Holland. Thus Jacob Polak (the Pole), the most eminent Talmudist at the beginning of the sixteenth century, introduced the Polish casuistical method of the study of the Talmud, known as Pilpul, to Prague, one of the most ancient and important communities in Central Europe.

A number of these Rabbis rose, however, above the prevailing objection to secular knowledge. Among such was Judah Löw ben Bezaleel, of Prague (d. 1609), who had gathered around him a circle devoted to philosophy and science. Most prominent among them was David Gans, author of a work on Jewish and general history entitled *The Branch of David* (*Zemah David*), who was in touch with Kepler and Tycho Brahe, and translated for the latter certain astronomical tables from Hebrew into German. An adept of profane learning was also Yom-Tob Lipman Heller (1579-1654), the most cultured German Jew in the Middle

Ages. Notable apologists of Judaism with a knowledge of Christian polemics were in the fifteenth century Yom-Tob Lipman of Mühlhausen, the author of *Victory* (*Nizahon*) and in the sixteenth century the Karaite Isaac of Troki, Lithuania, who achieved extraordinary fame by his *Strengthening of the Faith* (*Hizuk Emunah*), which attracted wide attention, and was hailed by Voltaire as an effective attack on the Christian faith. Zebi Hirsh Ashkenazi, known as Haham Zebi (1658-1718), was a great authority in his day, whom the Spanish and Portuguese congregation in London called in (1705) to decide as to the orthodoxy of certain philosophical utterances by their Haham (Rabbi) David Nieto, himself a man of varied accomplishments. Among the distinguished Rabbis of the eighteenth century must be mentioned Jonathan Eybeschütz (1690-1764), Chief Rabbi of Altona, who became involved in an accusation of Sabbathaian heresy which stirred the whole of Jewry in those days. That this race of Rabbinism could, even under adverse circumstances, produce spiritual leaders of enlightenment— not to speak of nobility of character, with which this period of Jewish history was no less rich than at other times—is evidenced by the life and work of Elijah of Vilna, named the Gaon of Vilna (1720-97), whose vast and critical range of Jewish learning did not exclude knowledge of secular subjects, such as astronomy and mathematics. A master of the Hebrew language was Moses Haim Luzzatto, of Padua (1707-1747), who might have inaugurated a new era in the national literature had his wayward genius not been lost in the mazes of the Cabbalah. But Judaism was saved from the dry rot which had set in generally by the rationalism and scientific investigation that arose in western lands and by the mystic movements which made their appearance in eastern Europe.

§ 14. *The Cossack Rising.* It was under the comparatively favorable conditions prevailing in Poland that in the middle of the seventeenth century the Jews received a staggering blow which affected very seriously the whole Jewish organism. The Catholic Poles, who ruled the so-called Saporogian Cossacks on the Dnieper, and endeavored to extract both material and spiritual advantages from these Greek Orthodox subjects, had handed over to Jews the collection of taxes which the Cossacks had to pay to their Polish lords. These taxes, odious as they already were, were made even more so by fees on all religious family ceremonies, such as baptism, marriage, or burial, according to Greek Orthodox rites, for the purpose of inducing the Cossacks to enter the Catholic Church. To enforce the payment of such taxes, the keys of the Orthodox churches were handed over to the agents of the Polish nobles, who happened to be Jews. It was a hateful business, which was to cost both Jews and Poles very dear. In 1648, a rebellion broke out and, led by Bogdan Chmielnicki, a Cossack of murderous temperament with a personal grudge against the Jews, the Cossacks swept over the country, and, with all imaginable ferocity, exterminated every Jew and Pole who fell in their hands, only those being spared who embraced the Greek Orthodox religion. Hundreds of large Jewish communities were wiped out of existence. The Poles were unable to offer effective resistance, and their troubles in the election of a king at that time gave the Cossacks still greater opportunities. The rebellion dragged on, with an interruption of a year and a half, from 1648 to 1651, but, even after the submission of the Cossacks, the troubles of the Jews were yet by no means at an end. At the instigation of Chmielnicki, Russia entered into war with Poland, and the Russian invaders exterminated the Jews without mercy. The campaign which the Swedes undertook against Poland made the lot of the hapless Polish Jews still more sad. Perhaps a half-million of Jews lost their lives in the Cossack uprising and the subsequent wars. The Jewish communities, east and west, became full of Polish refugees who had escaped the shadow of the sword. The ravages and butcheries of the Russian brigand gangs, known as Haidamacks, in the middle of the eighteenth century, filled again the cup of Jewish sorrow and misery to overflowing.

§ 15. *The Hassidim.* The wretched condition of the Polish Jews, increased by the troubles consequent on the rapid decay of Poland, found relief in a still more intense devotion to the comforts of faith. Especially in those parts which had been most severely visited by the terrible ravages of the Cossack rebellion, the harassed and despairing Jews turned eagerly to mystic hopes of better times. If the stagnant scholastic studies of the Talmudists brought little satisfaction to simple souls thirsting for a refreshing draught of the living waters of religion, it came to them in a large measure by the rise of a movement which at one time threatened the supremacy of traditional Talmudical Judaism among the masses in eastern Europe. The founder of this movement was Israel ben Eliezer, surnamed Baal Shem-Tob (the Master of the Good [Divine] Name), or, by his initials, Besht. He was born in Podolia about the year 1700, and lived in humble circumstances. He left no record of his views, but, by what can be gathered from the legends that have encrusted his fame, it is apparent that he was a mystical genius of a very high order, to which was added a heart of great humility and tenderness. He swept away the rigid formalism and the casuistic cobwebs which then overlaid the throbbing vigor that had once distinguished the Talmudical scheme of life. Israel Baal Shem-Tob cared little for the favorite studies, nor would he join in the somber views, of those Cabbalists who mortified the flesh as a service pleasing to God. He declared the immanence of God in man, and, therefore, saw God in all the acts and manifestations of life. This, the basic idea in the religious conceptions of the Baal Shem, was supplemented by his spiritual exaltation and the intense fervor of his ecstatic joy in his communion with the all-pervading Creator. There were some, the Righteous (*Zaddikim*), who, he felt, were in the counsel of the Eternal, and could influence the course of that constant miracle, the divine governance of the universe. Thus, all the forms and ceremonies were of little account compared to that spiritual abandon which bridges the gulf between mortal man and the eternal Spirit. The Baal Shem was, however, no mere pantheistic philosopher or mystic recluse; he entered into the joys and sorrows of his surroundings, and became famed far and wide as a thaumaturgic saint who could heal the bodily, as well as the spiritual, ills of mankind. His gracious intercourse with the common people, especially with "publicans and sinners," as well as many of his utterances and acts, remind the sympathetic, though unprejudiced, observer of the personality of Jesus of Nazareth, whom he strikingly resembled in several important respects. This is a suggestion which would have horrified the good Baal Shem, but it is no extravagant assumption that his pure and unselfish heart would have also most energetically repudiated the subsequent materialistic developments of his doctrines. Alas, for the spiritual growth of man! Israel Baal Shem-Tob became the founder of the Hassidim (Pietists), a cabbalistic sect which spread with lightning rapidity all over Poland, Hungary, Rumania, and brought for the moment a quickening influence, a comforting solace, to the weary existence of the Jewish masses. But the beautiful spiritual ecstasy of the chosen few degenerated into religious antics and perversions of the many; the Righteous who, by the purity of their souls, could see divine visions and intercede with the Almighty, became self-seeking pontiffs bent on their own aggrandizement. From the first, the apostles of the Hassidim were bitterly opposed by the leading Rabbis, headed by the famous Elijah, the Gaon of Vilna, but these "Opponents" (*Mithnaggedim*) could only hinder, not stop, the progress of Hassidism. The rationalistic ideas which subsequently found their way among the Jews of eastern Europe proved a more effective barrier. Yet at this day the Hassidim are still there a numerous and powerful force. The original leaders of the Hassidim founded various dynasties of the Righteous, popularly known as Rebbes (Rabbis), which still subsist in some splendor by the lavish offerings of their pious adherents and devotees. Apart from this local jurisdiction, the Hassidim form part of the general Jewish community, and readily merge their separatist doctrines and practices in different surroundings.

In recent times the specific spiritual values of a neo-Hassidism have been interpreted to western Europe by Martin Buber, the most profound Jewish religious thinker of the present generation, who has perceived in the Hassidic approach to the Divine an exalted emanation of the religious genius of the Jewish people. The researches of Simon Dubnow and Lazar Gulkowitsch, who have traced and elucidated the sources from which have arisen the ideas and doctrines of Hassidism, have given to this religious efflorescence a very notable place in modern Judaism.

§ 16. *The Rise of Tolerance.* It is an extraordinary coincidence that on the day following the expulsion of the Jews from Spain (2nd August 1492), Christopher Columbus set out for the discovery of the American continent, which was destined to play such a far-reaching part in the history of the persecuted Jews. It is a matter of interest, showing the part the Jews took in the great discoveries of Columbus, Vasco da Gama, and others of that time, that the money with which Columbus was provided for his memorable journeys was furnished by, or derived from, Jews; that astronomical charts and nautical instruments he used had been prepared by Jews, and that the first European to set foot on the American continent was one of a number of Jews who accompanied him, Luis de Torres (who was also the first to discover the use of tobacco). The New World did little at the beginning to help the Jews, except that a large number of crypto-Jews found a refuge there from the implacable hostility of the Inquisition, until that dread tribunal transferred its activities to that region also, and the sky over American soil was reddened by the flaring light of Jewish bodies burnt at the stake as an "act of faith" pleasing to God. These autos-da-fé, punctuated by the burning of Jewish books, were not, however, to last for ever. The enlightenment that came with the Renaissance, with the rise and spread of Protestantism, with the general rebellion against priestly authority, was to have its beneficent effects likewise on the Jews. It came indeed painfully slowly, but we can already discern its advent. In the darkness which enveloped the Jews at the beginning of the sixteenth century, the Dominican Jacob van Hoogstraten, instigated by the converted Jew Johann Pfefferkorn, of Frankfort-on-Main, brought up the old accusations against the Talmud, which was to be burnt again "by authority." The matter came before the Emperor Maximilian, and he referred it to the expert opinion of Reuchlin, one of the great humanists of Germany, who also possessed an extensive knowledge of the Jewish writings. Reuchlin's weighty pronouncement was in favor of the Talmud, and his bitter and successful struggle against his ecclesiastical opponent forms an interesting and important chapter in the history of human progress, and materially contributed to the ferment that brought about the Protestant Reformation in Germany. This incident drew the attention of the learned world to the value of post-biblical Jewish literature, and Christian scholars began to take an intelligent interest in the intellectual productions of the Jewish people. Hebrew was included in the New Learning for the purpose of arriving at the original text of the Old Testament; Rabbinical commentaries provided guides to the rational study of the Sacred Scriptures; the Talmud gave interesting and valuable information on the Jewish ideas and tendencies prevailing in New Testament times. Some, like Luther, ultimately turned in anger from the Jews, when they found that they would not see the truth in its Protestant Christian form; others, like Eisenmenger, the author of *Judaism Unmasked,* turned their Jewish knowledge into gall by collecting, with a zeal worthy of a better cause, every uncharitable and extravagant utterance in Jewish literature in order that the Jews might be irrevocably condemned to universal scorn and hatred; but Christian Hebraists like Bartolocci, the Buxtorfs, Lightfoot, Scaliger, Surenhusius, Wagenseil, Wolf, and others looked no longer at the post-biblical Jewish literature, and consequently at the Jews, with eyes of ignorant fanatics to whom the very Hebrew letters were magical forms. A work of high importance and considerable merit by a Christian divine was the *History and Religion of the Jews since Christ to the Present Day* (1706-11) by Jacob Christian Basnage.

The religious evolution effected by Protestantism, if it still retained a large measure of intolerance, brought gradually a change in the idea of uniformity which had been the grand passion of Catholicism. The first affected by the rising gleam of tolerance were the Dutch, who had liberated themselves from the Spanish yoke at such a tremendous cost of energy and blood. The Marranos in the Iberian Peninsula, in danger of the Inquisition, turned their anxious gaze to that little heroic people which, like the Jews, was battling with the mighty forces of fanaticism, and repeated attempts were made by these secret Jews to obtain a sure footing in Holland. After various dangerous and romantic attempts, they succeeded. Holland now became the most important place of refuge for those Jews of Spain and Portugal who were prepared to leave their country in order to throw off their religious mask, and in Amsterdam there arose a great community, a New Jerusalem, the fame of which spread over the whole Dispersion. In these neo-Jews we meet men of nobility in social station as well as in character; many who had played an important part in the commerce, politics, and literature of their native countries; not a few who, to escape the vigilant eyes of the Inquisition, had passed their days within the walls of a convent or church, or who had perhaps themselves sat in judgment on their detected fellow-Marranos; some even who had borne the priest's surplice or the friar's hood with becoming solemnity and outward piety. It was a strange company, these men and women, with the high-sounding names of proud hidalgos, who assembled in worship in some humble conventicle, and then, since 1675, in the noble synagogue which still forms the most interesting Jewish landmark in Amsterdam. Endowed with much of this world's goods as well as with high intelligence and education, their influence came to be of great service to their co-religionists abroad. In 1612 a community of Marranos settled in Hamburg under favorable auspices, and in 1622 King Christian IV of Denmark sent an invitation to Jews of Amsterdam to settle in Glückstadt, granting them above all full liberty of conscience.

It was from Amsterdam that one of its most eloquent and famous Rabbis, Manasseh ben Israel, a descendant of Marrano refugees, set out for England in 1655 to induce Cromwell to readmit the Jews into that country, where the race had been proscribed since the expulsion of 1290. The ground had already been prepared by the settlement in London of a number of Marranos, who had lived there outwardly as Catholic merchants, and by the religious ideas which agitated Puritan England at that time. Manasseh ben Israel was very kindly received by the Lord Protector, and a national conference met at Whitehall to consider the question of the readmission of Jews into England, but the commotion which the matter aroused rendered this assembly abortive. Nevertheless, the resettlement of the Jews in England was tacitly permitted by Cromwell (1657), who, with the eye of a statesman, saw the advantages that would accrue to the

British realm from the wealth, enterprise, and goodwill of the Jews. Manasseh ben Israel, who had influenced English public opinion in favor of the Jews by his able work *Vindiciae Judaeorum,* was dismissed home by Cromwell with a state pension of £100 a year, but he died on his way back to Amsterdam (1657). Charles II confirmed the Jewish position in England, and the Jewish community of London became gradually one of the most influential in the Dispersion. After worshiping in a private house in Creechurch Lane, off Leadenhall Street, the congregation of Spanish and Portuguese Jews, "Sahar Asamaim" ("The Gate of Heaven"), grew into such numbers that in 1701 they built the synagogue in Bevis Marks, which, as the oldest extant synagogue in England and associated with many proud memories, is still an object of great interest and importance. The Jewish activities that clustered around the sanctuary in Bevis Marks made this community for several generations the center of the intellectual and political life of the Jews in England and the connecting link between Europe and the Jews who had settled in the British colonies in America.

The Dutch and English conquests in Central and South America, which deprived the Spanish and Portuguese nations of many of their possessions there, brought to light considerable numbers of secret Jews, who, under milder regimes, openly acknowledged their Jewish convictions. Apart from the settlement of Jews in the Spanish and Portuguese colonies, the earliest references to which are to be sought in the transportation of forcibly baptized Jewish children from Portugal and in the local records of the Inquisition, the Jews found refuge in the various Dutch, French, and English colonies, and everywhere took a prominent and honorable share in the commercial and political activities of the New World. In 1642 about 600 Jews sailed from Holland to Pernambuco, Brazil, from which, however, they were expelled when Portugal retook it from the Dutch in 1654. A small number of the refugees found their way to New York (then New Amsterdam), where the Dutch governor Stuyvesant tried unsuccessfully to exclude them, and some of them settled in Newport, Rhode Island, the ancient Jewish cemetery of which forms the subject of one of Longfellow's best-known poems. The congregation of Spanish and Portuguese Jews, "Shearith Israel" ("The Remnant of Israel"), in New York, was established in 1655, and is still in a flourishing condition. In all these settlements the Spanish and Portuguese Jews played the leading part, even some time after the immigration of German and Polish Jews had set in, and the wealth, social standing, and public spirit of the first Jewish settlers largely influenced the favorable estimate which was formed of them in the early colonial days.

§ 17. *Spinoza.* Foremost among the numerous men of distinction in the new communities of the Spanish and Portuguese Jews in the seventeenth and eighteenth centuries was Benedict (Baruch) Spinoza (1632-77), who, in spite of his teachings and his life—or because of them—must be regarded as one of the glories of the people of Israel. Born in Amsterdam of Marrano descent, he was brought up in the schools of the Amsterdam Jewish congregation, and acquired under Manasseh ben Israel and other Rabbis a large measure of Jewish learning. In his mental equipment, Moses Maimonides, Levi ben Gerson, Hasdai Crescas, and other Jewish philosophers occupied the first place, but his bold mind led him into independent paths. Spinoza turned against the authority of Judaism, away from its conceptions and practices, and the leaders of the community, alarmed at his expressed views, first endeavored to placate him by an annual stipend of a thousand gulden, and, failing in this, they expelled him by excommunication (1656). It was one of those stern acts of self-purification which the Jews of Spain and Portugal had learned by their own bitter experience, though we may perhaps credit them with the legitimate fear that the dangerous views or acts of one of their number might seriously affect the slender basis of their newly won toleration. Spinoza took his excommunication resignedly and withdrew to The Hague, where he provided for his few wants by polishing lenses. If the fame of his genius spread already in his lifetime—he refused, among other tempting offers, the chair of philosophy at the Heidelberg University, as it would have fettered his independence—it was afterwards that his philosophy became one of the cornerstones of modern thought. High in the firmament of pure thought, Spinoza has his throne among the greatest master-minds of all time. The man who was once decried and dreaded as an atheist has been recognized as "a God-intoxicated Jew." He founded no school and left few disciples, yet Leibniz, Goethe, and other intellectual giants did not disdain to sit at the feet of this sage of the Amsterdam ghetto. Even more than this: serene as was the mind of Spinoza, so was also his life.

§ 18. *In the Middle of the Eighteenth Century.* While Europe was growing out of the swaddling clothes of ecclesiasticism and awaking to a sense of manhood; while the French encyclopaedists were accumulating the forces which were to burst and sweep away the dams of bigotry and servitude; even though the Jewish people itself had already contributed to civilization one of the greatest luminaries of modern thought, the Jews were still living in their Dark Ages. Not only in Catholic countries, but likewise among Protestant nations which had clamored and fought for the inalienable rights of the human conscience, the Jew was still an outcast for conscience' sake. By the middle of the eighteenth century, the Jews were yet everywhere a proscribed race, just as if Pope Innocent III, who had declared that the Jews were branded with the mark of Cain, were still the all-powerful master of Europe.

In spite of certain glimpses of light which had fallen on the Jewish people, its outlook was a very gloomy one indeed. The stray rays of toleration had reached mainly those few Jewish refugees from the Iberian Peninsula, who, owing to their wealth and extensive influence in all the great marts of the Old and New World, had become more or less welcome guests among the trading rivals of the Spanish and Portuguese nations. In Poland, the most populous Jewish center, the Cossack and other troubles had reduced the race to barbarism and misery; in neighboring Austria, the Jews were barely allowed to vegetate, and, in 1744, the Empress Maria Theresa hunted them out of Bohemia and Moravia. Where persecution was not in an active state, the Jews remained burdened with the general opprobrium with which contempt, the sickly offspring of the former religious fanaticism, had loaded them. Centuries of grinding oppression had brought the Jews very low. In Germanic lands there arose now and again a so-called court-Jew, who, entrusted with the financial affairs of one of the numerous princes, was perhaps at times able to secure some little administrative relief for his co-religionists. But, as happened in the cases of Lippold, the physician and financial agent of Joachim II of Brandenburg, and Joseph Süss Oppenheimer, the minister of Duke Charles Alexander of Wurtemberg (both of whom were executed with great ignominy on trumped-up charges in 1573 and 1738 respectively), the fall of the Jewish favorite usually dragged the whole community into his ruin. As a whole, the Jews remained a class of social pariahs, petty traders or artisans, speaking a mongrel German, with no ambitions outside their own small and despised circles. Their degradation was stamped officially by the Leibzoll, a special poll-tax which Jews had to pay in their passage from one into another of the numerous principalities; by the rigid institution of the "tolerated" and "protected" Jews; by the humiliating and vexatious regulations and limitations regarding the residence of Jews, and by the restrictions which were even placed on the number of Jewish marriages—all Pharaonic laws intended to repress the expansion of the Jewish communities and to break the spirit as well as the body of the Jew. Their intellectual condition had also sunk to a low ebb, and even the religiously obligatory instruction in Hebrew subjects was carried on in mean surroundings, in a mechanical manner, by men incompetent for any other calling. Religion still remained, but it had assumed the garb of its professors, and, in any case, it had lost that depth of interpretation and breadth of application which could alone ensure for Judaism the rank of a world-religion in modern civilization.

CHAPTER VI

THE ERA OF EMANCIPATION

§ 1. *The Modern Epoch.* By the middle of the eighteenth century, when the status of the Jews had reached its lowest watermark, they entered on a period of their history which, in its achievements and potentialities, was to rival, and, in certain respects, to eclipse, the most brilliant periods since the fall of the Jewish State. If the historian of the emancipation of the Israelites from the Egyptian yoke has had to have recourse to supernatural intervention, a more rationalistic age must seek in the extraordinary vitality and genius of the Jewish people for the causes of their rapid and marvelous evolution during the nineteenth century. Leaving aside the unproductive millions in lands of oppression, the enfranchised Jews have produced a remarkable host of men of international distinction in all walks of life, in science, arts, and letters. This progress is even more strikingly apparent in the field of politics, where Jews are naturally most exposed to prejudice and obstruction. The same generation that had been subjected in Germany to the degrading poll-tax, saw the rise of Heinrich Heine, the greatest lyrical poet of the German tongue, and of Ludwig Börne, the most prominent German political writer of the day. Already in 1848, Gabriel Riesser, the grandson of a Lithuanian Rabbi, was a Vice-President of the memorable German Parliament of that year, and a member of its deputation which offered to Frederick William IV the crown of the German Empire. Adolphe Crémieux, born in 1796, almost under the shadow of the medieval Jewish disabilities, became in 1848 a member of the Provisional Government of France, again of the Government of National Defence in the critical days of 1870-71; England received its greatest Imperialist statesman in Benjamin Disraeli, who, though nominally a Christian, was a Jew by inclination as well as by birth; in Rome, the conqueror of ancient Judea, the Italian army was commanded by a Jewish general, Giuseppe Ottolenghi; and at the same time that a Jew, Luigi Luzzatti, was Prime Minister of Italy, the capital of Catholic Christendom, where only forty years before the Jews were huddled together in a few miserable lanes and dark courts, was being administered by a Jewish chief magistrate, Ernesto Nathan. Not only did the Rothschilds and other Jewish bankers long maintain the leading, and a most honorable, position in international finance, but two Jews, Karl Marx and Ferdinand Lassalle, were the founders of Socialism, which became one of the greatest economic and political movements of modern times. Such a transformation of a scattered people of pariahs into one of the most progressive sections of western civilization, in spite of all the autocratic and ecclesiastical forces that were arrayed against them, in spite of all the ancient and deeply rooted social and religious odium and prejudice which still clung to them, is without parallel in modern history.

§ 2. *Moses Mendelssohn.* The revolutionary epoch-making change in the outlook and fortunes of the modern Jews was brought about in Germany, and by one who, both by his intellect and character, was well fitted to strike the generous imagination of the Christian world, and to usher in the social and political regeneration of his own people. Moses Mendelssohn (1729-86), to whom Jewry owes the initiative of its spiritual evolution from a strange element, out of touch with the interests and aspirations of its surroundings, into an integral part of European civilization, was born in Dessau as the son of a poor scribe of scrolls of the Law. At the age of fourteen, Moses, the son of Mendel (Mendelssohn), betook himself on foot from Dessau to Berlin in order to seek wisdom in the great city, where the poor Jew-boy was only admitted by referring to Rabbi David Fränkel, his former teacher, who had become Chief Rabbi of Berlin. Moses Mendelssohn, by sheer force of his own brilliant mind and the integrity of his heart, rose to the front rank of the German literary and philosophical world. He became an intimate friend of Lessing, who took Mendelssohn as his model in the fine type of a Jew he placed before the world in *Nathan der Weise*—a drama which represents a most effective plea on behalf of Mendelssohn's people—and among those who vied to do him honor was Kant, against whom Mendelssohn had successfully competed in a prize essay on a philosophical theme. The world looked with surprise at this Jew, who was one of the most polished German stylists and among its profoundest philosophers—and who yet remained true to the religious faith of the Jewish people. If Mendelssohn's *Phaedon,* on the immortality of the soul, which became one of the most fascinating books of the day, earned for him the title of the German Socrates, his work on behalf of his brethren-in-faith won him undying fame. Once more the Bible was to be the source of the rejuvenation of the people which gave the great Book to the world. Mendelssohn translated the Jewish Scriptures into German (transcribed in Hebrew characters), and thereby German became the medium for introducing the Jews into the rich literature of one of the great nations of modern Europe. From the Rhine to the Vistula and all along the Danube, Judaism now assumed a German hue; the devotees of the new-born Enlightenment (Haskalah) were followers of Mendelssohn, and its center was Berlin. But as Mendelssohn himself had imbibed his first philosophical conceptions from Maimonides' *Guide of the Perplexed,* and added to the German translation of the Bible a Hebrew commentary (*Biur*) by various hands, so also his disciples turned their attention to the ancient language and derived new strength by contact with an inspiring past. In his great work *Jerusalem,* Mendelssohn put before Jew and Christian a rationalistic conception of Judaism, showing the compatibility of its doctrines and practices with modern thought, and he also set out his religious ideas in *Morning Hours, or Lectures on the Existence of God* (1785). His high standing within and without the Jewish community made him the object of attack on the part of zealous Christians, but the loftiness and geniality of his personal character, no less than the reasoned steadfastness to his ancestral religion, inspired respect even among his opponents and reflected most favorably on his co-religionists. The emancipation of the Jews from the shackles of medieval barbarism and intolerance was thereby sounded in no uncertain tones, and they exerted their influence even beyond the confines of Germany. Thus the Jews entered on a new era in their history, and it was Mendelssohn who indicated the problems that have agitated Jewish life and thought to the present day.

The most extraordinary and original Jewish thinker in touch with Mendelssohn was Solomon Maimon (1754-1800). Born in a Lithuanian townlet, married at the age of twelve, earning a living as a dominie to the children of a village publican, Solomon Maimon resolved to satisfy his craving for knowledge by proceeding to Berlin. Less fortunate than Moses Mendelssohn, he was not admitted by the gate-keeper, and had to wander about for some time as a vagabond. He was, however, enabled to secure the desired protection of Mendelssohn, and with it he entered on those literary activities which were to ensure him a high rank in the realm of philosophy. Kant acknowledged that in *Die Transcendentale Philosophie* (1790) Solomon Maimon had shown himself the most penetrating of all his critics. His fame spread, and he received marked attention from Schiller, Goethe, and other lights of his time, but his intellectual genius could not replace the moral fiber he lacked, and this only accentuated the striking contrast he presented to Mendelssohn.

§ 3. *The Enlightenment (Haskalah) and Neo-Hebrew Literature.* The first direct effect of Mendelssohn's activities was the revival of Hebrew as a medium of modern culture. The circle that had gathered around him became the center of a general movement, the Enlightenment (Haskalah), the waves of which have not yet spent themselves. The purpose of it was to bring into the ghetto the best thought of the day in the ancient and acceptable language of the Jews, which had never been abandoned by them. The Hebrew commentary (*Biur*) on Mendelssohn's Bible marked the first step; a periodical, *Ha-measseph (The Collector)*, founded in 1784, grouped together a number of neo-Hebraists in Germany, Austria, and Poland, who became known by the name of *Meassephim.* These, as well as the Enlightened (Maskilim) generally, expended their literary efforts in the Hebrew translation or imitation of foreign classics, and in the criticism of the many superstitions and abuses which then disfigured Jewish life. Such attempts at reform created, of course, a cleavage between the old and the new order. Mendelssohn himself had to brave the determined opposition of those who feared that the new departure would bring about the extinction of the cherished faith of Israel, and their forebodings were justified by the lapse and apostasy of many of those who stood for the Enlightenment. These struggles filled out the intellectual life in eastern Europe for over a century, but eventually the modern Jewish humanists won the day. It is now recognized that traditional piety and general culture are not merely compatible with, but are essential to, Jewish welfare.

If the Enlightenment, in its cultural achievements, was but a pale reflection of the brilliant Spanish period, the Hebrew language gradually assumed a flexibility unexampled since

Biblical times. Abraham Mapu (1808-67) as a pioneer novelist, Leon Gordon (1831-92), a lyric poet, Kalman Schulman (1819-1899) as a prolific historian and translator of foreign literature, and Perez Smolenskin (1842-85), an influential publicist, stand high in the republic of Hebrew letters. Long before the end of the nineteenth century, there was no phase of modern literature that did not find expression in the Hebrew tongue, which again developed into a language for common use. Hebrew books of Jewish and general interest, as well as original works of belles-lettres and science, and a Hebrew press provided full accounts and discussions of political and social questions. In Palestine, stimulated by the lexicographer Eliezer ben Yehudah (1857-1922), author of an exhaustive though uncompleted dictionary, *Millon,* Hebrew became not only once more the vernacular of the Jews but one of the three official languages of the mandated country. The latest form of Hebrew literature has already produced several names of the foremost rank, such as the philosopher Ahad Ha'am (Asher Ginzberg, 1856-1927); the poets Haim Nahman Bialik (1873-1934), Saul Tschernichowski (1875-1943), Salman Schneour (b. 1887), the *littérateur* Nahum Sokolow (1861-1936), and the novelist Samuel Joseph Agnon (b. 1888)—to name but a few of literary genius—apart from a host of writers through whose talents Hebrew has, in spite of its hoary antiquity, entered once more into universal culture with all the elements and potentialities of a richly endowed modern language.

§ 4. *Yiddish.* As a *lingua franca* or folk-tongue, Yiddish (Jüdisch, Jewish) is widely current among the Jewish masses, being mainly spoken by the Jews of the whole of eastern Europe and their numerous emigrants in western Europe and the New World. It was originally the Teutonic vernacular of the medieval German Jews, who used the language of their native country, and, strange as it may seem, even produced in the thirteenth century Süsskind von Trimberg, a minnesinger of the German tongue. The great Jewish migrations from Germany to Poland during the crusades and the Black Death brought the German language also into eastern parts, but there the German was mixed up with Slavic expressions and grammatical turns, while the religious influence gave Hebrew an important part in shaping the language. This Jewish German was, however, so overshadowed by Hebrew that it long remained a stunted *patois,* and even those to whom Yiddish was the mother tongue did not accord it the respect due to one's native language. In its literary forms Yiddish was in its beginnings mainly a popular religious character, followed from the seventeenth century onwards by the characteristically Jewish "Story Book" (*Ma'asébuch*). With the growth of the Jewish publicistic activities in the nineteenth century, Yiddish was at last recognized as the only medium for reaching the masses, and a literature of some considerable dimensions grew up, both in permanent and ephemeral form. A number of writers of very high merit arose: Mendele Mocher Sepharim (1836-1917), aptly termed the Jewish Cervantes, Isaac Leib Perez (1851-1915), the classical interpreter of Hassidic life, and Shalom Alechem (1859-1916), with a characteristically Yiddish humor, as the foremost representatives of a remarkably rich literature that has not yet adequately found general appreciation. On the other hand, Shalom Asch has found wide recognition as one of the outstanding novelists of the present time. Yiddish plays, introduced by Abraham Goldfaden and developed by others, have also met with some success, especially in America. Hence Yiddish does not by any means deserve the opprobrium which has been meted out to it by Jews as well as by the outside world. Certainly, in some respects, as in invective and satire, Yiddish possesses an oriental exuberance not matched by any other European tongue (for such must Yiddish be acknowledged to be). In consequence of conditions that arose after the First World War, Yiddish in eastern Europe, particularly in the Russian border States, evolved into a recognized and, in certain respects, official language of the Jews. The Yiddish Scientific Institute, known as Yivo (founded in Vilna in 1925), became the center for the study and development of the Yiddish language and literature bearing particularly upon the life and thought of eastern Jewry. Owing to the war, this institute was transferred to New York, where it continues its activity. But in western lands Yiddish has to give way to the dominant language of the country, while the wealth, prestige, and dignity of Hebrew secure for this historic tongue the indisputable precedence in the affection, and even veneration, of the Jewish people.

§ 5. *The New Learning.* While the Hebrew Enlightenment took its course in eastern Europe, the Jews of Germany, attracted by the throbbing intellectual life around them, imbibed eagerly all that came within their reach. In an incredibly short time, they rose to a leading position in the literary world of Berlin. The daughters of Moses Mendelssohn, Rahel Levin, Henriette Herz, and other Jewesses, were now the brilliant hostesses in famous *salons* where the intellectual lights of Germany were wont to assemble. This rapid rise was not without its dangers. Bewildered and intoxicated, many of them lost their religious and moral bearings. Even the daughters of Moses Mendelssohn went over to Christianity; his son Abraham, though still remaining a Jew himself, had his son Felix, the future composer, baptized, admittedly not because of a belief in the truths of Christianity, but to smooth the way of his future career. The abnormal position of the German Jews, imbued as they were with the highest culture of the age, and yet condemned as political outcasts, shut out from all the benefits and favors of a bureaucratic State, led to conversions *en masse* to the dominant religion of the land. In a short space of time, about a third of the Berlin Jews, and that of the most wealthy and cultivated, entered the Christian fold. David Friedländer, the successor of Mendelssohn among the Jews of Berlin, applied on behalf of a number of fellow-Jews for admission into the Church on condition of not being obliged to subscribe to the divinity of Jesus or other dogmas of Christianity.

Whatever may be thought of any one solemnly forswearing his or her ancestral religion and publicly acknowledging an alien faith in which one does not believe, and whether worldly advancement is a sufficient condonation of what our better nature is sure to condemn, it must be admitted that very little had been done by the second quarter of the nineteenth century to strengthen the Jewish consciousness and to bring medieval Judaism into accord with modern thought. It began to be felt, however, that the great past of the Jewish people ought to be resuscitated from the dust of the ages, and presented to the inner circle as well as to the world at large as a picture worthy of all respect. A number of young men of eminent qualifications established a society, *Kulturverein,* for Jewish studies; but, alas! some of the most promising, among them the poet Heinrich Heine and the jurist Eduard Gans, left Judaism to be able to enter the service of the State or for some other materialistic reason. It was an unhappy beginning, but it was left to one of the small band of the faithful to carry through an herculean task with every success. Leopold Zunz (1794-1886) became the founder of what has been termed in Germany *Die Wissenschaft des Judentums* (the Science of Judaism), i.e. the scientific investigation and presentation of Jewish history and literature. With a marvelous industry and a remarkable instinct, Zunz collected and collated the ancient and scattered fragments of the extant Jewish documents, and brought order and beauty out of an apparently hopeless chaos. His masterly writings served to call forth the emulation of numerous other Jewish scholars. Among his contemporaries were the Galicians Nahman Krochmal and S. J. Rapoport, who combined the prodigious Talmudical erudition of the East with the critical sense of the West. Their labors brought forth an abundant harvest, especially in Germany. I. M. Jost (1793-1860), the first modern historian of the Jews; Abraham Geiger (1810-74), a Rabbi of encyclopaedic knowledge, and Heinrich Grätz (1817-91), the author of a monumental *History of the Jews* (also translated into English), stand out as the brightest stars in the galaxy of German-Jewish scholars and thinkers whose researches and penetrating minds have illumined the recesses of the Jewish past. Exceptional mention is due to Moritz Steinschneider (1816-1907), who, unlike other Jewish investigators, left the theological and historical highways and explored the rich contributions which the medieval Moorish and Spanish Jews made to the general advance of civilization.

From Teutonic lands the new Jewish Learning spread to other parts of Europe, and also to America. Samuel David Luzzatto in Italy (1800-65) and Salomon Munk in France (1803-67) were the chief pioneers in those countries. In eastern Europe, there arose a considerable number of Jewish scholars endowed with profundity of knowledge and a characteristically critical sense. Their most eminent representative has been Simon Dubnow (1860-1941), whose *Universal History of the Jews,* the most comprehensive of its kind, is based largely upon a record of the social and economic vicissitudes of the Jewish people, as distinct from its theological and literary aspects, and with a philosophy of Jewish nationalist autonomy in the Diaspora in addition to the Jewish national development in Palestine. As fruitful foster-grounds of modern Jewish studies must be accounted the various Rabbinical Seminaries, the first of which was established in Breslau in 1854. Similar theological colleges were established in Paris (a development of the Central Rabbinical School founded at Metz in 1830), London (Jews' College, founded in 1856), Berlin, Vienna, Budapest, Rome, Cincinnati, New York, but those in Berlin and Vienna were closed in the Nazi destruction of German and Austrian Jewry. In western parts they supplanted the Talmudical High Schools (Yeshiboth), which still continue their activities on a small scale in the Orient. The Judaistic Institute of the Hebrew University of Jerusalem is potentially the most important center of research in the Jewish past amidst the vital developments of the Jewish spiritual forces of the present age. The Rabbi Isaac Elhanan Yeshibah College in New York (opened in 1928), commemorating Rabbi Isaac Elhanan Spector, of Kovno (1817-96), the most famous Russian Rabbinical authority in the second half of the nineteenth century, is the first comprehensive effort to combine in the same institution traditional Jewish learning with a university training.

§ 6. *The Reform of Judaism.* The revival of Jewish Learning, no less than the imperative call of the times, brought a change in the current conceptions of Judaism. While medievalism had practically confined the Jews to the Talmud and the ritual codes that had been elaborated by Moses Maimonides and Joseph Caro, the all-absorbing effort to maintain Judaism against the numerous subversive influences that threatened its very existence led to the neglect of the study of the inspiring Biblical epoch, of all the philosophical developments of Judaism, its wealth of ideas, the profundity of its social ethics and the grandeur of the world-mission of Israel. A critical examination laid bare the strength as well as the weaknesses of Judaism. It showed that Judaism was not a religion bounded by the circumscribed outlook of medieval Rabbis, but that the Jews were still in possession of those sources which had given the ethical monotheistic idea and the prophetical inspiration to the world. It was only necessary to clear away the accumulations of scholasticism and narrow-minded pietism in order to make the living waters accessible to all.

The Reform of Judaism, which took its rise in Germany, the intellectual center of Jewry, was not a moral revolt, like the Protestant Reformation of Christianity in the sixteenth century, but was primarily liturgical and ceremonial in character. The prayers, which had grown to inordinate length, were curtailed and certain customs abolished, not through any wanton desire for destruction, but because historical investigations had shown what was truly ancient and essential and what was a later and unnecessary accretion. The Divine Services were beautified, because the growth of the aesthetic taste demanded that a greater decorum and dignity should be introduced into the synagogue, which had hitherto been utilized as the ordinary house of assembly in the Jewish community. Religious instruction from the pulpit, which had been long neglected, became again an integral feature of the Divine Service, and the vernacular was more and more introduced among the prayers. Throughout there was a general tendency to do away with the oriental and separatist aspects of Judaism, and to bring into bold relief the universalistic and ethical mission of the Jewish people.

The first effort to introduce liturgical and ceremonial reforms in the synagogue was made by Israel Jacobsohn, who, in 1810, established at Seesen, near the Harz Mountains, a synagogue on those lines. In 1818 another such synagogue was founded in Hamburg, and many of the outward improvements adopted there were introduced later on in the Jewish houses of prayer throughout western Europe; but those places where doctrinal changes were acted upon became known as Reform Synagogues, or Temples, which spread all over Germany and found their fullest development in the United States of America. The first Reform Synagogue in London was established in 1841, and was then followed by similar synagogues in Manchester and Bradford, and recently in other parts of the country.

Among those Rabbis who worked in the cause of Reform Judaism in Germany were Samuel Holdheim (1806-60), a thorough-going Radical, whose synagogue in Berlin boldly transferred the Sabbath from Saturday to Sunday; Abraham Geiger, whose great learning gave historical support to progressive ideas; Samuel Hirsch (1815-89), who elaborated a philosophical basis for the new movement; Ludwig Philippson (1811-89), whose *Allgemeine Zeitung des Judentums,* long the most important German-Jewish periodical, spread the cause of reform far and wide. In the United States, the remarkable organizing abilities of Isaac M. Wise (1819-1900) rendered Reform the dominant feature of American Judaism. Rabbinical Conferences in Germany in the middle of the nineteenth century, and in America during its last decades, brought about definite pronouncements on the Reform attitude on vital problems of Judaism and their relations to modern thought and conditions.

The cause of Conservatism, or Orthodoxy, was upheld in the first place by Rabbis of the old type, who saw in Reform the dissolution of Judaism, and by scholars and thinkers who, recognizing the need for some definite action to counteract the growing indifference and apostasy, sought to preserve the ancient structure of Judaism while effecting such alterations as were undoubtedly demanded by the changed times. It was the latter attitude which stemmed the tide of Reform in Germany and elsewhere. Zecharias Frankel (1801-75), the principal of the Breslau Theological Seminary, brought about a tendency, the so-called Breslau school, which, proclaiming the well-established freedom of Jewish thought, emphasized the continuity—or the positive-historic aspect—of Judaism. Samson Raphael Hirsch (1808-88), of Frankfort-on-Main, exercised a marked conservative effect on those who came under his immediate influence, while

Israel Hildesheimer (1820-99), by his Rabbinical Seminary in Berlin, created a living center of traditional Judaism. In addition, the somewhat disappointing results of the high hopes of Reform in Germany, and the common and pressing problems which affected the Jews of all parties, acted as checks to the progress of Reform, while the reckless radicalism of some Rabbis on the one hand, and the rally of the orthodox on the other, brought about a general reaction towards moderate conservatism. Perhaps the most striking feature in the re-orientation of Reform Judaism was the change of attitude in favor of Palestine as the Jewish national as well as spiritual center and the consequent merging of the universalist and particularist elements of Judaism in accordance with the ideals of the ancient Hebrew prophets.

§ 7. *The Struggle for Emancipation.* While internal problems, religious and social, stirred western Judaism out of its long lethargy, the growing intellectual advancement of the Jews called for the abrogation of those medieval enactments with which bigotry and prejudice still fettered all the efforts of the Jews. Even in Holland, England, and in other parts of Europe, where the Jews had found a refuge, they were tolerated as aliens rather than recognized as full-fledged citizens. To attain this latter object was the determined effort of the Jews during the last century. The first modern European ruler to recognize the fact that the Jews might be turned into useful members of the State by according them the means of self-development was Joseph II of Austria, who, in 1782, issued a number of liberal laws affecting the Jews, but they proved of little practical effect under the inimical governments of his successors, and it was only in 1848, the year of fateful commotions on the European Continent, that the Austrian Jews achieved some measure of freedom. In 1866 the Jews of Austria were completely emancipated from all legislation directed against them. The French Revolution, which proclaimed the equality of all men, could not well have excluded the Jews from this fundamental principle. Napoleon I, who had his own opinions, was at first inclined to question the general idea of equality in its application to the Jews; but, to settle his doubts, he convened in 1806 an assembly of representative Jews, grandiosely termed a Sanhedrin, which was called upon to answer a series of questions relating to the attitude of Jews towards the State and their non-Jewish fellow-citizens. The only concrete result of these deliberations was the establishment of a consistory of the Jews of France. The Revolution of 1830 crowned the citizenship of the Jews by including Judaism among the religions officially recognized and subventioned by the State. In spite of revolutions and social convulsions, the emancipation of the French Jews has remained intact. A considerable number of them have attained to the highest political offices, the Socialist leader Léon Blum (1872-1950) having occupied the position of Prime Minister of France three times. France, which thus led in the emancipation of the Jews in Europe, brought the same boon to the Jews of all the States that came under its rule, or even influence, in the great conquests of the Revolution and the Empire. But when the French receded from their positions in western Germany, many of the old laws were again put into force against the Jews; and although the Congress of Vienna confirmed the rights granted to the German Jews during the French occupation, this was made invalid by the trickery and chicanery with which it was interpreted by the authorities. The leading Jewish champion in the struggle for the emancipation of the German Jews was Gabriel Riesser (1806-63), who claimed the liberation of the German Jew as a German patriot to whom the name and fame of his fatherland was as dear as the welfare of his co-religionists. The upheaval of 1848 proved a turning point in the political fortunes of the German Jews, whose emancipation was completed in the creation of the German Empire in 1871. In Hungary, the Jews were emancipated with the grant of the constitution in 1867, and in Italy the last vestiges of Jewish disabilities were swept away with the entry of the Italian army into Rome in 1870.

§ 8. *Emancipation in England.* The history of the Jews in England since the Resettlement in the middle of the seventeenth century is one of organic development from a trading body of aliens domiciled in England to one of the many integral elements of which the British Empire is composed. The Jews in England had not to battle against a medieval anti-Jewish legislation, as was the case on the Continent, but the Christian character of the English State precluded the incorporation of the Jews into the body politic. The disabilities which were thereby created rendered necessary a lengthy struggle to bring about the enfranchisement of the British Jews. The fact that already at the beginning of the eighteenth century Jews took a prominent part in the financial affairs of the nation, such as the assistance rendered by Antonio Lopez Suasso (Baron Avernas de Gras) to William III in his descent on England, by Sir Solomon de Medina (the first Jew to be knighted in England) to the Duke of Marlborough, or the loyal support of the Jews during the Jacobite insurrection, predisposed the king and the Government in their favor. In 1723 the words, "On the true faith of a Christian," were removed from Jewish oaths, though the phrase was to prove a very serious obstruction to Jewish political progress. In 1753 a Jewish Naturalization Bill was passed both in the House of Commons and the House of Lords, but this created such opposition that it was repealed in the following year. With this the civic emancipation of the Jews was delayed indefinitely. Even more than on the Continent, the intellectual and social had preceded the political emancipation of the Jews, and increased the discontent and impatience of those who yearned to shine in the larger life of the nation. Hence a great number of the wealthy and cultivated Spanish and Portuguese Jews—descendants of those who for their religion's sake had braved the dangers of the Inquisition—entered into the coveted equality through the portals of the Church. The families of D'Israeli, Basevi, Bernal, Ricardo, Ximenes, Lopez, etc., who afterwards rose high in British public and social life, gradually severed their connection with Judaism. But the Jewish community nevertheless increased in numbers and influence, and the demand for civic rights thus became only more urgent. In 1833 a Bill for the removal of Jewish disabilities was passed by the House of Commons, but it was rejected by the House of Lords, and this procedure was repeated no less than ten times. Following the line of least resistance, relief was obtained meanwhile by the repeal of disabilities connected with municipal life, and David Salomons (afterwards created a baronet) was in 1835 elected sheriff of London. (In 1839 he was high sheriff of Kent, and in 1856 the first Jewish Lord Mayor of London.) Admission to Parliament was, however, still barred by the Christian oath of allegiance. To force events, the City of London elected in 1847 Baron Lionel de Rothschild a member of Parliament, but he could not take his seat, although re-elected in 1850. In 1851 David Salomons, on being elected for Greenwich, took the bolder course of voting and speaking in the House, even against the Speaker's ruling. He was nevertheless obliged to withdraw, and to pay a fine of £500 for each of the three times he had sat in the House. It was only in 1858 that, as a compromise between the Upper and the Lower House, it was decided that the oath could, by a special resolution, be modified, and it was under such a resolution that Baron Lionel de Rothschild, as the first professing Jew, entered Parliament in that year. In 1860 the Parliamentary oath for both Houses was permanently amended, and in 1885 Sir Nathan Mayer de Rothschild took, under the title of Lord Rothschild, his seat in the House of Lords as the first Jewish peer. The highest offices have been occupied by Jews in the Empire, Rufus Daniel Isaacs, the Marquess of Reading (1860-1935), having risen to the positions of Lord Chief Justice and Viceroy of India (1921-6), and Sir Isaac Isaacs (1855-1948) to those of Chief Justice of the High Court of Australia and Governor-General of Australia (1931-6). Herbert Samuel (b. 1870), now Viscount Samuel of Mount Carmel and Toxteth in the city of Liverpool, and Alfred Mond, Lord Melchett (1868-1930), were in the British Cabinet during the First World War; Edwin Montagu was Secretary for India, 1917-22; Arthur Michael Samuels (Lord Mancroft) was Financial Secretary to the Treasury; and Leslie Hore-Belisha and Sir Philip Sassoon were members of the Government in 1939. While Edwin Montagu was opposed to Jewish national aspirations in Palestine, Herbert Samuel, who became the first British High Commissioner for Palestine (1920-5), and Alfred Mond were actively associated with the adoption by the British Government of the Zionist claims. The Labor Ministry of 1945-50 included Mr. Emanuel Shinwell, first as Minister of Fuel and Power and then as Secretary for War; Lord Nathan as Minister of Civil Aviation; Mr. Lewis Silkin as Minister of Town and Country Planning; and Mr. George Strauss as Minister of Supply. Mr. Attlee's second Ministry included Mr. Shinwell as Minister of Defence.

For a century, British Jews have held politically an exceptional position in the Jewish world. The missions of mercy by the Anglo-Jewish philanthropist, Sir Moses Montefiore, which, from 1840 to 1872, he undertook to the Orient and various parts of Europe with the benevolent interest of Queen Victoria and the diplomatic support of the British Government, created a tradition which has been maintained by British Governments through the representative body of the Anglo-Jewish community, the Board of Deputies of British Jews (established in 1760), uninterruptedly ever since.

The number of Jews in Great Britain and Ireland, about 60,000 before the large Russo-Jewish immigration that began in 1881, has increased to about 400,000, of which London has a population of over 230,000. The insular position of British Judaism towards the end of the nineteenth century has changed with the advent of new elements from abroad which have given it new orientations. The Chief Rabbinate of Nathan Marcus Adler (b. in Hanover in 1803, d. 1890) and of his son Hermann Adler (1839-1911) created for English Judaism special characteristics, which have been developed on broad, albeit conservative, lines by Joseph Herman Hertz (1872-1946), who assumed the office of Chief Rabbi of the United Hebrew Congregations of the British Empire in 1913. The community of Spanish and Portuguese Jews is under the independent ecclesiastical jurisdiction of a Chief Rabbi, entitled Haham—a position which has been held by preachers and scholars of eminence: Raphael Meldola (1754-1828), Benjamin Artom (1835-79), and Moses Gaster (1856-1939). Reform Judaism has made some progress since the end of the nineteenth century, mainly through the influence of Claude Goldsmid Montefiore (1858-1938), a Maecenas of Jewish scholarship in all its aspects. Jewish learning has advanced under the guidance of Michael Friedländer and Adolphe Büchler (principals of Jews' College), of Solomon Schechter and Israel Abrahams, while, by the establishment of the Jewish Historical Society of England in 1893, Joseph Jacobs and Lucien Wolf laid the foundations for the study of the colorful Jewish past in this country.

In the British Dominions, where many positions of political dignity have been held by Jews, they have been among the earlier pioneers in the development of those territories from colonies to self-governing States of the British Commonwealth of Nations. In Canada, the settlement of Jews dates back to the British occupation of 1760, in which some of them took a notable part. There is in Canada not only a vigorous Jewish life, but the Dominion has become a home for large numbers of Jews who had to leave their native lands in the Old World. South Africa, which owes a great measure of its development to the enterprise of Jewish pioneers, has a Jewish population unrivaled in its intensive devotion to the spiritual ideals of the brotherhood of Israel. In Australia and New Zealand, the thriving Jewish communities have contributed an exceptionally large proportion of public men of distinction who have advanced the material and moral interests of their country. In New Zealand Sir Julius Vogel was Premier (1873), Sir Arthur M. Myers Minister of Finance and Defence (1912), and Sir Michael Myers Chief Justice (1929-46). The Legislative Assembly of New South Wales has had two Jewish Speakers, John Jacob Cohen (1917-19) and Sir Daniel Levy (1919-37, with two brief intervals).

§ 9. *Russia.* At the beginning of the twentieth century, all the important States of Western civilization recognized, at least in principle, the equality of the Jews with their fellow-citizens, but the Jews in Russia, who comprised about a half of the Jewish people, still remained subject to all the tyranny and whims of medieval legislation and administration.

In large tracts of modern Russia, Jews were already settled long before the appearance of the Russian conquerors, and the conversion of the Chazars to Judaism brought a large part of southern Russia under Jewish influence. But owing to the religious exclusiveness of the Muscovite grand dukes as well as to the spread of a remarkable Judaizing heresy, which was formed in Novgorod towards the end of the fifteenth century, and affected the highest circles in the land, the Jews were barely suffered on Russian territory. Ivan the Terrible refused to consent to the proposal of King Sigismund Augustus of Poland to admit Jews into Russia, and this attitude was continued by Ivan's successors, who in effect adopted the famous words of the Empress Elizabeth (1742), "I will not derive any profit from the enemies of Christ." Catherine II, who affected the airs of an enlightened sovereign, confirmed the exclusion of Jews from Russian soil; but with the first division of Poland in 1773, when a large number of Jews came under Russian rule, she had to content herself by issuing certain restrictive laws against them. This policy of discrimination against the Jews became the standing policy of the Russian Tsars, and it was only now and again interrupted by some countervailing decrees designed to alleviate the too manifest misery of the Jewish lot or to incorporate them into the Russian national life. Attempts made in this latter direction, which were usually carried out with a brutal disregard of Jewish susceptibilities and with the ulterior motive of converting the Jews to the Orthodox Church, aroused their justified suspicions, and defeated even the well-intentioned objects of the central Government.

That the Russian Jews were more amenable to genuinely tolerant measures was proved in the hopeful reign of Tsar Alexander II. The Russian defeat in the Crimean War, which led to general reforms, also affected favorably the welfare of the Jews. A relaxation of the restrictions imposed on their movemnts and social developments was all that was necessary to bring about a great forward stride in their Russification. In literature and art, in industry and commerce, Russian Jews rose very rapidly to honorable positions. Anton Rubinstein, one of the most famous musicians, and Marc Antokolski, the greatest sculptor produced by Russia, stood for a host of Russian Jews who added to the renown of their fatherland, while the intelligence and enterprise of Jewish merchants and manufacturers contributed to its wealth.

Even the reaction that set in during the latter part of the

reign of Alexander II did not check the progress and all-round expansion of Russian Jewry. But everything came to a sudden standstill with the shock occasioned by the assassination of the Tsar-liberator and the accession of Alexander III. The growing revolutionary sentiment was arrested by a merciless proscription of every liberal idea, and, to save the Asiatic despotism and Byzantine bureaucracy peculiar to Russia, the Jews were thrown to the reactionary wolves. The civilized world was horrified by the widespread anti-Jewish riots which occurred all over southwestern Russia, and threatened to engulf the Russian Jews. Then sweeping measures were taken to cripple the economic and intellectual development of the Jewish population. On the 3rd May 1882, Count Ignatiev issued certain "temporary" regulations, known as "May Laws," which, in spite of the recommendations of an imperial commission favorable to the Jews, remained in force. The Jews were cooped up in Poland and in towns of certain specified provinces in northwestern Russia, designated as the Pale of Settlement. The Jews outside this Pale of Settlement were mercilessly driven out, bag and baggage. With some notable protests, particularly in London in 1882 and 1891, civilization had come to the end of its resources, and the Russian Government, of which Pobiedonostzev, the procurator of the Holy Synod, was the leading spirit, had its own way. This policy (summed up in Pobiedonostzev's ideal solution that a third of the Russian Jews would emigrate, a third become converted, and a third die of starvation) was continued under Nicholas II, whose reign was marked in 1905 by the most violent anti-Jewish atrocities that had taken place since the Cossack uprising in the seventeenth century. In spite of the mocking hopes of a constitution and a Duma, the Russian Jews remained in a state of bondage, which was only broken by the cataclysmal upheaval that followed the Revolution and shattered the proud and mighty Empire of the Tsars.

§ 10. *The United States of America.* In striking contrast to Russia stood the United States of America, where the stream of Jewish emigration from eastern Europe found an easy and beneficent outlet. If, according to the oft-quoted saying of the Jewish novelist, Karl Emil Franzos, every country has the Jews it deserves, we may extend the application by the remark that every people has the government worthy of it. From the time when the Spanish and Portuguese Jews, hunted out of priest-ridden countries, found a refuge in North America, it has received all manner of Jews, who have proved citizens of value and worth to their new country. Although barely 2,000 all told at the time of the War of Independence, the American Jews took an appreciable part in the revolutionary struggle, Colonel Solomon Bush being among those who particularly distinguished themselves. The most notable of the patriots was Haym Salomon (1740-85), a Polish Jew, who unselfishly served in a variety of important financial capacities and spent his own large fortune for the benefit of his adopted country. Although the Jews in some of the States, like their co-religionists in England, had to contend against certain Christian formulas which shut them out from public offices, the Declaration of Independence (1776) and the Constitution (1790) of the United States removed every legal ground for political discrimination. In the spirit of the Hebrew Bible, which originally moved the Pilgrim Fathers and afterwards proved a beacon to the leaders of the new Republic, George Washington expressed in 1790, in a letter to the then important Hebrew congregation in Newport, Rhode Island, the characteristically worded hope: "May the Children of the Stock of Abraham, who dwell in this land, continue to merit and enjoy the goodwill of the other inhabitants, while every one shall sit in safety under his own vine and fig-tree, and there shall be none to make him afraid." The foundation in 1655 of congregation "Shearith Israel" in New York City, and in

1782 of congregation "Mikveh Israel" in Philadelphia, under the religious guidance of Gershom Mendes Seixas (1745-1816), known as the patriot Jewish minister of the Revolution, were milestones in the development of American Jewry. The hegemony which, until the middle of the nineteenth century, was held by the Spanish and Portuguese section, then passed to the "Germans" who had come in considerable numbers from central Europe, especially after the abortive revolutionary upheavals of 1848. The outbreak of the Russian riots in 1881 caused, however, the beginning of a new wave of Jewish immigration, which, impelled by the unrelenting persecution under the Tsarist regime, assumed proportions unprecedented in Jewish history. The net number of Jewish immigrants to the United States during the years 1881 to 1947 amounted to over 3,000,000 souls. The somewhat placid course of Jewish life in America was thus gravely disturbed by the momentum of the rapid and continuous flow of new arrivals on its hospitable shores. The congestion created by the settlement of the Russian, Rumanian, and Galician Jews in a few centers in the eastern States did not only produce economic evils, such as the so-called sweating system, but created new problems of a social, political, and religious nature. One of the most remarkable features of the ensuing Americanization and social advancement of the Russo-Jewish immigrants is, however, to be found in the striking fact that the relatively small community of Jews which received and absorbed them proved, in capacity and self-sacrifice, equal to its formidable task. In almost all respects the various strata of American Jews, irrespective of their lands of origin, tend to merge into one body with common aspirations.

The active participation of the Jewish citizens in American national life is a pronounced feature in their comparatively short record. Of those who, in the nineteenth century, rose to distinction, particular mention may be made of Commodore Uriah P. Levy (1792-1862), who brought about the abolition of corporal punishment in the navy, and Judah P. Benjamin (1811-84), the most able minister of the American Confederation. In 1906, Oscar Solomon Straus (1850-1926) was appointed by President Theodore Roosevelt as Secretary of Commerce. In more recent times a considerable number of Jews have attained high office, and have contributed to the honorable role played by America in international affairs. Indicative of the standing of American Jews among their fellow-citizens is the fact that the United States Supreme Court has had simultaneously two Jewish members—Louis D. Brandeis and Benjamin Nathan Cardozo, who, on his death in 1938, was succeeded by Felix Frankfurter.

In spite of their freedom from legal disabilities, the Jews in the United States have shown a remarkable tendency to racial cohesion. A notable figure in American Israel was the versatile Mordecai Manuel Noah (1785-1851), who, endowed with an imagination ranging beyond his age, attempted in 1825 to creat a Jewish State on American soil in anticipation of the ultimate restoration of the Jewish people to its ancestral land. Simon Wolf (1836-1923) was one of the most public-spirited representatives of the American Jewish community, especially as chairman of the Board of Delegates of Civil and Religious Rights. In more recent times American Jews created various bodies for international action—notably the American Jewish Committee (founded 1906) and the American Jewish Congress (1916). In the former, Mayer Sulzberger (1843-1923), Jacob H. Schiff (1847-1920), Louis Marshall (1856-1929), and Cyrus Adler (1863-1940) were foremost in their activities on behalf of their co-religionists in foreign lands, while in the latter body, led by Rabbi Stephen S. Wise (1874-1949), the more democratic and nationalist elements combined in the defence of Jewish rights.

In a spiritual direction, too, there has taken place on

specifically American lines an evolution of Jewish religious values. As was to be expected, attempts at radical changes in traditional ritual and practice, which began in 1824 with the establishment of the Reformed Society of Israelites in Charleston, South Carolina, found a receptive soil in the new and scattered communities cut off from the main stream of Jewish life and lacking the unifying force of a recognized authority, either personal or of a religious code. The Union of American Hebrew Congregations, which came into being in 1873, and the Central Conference of American Rabbis (1889) brought about a certain cohesion in the ranks of Reform Judaism. On the other hand, there has been a continuous effort on the part of the leaders of traditional Judaism to give it that spiritual content which would enable the old ideas and forms to thrive and bear fruit in a strange and uncongenial environment. Among the earlier protagonists of orthodoxy were Isaac Leeser (1806-68), possessed of boundless energy allied to discriminating zeal, and Sabato Morais (1823-97), whose ardent personality proved of decisive influence. An abiding inspiration was the association with the conservative Jewish Theological Seminary in New York of Solomon Schechter (1850-1915), a rabbinical sage, who in his teachings blended most happily the rationalism and aesthetics of the West with the mystical genius of eastern Judaism. The Jewish Publication Society of America and the American Jewish Historical Society, established in 1888 and 1892 respectively, have been important agencies in promoting an interest in contemporary Jewish life as well as a knowledge of the Jewish past. The virgin soil of America has thus brought forth religious and intellectual developments of Judaism adapted to the new conditions, though history must still reserve its verdict on their ultimate effect. In any case, the Jews in the United States of America, comprising about five millions—nearly one half of the whole

Jewish people—are called upon to play an increasingly decisive part in the fortunes of modern Israel.

§ 11. *Cultural Progress.* The Jewish religious genius gave through Christianity and Mohammedanism the immortal gift of ethical Monotheism to the world, and has thereby contributed one of the main constituents of European civilization. Law and loving-kindness, the essential elements of the fabric of Judaism, became the foundations of human society as evolved in the course of time. The Jews in the Middle Ages, who were the first to mediate between East and West, ushered in the Renaissance, though they were then engulfed in an Age of Darkness during which they were excluded from participation in the cultural values they had helped to bring into being.

The civic emancipation of the Jews gave a new impetus to the creative intellectual forces which had lain dormant amidst the intensive and long-drawn-out religious disputations and the quest for God that then characterized the Jews. Many of the *Yeshibah Bahurim* (students of Talmudical academies) applied their perfected dialectic skill to the acquisition of secular knowledge with phenomenal results. The grudging admission of Jews to high schools and colleges and the bar placed against their academic advancement proved no effective obstacle to Jewish aspirants to knowledge, many of them autodidacts who succeeded in spite of the economic as well as cultural difficulties in their way.

Men of Jewish origin have contributed to all aspects of European civilization far beyond their numerical proportion, some of them as leaders in their particular field of intellectual progress and human welfare. Albert Einstein in mathematics; Heinrich Hertz in electricity; Fritz Haber and Richard Willstätter in chemistry; Paul Ehrlich and Waldemar Haffkine in medicine; Albert Michelson, Gabriel Lippmann, Simon Flexner, Jacques Loeb, Ludwig Mond in physics; Jacob Epstein in sculpture; Jozef Israels and Max Liebermann in painting; hosts of men distinguished in music, law and literature, commerce and industry, technical inventions —these stand to the credit of a race that has only with infinite difficulty found its way back to European culture. International understanding has been fostered by the press agency established by Baron Paul Julius Reuter (1821-99, originally Josephat), and the Polish Jew Ludwig Zamenhof has through Esperanto created a means of friendly intercourse between the most diverse nations. Among the disproportionately large numbers of Nobel prize-winners of Jewish origin (twenty-three Jews and three half-Jews) there have been two—Tobias Asser and Alfred Fried—who received the prize for peace. A Jewish generation that could produce philosophers of the caliber of Samuel Alexander in England, Henri Bergson in France, Hermann Cohen in Germany, Sigmund Freud in Austria, has indeed justified the claim for the intellectual eminence of the Jewish people.

§ 12. *Self-Emancipation*. While during the struggle for political enfranchisement in the various lands of civilization the Jews were left to work out their own salvation, the collective Jewish conscience responded to appeals for aid from all parts of the Dispersion. Apart from the measures of relief extended to the Jewish refugees from eastern Europe, it was particularly the Jews of the Orient who called for the intervention of their more favorably situated co-religionists.

While the Jews on Ottoman territory, largely descendants of refugees from the Iberian Peninsula, enjoyed a relatively fair measure of toleration, the despotic and corrupt regime in the extensive but decaying Empire subjected the Jews to the rapacity and arbitrary caprice of the local potentates. This unhappy state of affairs prevailed all over the Moslem east, from Persia to Morocco, and exposed the Jews to oppression and to personal indignities which were only mitigated by the presence of diplomatic representatives of the Western Powers.

The first concerted Jewish public action was aroused in 1840 by an accusation against a number of Jews in Damascus that they had killed a Franciscan monk in order to use his blood for religious purposes. This Damascus Affair, which excited great interest and sympathy at the time, raised up two men who headed the struggle for the liberation of the whole Jewish race. Sir Moses Montefiore (1784-1885) and Adolphe Crémieux (1796-1880), both men of high distinction in England and France, accompanied by Salomon Munk and Louis Loewe, orientalists of note, set out for the East on a mission against the forces of religious bigotry. They were supported by enlightened public opinion, and were not only instrumental in freeing the accused, but also in obtaining a firman from the sultan of Turkey condemning the charge of ritual murder as a baseless fabrication. Still more important was the example and stimulus this gave to future public action on similar occasions. Such an instance occurred in 1858, when a six-year-old Jewish child, Edgar Mortara, of Bologna, was forcibly taken from his parents by papal guards on the ground of his having been surreptitiously baptized by a servant four years previously. The world was up in arms. The Emperors Francis Joseph and Napoleon III intervened personally with Pope Pius IX, and Sir Moses Montefiore went on a mission to Rome, but it was all of no avail, and Mortara was afterwards brought up as a Catholic priest. The indignation aroused in this matter contributed much to the odium which surrounded the last days of the Papal State, and gave the impetus for the establishment, in 1860, of the Alliance Israélite Universelle, for some years the most important international Jewish body. The Alliance was to act as the accredited representative of the Jewish people wherever it suffered for conscience' sake. This function was exercised with marked effect in oriental countries, where the prestige of the Alliance was supported by the representatives of France and other civilized Powers. At the Berlin Congress of 1878, the Alliance submitted a memorandum urging the emancipation of the Jews in the Balkan States, but the persistence and impunity with which Rumania evaded its undertaking in this respect, and the helplessness of the Alliance during the Russian troubles in 1882, led to a subordination of political activity in favor of a vast educational work for the betterment of the oriental Jews. This was largely made possible by the munificence of Baron Maurice de Hirsch (1831-96) and his equally noble-hearted widow, Clara de Hirsch (1833-99). The educational work of the Alliance has been supported by the Anglo-Jewish Association (founded 1871), and in 1901 there was established in Germany the Hilfsverein der Deutschen Juden to serve the Jewish cause in eastern parts. An interesting development of Jewish self-help is the international humanitarian organization of B'nai B'rith (Sons of the Covenant), established in New York in 1843, which has particularly taken a leading part in Jewish affairs in America.

The Central Union of German Citizens of the Jewish Faith, established in Berlin in 1893, rendered valuable service in stemming the tide of German anti-Semitism until it overflowed the banks of reason forty years afterwards. A body of ultra-orthodox Jews, named Agudath Israel, was formed in 1912 under the guidance of Jacob Rosenheim for the promotion of Judaism on uncompromising religious principles. Reform Jews in both hemispheres grouped themselves together in 1926 into the World Union for Progressive Judaism, the *spiritus rector* of which has been the Rabbi-statesman Leo Baeck, of Berlin. Sephardi Jews, who lacked a religious or cultural center, also organized themselves on the initiative of Rabbi Nissim Ovadia, of Paris, in the Union Universelle des Communautés Séphardites, with the object of advancing the spiritual aspirations of Sephardi Jews in the general revival of Judaism, and held their first international conference in London in 1935. Representatives of Jewish communities of East and West who, in 1919, met during the Peace Conference in Paris, were organized by the Zionist leader, Leo Motzkin, for the defence of general Jewish interests into the Comité des Délégations Juives, with Judge Julian Mack, President of the Zionist Organization of America, as its first chairman. Its successor, the World Jewish Congress, which arose out of the strain and stress of the German persecution, and which held its first session in Geneva in 1936, has its head office in New York and branches in many countries.

Philanthropy, which formed the most prominent feature in Jewish public life during the second half of the nineteenth century, found its highest representative in Sir Moses Montefiore, who not only gave generously of his own wealth, but intervened personally, and with some success, with the rulers of Turkey, Russia, Rumania, Morocco, and Rome, in order to right Jewish wrongs and to alleviate the unhappy lot of his oppressed co-religionists in those countries. Of more permanent effect was his promotion of Jewish colonization in Palestine, of which he was the foremost pioneer among western Jews. The culminating point of philanthropic effort was reached when in 1891 Baron Maurice de Hirsch conceived the titanic scheme of transplanting the Jews from Darkest Russia into the light and freedom of the New World, and for this purpose created the Jewish Colonization Association which he endowed with a fund of about £9,000,000. Its colonizing activities, which have largely been carried on in the Argentine, were, however, found to be of slow growth, and the authorities of the Jewish Colonization Association therefore thought it advisable to utilize a considerable part of its resources for the economic and educational relief of the overwhelming Jewish misery in various parts of the world. Of exceptional importance in these respects is the part played by the American Joint Distribution Committee, which, established in October 1914, immediately after the outbreak of the First World War, has rendered untold benefit to the economic and cultural reconstruction of the Jews of eastern and central Europe. Organizations of Russo-Jewish origin termed Ort and Ose are maintaining trade schools and developing productive activities and health services among the distressed Jewish populations in those parts. Even as it is, only a fringe of the vast problem can be touched by philanthropy, which has proved a mere palliative to meet the tragic problems with which the Jewish people are faced.

§ 12. *Anti-Semitism.* The outburst of national feeling consequent on the Franco-German War in 1870-1871, brought a new phase of Jew-hatred into regions where emancipation had already been achieved. Conformably with the character of the age and the country of its origin, the Jew-hatred that made its appearance in Germany was stripped of its old religious fanaticism, and clothed in a new scientific garb. It was now discovered that the Jew was constitutionally of an inferior moral nature by reason of his so-called Semitic descent, and could not, therefore, claim equality with the higher Aryan race. Anti-Semitism, as this "scientific" Jew-hatred came to be called, found great favor among the impressionable academic youth, and was spread among the people by demagogues, like the court chaplain Stöcker, and by politicians in search of a battle cry. In Germany and Austria there arose anti-Semitic parties in all legislative and municipal bodies, which, supported from above by the prevailing feudal and clerical elements, seriously threatened the hardly acquired citizenship of the Jews. In 1882, the theories of anti-Semitism were translated into wild riots in Russia, and accusations of ritual murder by Jews, that claimed wide attention, were made in various parts of Europe. But the greatest effect of anti-Semitism, one of the most remarkable incidents at the end of the nineteenth century, was the Dreyfus Affair in France (1894), in which Alfred Dreyfus, a Jewish officer, was falsely accused of treason and condemned for the purpose of ousting Jews from the higher ranks of the French army. The Dreyfus Affair, which convulsed France to its very depths, was largely responsible for the anti-clerical policy and the separation of Church and State following on the conflict that ended with the release and rehabilitation of Captain Dreyfus.

Since then, however, anti-Semitism has assumed a character and proportions inconceivable at the end of the nineteenth century. The anti-Jewish developments are best indicated by the widespread publication of a grotesque forgery entitled *The Protocols of the Elders of Zion,* which charges the Jews with the conspiracy to destroy the existing state of society and to set up their own world-dominion.

§ 13. *Zionism.* The rise of virulent anti-Semitism in cultured Germany and Austria, and the savage anti-Jewish outbreaks in Russia, brought about a revulsion of feeling and hope within the Jewish ranks in eastern Europe, while the Dreyfus Affair in enlightened France led to a partial revision of the Jewish outlook in western lands. It came to be recognized by ever-growing numbers that however desirable political emancipation had been at one time, this had not, and could not, achieve the object that formed the *raison d'être* of the Jewish people, viz., the full and unfettered development of its own innate forces, and that a purely legal enfranchisement could afford no solution of the Jewish social and economic problems *so long as the Jews were subject to the will and power of a necessarily dominant majority of the non-Jewish population.* It was found that anti-Semitism is a growth of envy and malice which knows no frontiers; that even in free countries the Jews are subjected to intellectual and moral pressure ultimately entailing the loss of many valuable members; that the very Liberalism that stands up valiantly for the rights of the Jew hopes for the dissolution of Judaism; that this dissolution, forced by the identification of the Jewish citizens with all the aspects of the national life surrounding them, is in actual progress and a serious menace to the perpetuation of the Jewish people. These thoughts, and the consequent necessity for the regathering of the Jews in their ancient land as a political entity, were already elaborated by the German publicist Moses Hess in *Rome and Jerusalem,* in 1862, during the throes of the emancipation movement, but the Russian atrocities in 1881 initiated an organized effort for the realization of this idea. Groups of people, known as Hovevi Zion (Palestinophiles), were formed for the purpose of resettling Jews in their ancestral home. Of far-reaching effect was the anonymous publication at that critical time of a pamphlet *Auto-Emancipation* by Leon Pinsker, of Odessa, with his plea for a territorial solution of the Jewish Question, and especially the lead he gave for the assembly of an international conference of Hovevi Zion at Kattowitz (1884), and subsequently the establishment of a popular Russo-Jewish society for assisting artisans and rural settlers in Palestine. A great success was achieved when these aims received the support of Baron Edmond de Rothschild (1845-1934), of Paris, who, with a generous heart, provided large resources for the creation of Jewish agricultural colonies in that country. By the beginning of the twentieth century, the continuous stream of immigration had introduced into Palestine once more a flourishing agricultural population passionately attached to the soil, and again turned Jerusalem numerically into a Jewish city. While the movement had thus gathered strength in the East, there arose in the West a new star which shed a brilliant light on the whole Dispersion.

Theodor Herzl (b. in Budapest, 1860; d. at Edlach, Austria, 1904), an heroic figure, recalling one of the Judges of Israel of ancient days, may be said to have inaugurated a new era in Jewish life. Whereas since the days of Moses

Mendelssohn it had become the aim of the Jews to achieve political and social equality by assimilation with their fellow-citizens short of religious dissolution, the movement known at Zionism set on foot by Herzl by the publication in 1896 of a brochure, *Der Judenstaat,* declared the inadequacy of the old ideal for the preservation of the Jewish individuality, and raised the necessity for the national rebirth of the Jewish people as a self-governing body into an object and ideal worthy of labor and achievement. Since its inception at an international congress, held in Basle in August 1897, the object of Zionism—the creation of a Jewish national home in Palestine secured by public law—has received the suffrages of the largest number of Jews ever permanently united for a definite purpose since the days of Jewish independence.

CHAPTER VII

REACTION

§ 1. *The First World War.* The War of 1914-18 that
shattered mighty empires and led to the political resurrection
of a host of nations had a profound and far-reaching effect
on the fortunes of Israel. The Jews had to pay with their
lives and treasure for the age-long contests between Teuton
and Slav and Frank; for the vainglory of emperors; the in-
competence and corruption of military commanders. The
clash of arms, which in eastern Europe was fought out
largely on territories thickly populated by Jews, brought
face to face the whole manhood of the Jewish people, tragi-
cally divided in allegiance between the two hostile forces.
Over the whole world-wide battlefield Jews paid their toll of
death and, to a disproportionately greater degree, shared the
fate of the non-combatants in the afflicted war areas. The
youth and manhood of the six millions of Jewish inhabitants
of Tsarist Russia fought in the ranks as common soldiers
for a fatherland which denied them the elementary rights of
citizenship. They suffered with their compatriots not only
the defeat of armies that were ill led and worse equipped,
but had to witness the ruthless brutalities and wholesale
deportations as far as the regions of the Ural Mountains
and the wastes of Siberia inflicted upon the Jewish civil
population by advancing and receding armies under cover of
measures of military necessity. The Jews in Austria-Hun-
gary, numbering over two millions, found themselves entangled amidst the mutually hostile and treacherous elements
in which the armed forces of the monarchy were ultimately

dissolved. The wavering conflict between the Romanovs and the Hapsburgs raged on battlegrounds in which the dense Jewish population was generally treated as untrustworthy and, therefore, subjected to exceptional and undiscriminating hostility by both sides.

On the other hand, the Jews of Germany, though still regarded with a sense of superiority by the dominant Junker class and practically excluded from the commissioned ranks, joined in the armed struggle with the consciousness that their German fatherland was entitled to the supreme sacrifice they could lay on the altar of patriotism. Of the 600,000 Jews in Germany, 100,000 were combatants, 80 per cent of them at the front. About 12,000 were among the fallen and the missing; 35,000 received decorations, and close on 2,000 were promoted to the hitherto closed caste of officers.

The small Jewish population of France—in 1914 they numbered about 95,000, of whom 65,000 were of French origin—produced an extraordinarily large number of officers of high rank. When the War broke out, there were two Jewish generals on the active list, and four in the reserve resumed service; in the course of the War, eight more Jewish officers were promoted to the rank of general.

In England the call for volunteers before conscription came into force received a response from about 10,000 Jews, of whom 1,140 were officers. In the British Dominions the number of Jews who enlisted was exceptionally high. Out of the 19,000 Jews in Austria 1,800 enlisted and 250 fell in action. In the British forces 316 Jewish officers and 2,008 non-commissioned officers and men fell in action or died in active service. Five Jews gained the Victoria Cross. Lieut.-General Sir John Monash (of East Prussian Jewish ancestry), who was in command of the Australian forces on the western front, proved one of the most successful military leaders of the Allied armies.

In the United States of America, the number of Jews on

active service is computed to have been over a quarter of a million, of whom approximately 8,000 were officers. About 3,500 American Jews fell in action and 12,000 were wounded.

A touch of heroic romance in the mobilization of Jewish man-power in the struggle of 1914-18 was provided by the formation of the Jewish military units composed of volunteers for service in Palestine from various parts of the world, who first served as the Zion Mule Corps in Gallipoli and then as separate battalions, officially styled "Judeans" and referred to as "Jewish troops," in Lord Allenby's conquest of Palestine.

§ 2. *The Aftermath.* The effects of the First World War proved a major catastrophe to the Jews of Europe. The political and social chaos which ensued after the collapse of the Romanov and Hapsburg monarchies placed the Jews between the hammer and the anvil of the fiercely contending nationalities. The grim contest between the various Russian parties that fought for mastery led to pillage and massacre on such a large scale that they aroused pity and horror even in an age that had grown accustomed to bloodshed. The Ukraine, which, since the days of Chmielnicki in the seventeenth century, had an unenviable record in this respect, became under the hetmans Skoropadski and Petliura during the civil war of 1918-20 the scene of untold savagery, which spread to Poland, whose newly found independence was marked by anti-Jewish excesses on an extensive scale. The most tragic feature of the wave of pogroms that swept across a large part of Europe after the war was the ferocious attacks on the Jews in Hungary after the Communist revolt in 1919 and the Rumanian spoliation, when the humiliated Magyars revenged their defeat on the intensely patriotic Jewish inhabitants of the country.

In addition to the legacy of the hatred that had been engendered and cultivated during the war there now arose in the new States a chauvinism that came to be regarded as essential to the assertion of a national individuality from which the Jews, as an ethnical and religious minority, were to be excluded even though, as in many cases, they had helped to bring those States into being. The liberal professions were gradually closed to the Jews by the adoption of a *numerus clausus* at the universities, which was reinforced by the turbulent demands of non-Jewish students for the total exclusion of Jews. The economic boycott of Jewish traders on the part of the non-Jewish population was made effective by the increasing nationalization of commerce and industry from which the Jews, who had been largely engaged in them, were ousted by the State. The establishment of co-operative stores in order to eliminate Jewish middlemen led to their ruin, which was accelerated by the encouragement which the State afforded to every enterprise by which the Christian peasant and workman could supersede their Jewish neighbors or competitors.

This process of exclusion of the Jews became more drastic as the years went on, and one country vied with the other in adopting more rigorous measures to eliminate the Jew from profitable occupations. As nationalized commerce and industry, especially in the form of autarky, proceeded apace, the scope of Jewish development contracted, and the pauperization of the Jewish masses became intensified. Since the former outlet for mass-emigration was now practically closed, there arose in Poland and in other lands of eastern Europe the view that the most effective way of reducing an undesirable "surplus" of Jews was to curtail their means of livelihood. Even in Hungary, which had gradually been adopting a more liberal attitude towards the Jews within its shrunken borders, the Government adopted a policy of discrimination against its Jewish citizens by limiting severely their employment in all branches of the professions, industry, and commerce. Economically as well as politically the Jews in those countries became unwanted stepchildren of their fatherland.

§ 3. *Jewish Minority Rights.* The peace treaties (which bear the signatures of two Jewish Ministers of State, Edwin Montagu for India and Lucien L. Klotz for France) between the Allies and the defeated States (excepting Germany) took account of the Jewish problem by the provision of minority rights to which the Jews, on the grounds of race, language, and religion, were to be entitled. In spite of the resistance of Poland, Rumania, and other States that benefited by the victory of the Allies, the minority rights were likewise imposed upon them. The creation of the League of Nations, which held out the prospect of a new moral order in international relations, appeared to give to the Jews, not only individually but collectively, guarantees which in effect amounted to such Jewish religious and cultural autonomy as was compatible with the sovereignty of the State. The beginnings of this new status of the Jews in eastern Europe were hopeful, even though, as in Poland, waves of pogroms made these rights illusory. In Lithuania, which owed its independence to a considerable extent to Jewish influence, there was created a Ministry for Jewish Affairs which, from 1919 to 1922, was held by Max Soloweitschik, and then, for a short period, by Simon Rosenbaum. In the Ukraine Jewish affairs were placed in 1918 under the charge of a Jewish minister, Jacob Wulf Latzki. But the national autonomy of the Jews manifested itself more particularly and effectively in the cultural rather than in the political field. The assertion of the Jewish national consciousness gave to Yiddish, as the tongue spoken by the Jewish masses, a new dignity, and made it the vehicle of Jewish education together with Hebrew as the classical language of the whole Jewish people. In Poland and Rumania, as well as in the Russian border States in northeastern Europe, the Jews became national entities, while in the succession States of the Austro-Hungarian monarchy the Jews, deprived of their former political co-hesion, were thrown back on their separate cultural resources. In certain parts of the Jewish Diaspora, at least, the Jews had the prospect of being able to develop a culture of their own enhanced by the dignity of their political enfranchise-ment as a recognized minority under the protection of the League of Nations. These minority rights, which had been solemnly guaranteed in the peace treaties, lapsed, however, after some years. Poland was the first to refuse formally to be bound by those conditions which it had agreed to ob-serve towards its minorities, and other States followed suit, without any effective protest being raised against this flagrant repudiation of one of the most beneficent results of the great struggle for the freedom of humanity.

§ 4. *In Soviet Russia.* The collapse of Tsarist Russia brought about, paradoxically, the ruin of the Jews within its borders. The breakup of the Empire by the loss of Poland and other adjoining regions split Russian Jewry into a num-ber of disjointed communities, divided not only by political allegiance but by impassable spiritual and cultural frontiers.

The Jews of Russia experienced a vast upheaval when, mainly by order of the Russian commander-in-chief, Grand Duke Nicholas Nicholayevitch, they were, suspected as an unpatriotic and unreliable element, ruthlessly deported *en masse* from Lithuania and other regions bordering on enemy territory to distant parts of the country from which they had hitherto been rigorously excluded. At the time of the revo-lution in March 1917 there was in Russia proper about a half of the Jewish population of the former Empire, which was over-ripe for the change that was to transform that land beyond recognition. The Jews were accorded full civil and political emancipation, and, by the literacy which distin-guished them from the mass of other sections of the popula-tion, were able to assume a leading part among their compatriots. As a community, the Russian Jews demanded a national, as distinguished from a territorial, autonomy within the State. In the self-governing territory of the Ukraine the establishment of a Ministry for Jewish Affairs placed the Jews there on an equality with the other important nationalities. The Bolshevik Revolution of November 1917 and the civil wars that followed it proved, however, disastrous to the Jews, who suffered from merciless orgies of murder and pillage on both sides. The Communist upheaval no less than these pogroms brought the whole Jewish population to the verge of beggary. The prominent participation of a number of Jews in the establishment of the Union of Soviet Socialist Republics—notably that of Leon Trotsky, one of the most outstanding and dynamic of the Bolshevik leaders—gave to the new regime a Jewish coloring which the enemies of the Jews have unscrupulously exploited by ascribing Bolshevik propaganda almost exclusively to Jewish influences. Though a considerable number of Jews became leaders of the new dispensation, they had ostentatiously dissociated themselves from their racial kinsmen and, moreover, had manifested this by a peculiarly virulent agitation against the Jewish bourgeoisie and Jewish tradition generally. In addition, there was a sectarian enmity between the Bolsheviks and the Mensheviks of Jewish origin which has never healed. From mere self-interest the Jewish petite bourgeoisie, comprising the majority of the Jewish population, was hostile to the Bolshevik economy, which had completely wiped out the trader and middleman. The course of time has brought about remarkable economic changes among the Jewish population in Soviet Russia, but politically the Jews have ceased to play a leading part. The ruling policy of Stalin has led to the elimination of almost all the Jewish fathers of the revolution, though one of the foremost offices is now held by Lazar Kaganovitch as Commissar for Transport.

The Jews in the U.S.S.R. enjoy not only all the rights of

citizenship but are encouraged to develop a national life within certain limits. There are various districts in White Russia, the Ukraine, and the Crimea where Jews form cohesive groups with their own Soviets and with Yiddish as the official language of the law courts and educational establishments. The attempts to colonize Jews on the land as self-governing units of Soviet Russia have been supported by the central authorities with the financial help of American Jews. An extensive territory in Biro-Bidjan on the Amur River, near Manchuria, was set aside in 1928 for the creation of an autonomous Jewish region, but it has failed to achieve its ambitious purpose.

In spite of their complete political emancipation, however, and the economic opportunities afforded to Jews in Soviet Russia, they represent a branch of the Jewish people that has been cut off from its stem and is withering away for lack of vitality. The once hopeful colonizing projects have ceased to attract new settlers to any considerable extent. The Jewish Socialist culture lacks inspiration. The Yiddish language of the masses is giving way to the dominant Russian. Intermarriage with non-Jews is increasing very rapidly. Indeed, there is no reason why the Russian Jews, spread over the vast territory of the Republic, should endeavor to survive as a national or even cultural entity. As it is, the former Jewish Department, Yevsectsia, which was specially created by the central Government to direct the development of the Jewish population, signed its own death-warrant by an uncompromising hostility to every phase of Jewish life reminiscent of Jewish traditions. The Jewish faith and Jewish religious instruction were outlawed in accordance with the general policy governing religion in the Republic. There is a ban on Hebrew, and any association with Palestine and Zionism is treated with the rigors attaching to counter-revolutionary activities. The Jews in the U.S.S.R., now reduced from three to two million, have thus been cut off, even culturally and socially, from every contact with their people abroad. The ancient Jewish traditions of learning and faith, of the sanctity of personal relations between man and wife and between parents and children, of classless compassion for suffering mankind—these ethical characteristics are being wiped out by an intensive process of anti-religious propaganda which has coarsened the Jewish fiber. It may be expected that, if the present system should continue for several generations, the Jews in the mass will survive as one of the many ethnic groups in the Republic, but that Judaism as a spiritual force will be doomed to extinction. This eventual loss to the Jewish people can in the vastness of extent only be compared to the disappearance of the ancient Ten Tribes of Israel.

§ 5. *In Nazi Germany*. The defeat of Germany in the First World War, which marked the eclipse of the military caste and the creation of the Weimar Republic, led to a remarkable change in the Jewish situation in that country. The Jewish political forces, which had hitherto been mainly spent in opposition, were now utilized in the service of the democratic State. Among those who helped to bring the Republic into being by the formulation of its constitution was Hugo Preuss, who in 1918, after the outbreak of the revolution, became Secretary of State, then Minister of the Interior. Walther Rathenau, one of the great statesmen of his time, was appointed in 1921 Minister for Reconstruction and in 1922 Minister for Foreign Affairs; but his efforts to arrive at an understanding with France led to his assassination by German Nationalists. Among others who held high office was Rudolf Hilferding, who in 1923 and 1928 occupied the position of Minster of Finance. Max M. Warburg, as a banking expert of high repute, represented the interests of Germany in connection with War Reparations. As subsequent events proved, the rise of Jews to political power in Germany and a Communist rising in Bavaria in which certain Jews took a prominent part gave to reactionary and chauvinistic elements additional opportunities for attacks on the hated "Jew Republic." Events moved fast as the economic conditions, complicated by the French invasion of the Ruhr, led to an organized inflation of the currency that ruined the German economy and brought about unemployment on an increasingly vast scale.

It was in such circumstances that, among other anti-Semitic groups, the National Socialist Workers' Party (Nazis) found a fruitful field for a campaign of unexampled violence in which the Jews were used as the scapegoats for the ills that had befallen Germany. This party, led by Adolf Hitler, adopted an anti-Jewish program on the lines elaborated by the Austrian Pan-Germans in the 'eighties of the nineteenth century; the movement, gathering force from other elements hostile to the democratic Republic, made rapid strides, and in 1933 Hitler became the Leader of the Third Reich. His dictatorship, in which anti-Semitism became the pivot of the policy of a Great Power in the heart of Europe, proved the tragic collapse of the canons of civilization not only in so far as the Jews are concerned. To understand the Nazi mentality, it is necessary to go back to the ages of witchcraft and to primeval tribal taboos—now stirred up frantically by the latest technical devices of the human mind. The public burning of books by authority in the capital of this European Empire and in other centers of German Kultur, and the ceremonial incantations which accompanied these fantastic spectacles, the savage hunt for the distant racial origins of every inhabitant of that land, the utter absence of scruple or mercy or of any ethical considerations in its government, not only characterize but explain the otherwise incredible policy towards the hapless Jews within the grim and all-embracing tentacles of Nazism. The Nazis fully emulated the terror which the Huns under Attila, "the scourge of God," spread in their invasion of

Europe. The *furor Teutonicus,* with which Kaiser William II once threatened the Chinese after the Boxer Rebellion— that they would remember the effects of German vengeance after a thousand years—was let loose with unbridled fury against the Jews in Nazi Germany, then in Austria, and next in Czecho-Slovakia. Their temples were destroyed by dynamite or deliberately devastated, and the scrolls of the Law defiled; the State confiscated their property and deprived them of the means of livelihood; they were suddenly and callously driven from their homes like dumb cattle and confined to the meanest streets; they were banned like pariahs from the society of their non-Jewish neighbors with a cynicism that was alien to the persecution of the Jews in the darkest ages of faith. It was openly avowed by Nazi spokesmen that the Jews were thereby meant to be turned systematically into beggars and criminals so that they should then be exterminated with fire and sword.

It may be that the verdict of Jewish history, in the spirit of the ancient Jewish seers, will record as the besetting sin of German Jewry that it was, almost to the very last, much more Teutonic than Hebraic. It is the dramatic irony of events that, with hardly an exception, the German Jews were the most chauvinistic group of their race, not in pursuit of Jewish ideals but in their pride of German achievement. Their immense contributions to science, the arts, and economics have been credited to Germany; indeed, until they were cast out by their German fellow-citizens into outer darkness, those Jews who had shed luster on Germany and had promoted its intellectual and economic progress were justly imbued with the consciousness that their achievements had served their German fatherland. In this, too, they shared the Jewish destiny, *das Judenschicksal,* from which only the few have been able to escape.

Now that the devastation wrought under the shadow of the swastika is over, it is well to recall the glory that was

German Jewry. It was in the vanguard of that universalist humanism which has been the immortal contribution to civilization by the Jewish prophets and sages. They gave birth to, and cultivated, Jewish learning which has spread its light all over the Jewish Diaspora. In a material sense, the well-ordered Jewish life in Germany set a public-spirited example to Jewish communities all over the world. Now that German Jewry has partly gone into exile and partly perished, it should be remembered to them for good that the Jewish emigrants who, for many decades, passed from the lands of oppression in eastern Europe to the freedom of western lands and the New World, were comforted and aided on their way through Germany by the never-failing sense of Jewish brotherhood manifested by their German fellow-Jews. Perhaps the highest tribute that posterity will pay to the German Jews in their agony will be the recognition of the noble fortitude of faith—paralleled only by the Spanish Jews in the great Expulsion of 1492—with which they steadfastly faced the bitter humiliations which were designed to degrade them below the human kind.

§ 6. *In Fascist Italy.* The bimillennial history of the Jews in Italy—which dates back to pre-Christian times, when in about 144 B.C.E. the Maccabean Jonathan sent an embassy from Jerusalem to Rome, has undergone many vicissitudes, but no persecution so characteristically arbitrary as was suddenly decreed against them by Benito Mussolini in the year 1938. Even in medieval times, the Jews who lived in the shadow of the majesty of the Vatican were relatively tolerated, and enlightened rulers gave asylum to Jewish refugees, like the Spanish exiles in 1492 with Don Isaac Abravanel at their head, who landed on the Italian shores. Since the Jewish emancipation in 1870, Italy was, politically and socially, entirely free from anti-Semitism. Amidst its Mediterranean population and culture, the Italian Jews—numbering barely 50,000 souls—were hardly distinguishable

from their non-Jewish compatriots. Luigi Luzzatti, as Prime
Minister (1910-1911), General Giuseppe Ottolenghi, Leone
Wollemborg, Carlo Schanzer, Sidney Sonnino, and Guido
Jung were Ministers of State of whose devoted services to
their country, as of those by many other eminent Italians of
Jewish origin, there was no question until Mussolini's Nazi
enactments for "the defence of the race" on biological
grounds.

The eclipse of Jewish emancipation in Nazi Germany thus
had its sequel in Fascist Italy. Though numerically the
Italian Jewish problem was of much less account than that
in Germany, the implications were historically far-reaching.
For it was in the home of the Papacy that Mussolini had
introduced the racial paganism which the masters of Nazi
Germany had adopted to supplant "Jewish" Christianity.

The traditional foundation of the Catholic See of Rome
by the Jew Simon Cephas, known as St. Peter, and the
Epistle to the Romans by Saul of Tarsus, or St. Paul,
brought the Jews and Rome early into close association.
There was a further connection between Judaism and Roman
Christianity by reason of the fact that the early Jewish communities in Italy were largely composed of proselytes, many
of whom subsequently joined the nascent Church. Following
the attempted break by the secular State with the fudamental
constitution of the Catholic Church as a universal body,
there was decreed a definite division between Italians and
Jews, not because of their difference in faith but solely on
account of their blood. The race of Jesus of Nazareth, of
St. Peter and St. Paul, was declared to be humanly so inferior that it was rigorously excluded from the Italian nation.
The pseudo-scientific theory of the distinction between so-
called Aryans and non-Aryans, which had been adopted as
part of the constitution of the German Reich, was, overnight,
declared in Italy the official policy of Italian Fascism. It was
significant that, as in Germany so in Italy, the Catholic

Church, headed by the late Pope Pius XI, sensed the danger which the anti-Jewish racialism of those States had for the future of Christianity in Europe—an unprecedented fellowship between the Synagogue and the Church in defence of the Messianic ideals common to both of them.

CHAPTER VIII

THE JEWISH NATIONAL HOME

§ 1. *The Foundations.* While the most remarkable developments of Jewish life in the Diaspora within the inter-war period were the virtual elimination of Jewish life in Soviet Russia and the continuously extending disfranchisement of the Jews as a racial, or so-called non-Aryan, minority over a large part of Europe, Palestine developed as a factor destined to change fundamentally the course of modern Jewish history. The intimate, indissoluble connection of the Jewish people and its religion with its original homeland is not only unique but has dramatically reasserted itself; for despite the physical severance between Israel and the territory already referred to in the days of Joseph as the land of the Hebrews or, from the conquest of Joshua, as Erez Yisrael (the Land of Israel), there has been no spiritual break during the whole course of three millennia. Indeed, the complete destruction of the Jewish State intensified the religious emotions of which the Return to Zion became the central motive of the Messianic hopes of that dispossessed, homeless nation.

It was only in the course of the struggle for civic and political emancipation during the nineteenth century that the primacy of Palestine in Jewish sentiment gave way to local patriotism, and Judaism assumed religious aspirations in which the traditional nationalist elements were reinterpreted into the spiritual universalism of the ancient Hebrew prophets. But the Zionist Movement, at first tentatively and then, impelled by external circumstances, fast gathering force, returned to the old national orientation of Jewish hopes in

Palestine. While Theodor Herzl failed in his negotiations with Sultan Abdul Hamid for the grant of a Charter for a large-scale Jewish immigration into Palestine under Turkish sovereignty, and Zionist efforts to obtain a recognized foothold under the subsequent regime of the Young Turks proved abortive, there continued a steady influx of Jews into Palestine who, despite legal restrictions by the Turkish authorities, were able to develop on national lines. The Zionist Organization, led after Theodor Herzl's death by David Wolffsohn (1856-1914) and then (1911) by Otto Warburg (1859-1937), and stimulated politically by Max Nordau (1849-1923), with his unequaled prestige as a Jewish tribune and Herzl's closest comrade-in-arms, gave a plan and direction to Jewish colonization, even though on very modest lines. The establishment by the Zionist Congress in 1901 of the Jewish National Fund as the land-purchasing agency of the Organization and the creation in 1908 of a Palestine Department under Arthur Ruppin (1876-1943) proved the beginnings of a Jewish national colonization in Palestine, in addition to the great philanthropic effort of Edmond de Rothschild and the private enterprise of many settlers. The special significance of that national colonization lay in the fact that it was built on the soil of Palestine, nationally owned by the Jewish people and inalienable, and tilled by Jewish hands only.

§ 2. *Zionist Leaders.* Zionism has been fortunate in its leaders as well as in the endurance and faith of their followers. Chaim Weizmann, on whom has fallen the mantle of Theodor Herzl, stands out as the foremost Jewish figure in the momentous events that led to the establishment of the Jewish National Home in Palestine. In certain respects, he represents an antithesis to that illustrious founder of Political Zionism, who was led to this attempt at a solution of the Jewish Question by intuition and who, paradoxically, found his strength in his previous detachment from Judaism and

Palestine. Weizmann (born in 1874 near Pinsk, northwest Russia) was bred in an east European Jewish atmosphere, and is, spiritually, profoundly rooted in Jewish tradition. While Herzl's intellectual bent was denoted by the fact that he was one of the leading Viennese feuilletonists, Weizmann is an eminent man of science. Indeed, we have it on the testimony of Lloyd George that, as Minister of Munitions in the First World War, he "felt a deep debt of gratitude, and so did all the Allies, to the brilliant scientific genius of Dr. Weizmann." The dynamic and commanding personality of Chaim Weizmann, no less than the political resourcefulness and constructive statesmanship he has displayed amidst well-nigh insuperable obstacles, both Jewish and non-Jewish, are all the more remarkable when the weak material forces of Zionism at his disposal are compared with its historic achievements under his leadership.

Nahum Sokolow (1861-1936) was the most representative of the Zionist leaders. Combining an encyclopaedic grasp of the problems of Jewish life and thought with a delicate perception of the currents of European politics and culture, one of the master-builders of modern Hebrew literature and a polyglot publicist of an extraordinarily wide range, Sokolow was also endowed with the serene judgment of men and affairs that made him an ideal diplomatist. Apart from his close collaboration with Weizmann in Zionism, he was at the head of the movement for the recognition and maintenance of Jewish minority rights in eastern Europe, thus joining Jewish Nationalism in the Diaspora with the Jewish National Home in Palestine.

Louis Dembitz Brandeis (1856-1941), Associate Justice of the United States Supreme Court, was one of the noblest figures in American Jewry, whose devotion to the Zionist ideal proved of the greatest influence on the pro-Jewish sympathies of President Woodrow Wilson in the Peace settlement of 1919. His active participation in Jewish affairs proved of no less far-reaching consequence in a Zionist direction among the American Jews.

Fundamentally, the greatest intellectual force in Zionism has been Asher Ginzberg, best known by his pen-name as Ahad Ha'am. More than any one, he was able to give a philosophical and cultural content to modern Jewish Nationalism; and though he formulated the object of Zionism as the creation of a Jewish spiritual center in Palestine and thereby found himself in opposition to Herzl and Nordau, the foremost leaders of Political Zionism, Ahad Ha'am participated in the Zionist political efforts in the latter period of the First World War.

Among those who exercised the most potent influence on the achievement of the Zionist political objective was also Jehiel Tschlenow (1864-1918), the recognized leader of the Russian Zionists, who belonged, like his compatriot, Menahem Ussischkin (1863-1941), to the Old Guard of pre-Herzlian Zionism.

§ 3. *The Balfour Declaration.* While the Jewish Settlement in Palestine (known by its Hebrew designation as the Yishub) was gradually germinating even under the most unfavorable conditions of Turkish rule, the outbreak of the First World War in 1914 caused the Zionist Organization, with its central seat in Berlin, to be broken and put out of action. The Organization had already been seriously weakened by the apparent hopelessness of the Zionist expectations in Palestine under the Turks. An offer to the Zionists in 1903 by Joseph Chamberlain, as British Colonial Secretary, of a territory in British East Africa (on the Guas Ngishu plateau, commonly referred to as Uganda) for an autonomous Jewish settlement—indirectly a notable Zionist achievement—and its rejection by a Zionist Congress led to the formation of the Jewish Territorial Organization under the leadership of the Anglo-Jewish *littérateur* and Zionist protagonist Israel Zangwill (1864-1926). Its object was "to procure a territory upon an autonomous basis for those Jews who cannot or will not remain in the lands in which they already live." The Jewish Territorial Organization, though based on the Zionist ideal of Jewish autonomy, was able to attract influential non-Zionist elements, but was nevertheless not successful in its search for a suitable territory for Jewish colonization, and in 1925 was formally dissolved. But while, on the one hand, the secession of many prominent Zionists to that rival body had materially weakened the Zionist Organization, the renewed political contacts with the British Government, on the other hand, thereby developed the biblical, pro-Jewish sympathies which already centuries ago had become manifest in Puritan England.

It was in the tragic years of the First World War that, amidst the pain and travail to which the Jews were subjected, both as victims of discrimination and as combatants, a ray of light of unhoped-for splendor shone upon them. After having consulted all shades of Jewish opinion and supported by all principal Allied and Associated Powers, the British Government declared itself in favor of the establishment in Palestine of a national home for the Jewish people in the following letter, which was addressed to (the second) Lord Rothschild by Arthur James Balfour, the Secretary of State for Foreign Affairs:

FOREIGN OFFICE.
November 2, 1917.

DEAR LORD ROTHSCHILD,

I have much pleasure in conveying to you, on behalf of His Majesty's Government, the following declaration of sympathy with Jewish Zionist aspirations, which has been submitted to, and approved by, the Cabinet.

"His Majesty's Government view with favor the establishment in Palestine of a national home for the Jewish people, and will use their best endeavors to facilitate the achievement of this object, it being clearly understood that nothing shall be done which may prejudice the civil and religious rights of existing non-Jewish communities in Palestine, or the rights and political status enjoyed by Jews in any other country."

I should be grateful if you would bring this declaration to the knowledge of the Zionist Federation.

Yours sincerely,

ARTHUR JAMES BALFOUR.

The Balfour Declaration (as this communication came to be termed) was hailed by the Jews all over the world as an act of national liberation comparable to the decree of Cyrus of Persia which led to the re-establishment of the Jewish Commonwealth in Judea after the Babylonian Captivity. The instinct for self-preservation evoked among the Jews of all lands a collective consciousness and cohesion that broke down national barriers and ideological divisions, and gave to the Messianic ideal of the Restoration to Zion an actuality that captivated the Jewish mind.

§ 4. *The British Mandate.* The Balfour Declaration became practical politics when, after Lord Allenby's conquest of Palestine, it came under British administration, and was ultimately incorporated in a mandate to Great Britain by the Council of the League of Nations, which was formally approved on July 24, 1922. The preamble to the mandate, which incorporated the Balfour Declaration, states that "recognition has thereby been given to the historical connection of the Jewish people with Palestine and to the grounds for re-constituting their national home in that country"; and in article 2 it is stipulated that "the Mandatory shall be responsible for placing the country under such political, administrative, and economic conditions as will secure the establishment of the Jewish national home." With this international acknowledgment of the Jewish title to Palestine, the Zionist Movement, a quarter of a century after its First Congress, achieved the recognition of its main object, viz. "to create for the Jewish people a home in Palestine secured by public law."

The policy of the Jewish National Home as provided in the mandate was challenged in certain British quarters and violently opposed by Arabs in Palestine and outside that country. It was, however, formally reaffirmed by successive British Governments on the basis of an authoritative interpretation in a British Statement of Policy issued in June 1922, just before the mandate was approved by the Council of the League of Nations. In that Statement it was set out that the Jewish community in Palestine,

with its town and country population, its political, religious and social organizations, its own language, its own customs, its own life, has in fact "national" characteristics. When it is asked what is meant by the development of the Jewish National Home in Palestine, it may be answered that it is not the imposition of a Jewish nationality upon the inhabitants of Palestine as a whole but the further development of the existing Jewish community, with the assistance of Jews in other parts of the world, in order that it may become a center in which the Jewish people as a whole may take, on grounds of religion and race, an interest and a pride. But in order that this community should have the best prospect of free development and provide a full opportunity for the Jewish people to display its capacities, it is essential that it should know that it is in Palestine as of right and not on sufferance. That is the reason why it is necessary that the existence of a Jewish National Home in Palestine should be formally recognized to rest upon ancient historic connection.

§ 5. *Culture and Economics.* The Jewish National Home rested upon a spiritual basis, and it has been well said that the Jewish mandate for Palestine is the Bible. In addition to their former religious establishments, the Jews have created in Palestine a network of educational institutions which, from the village kindergarten to the Hebrew University in Jerusalem, are adapted to the national development of the

Jewish people. The most remarkable achievement of the Jews during the last half-century has been the miraculous revival of Hebrew as the vernacular of the Jewish masses in Palestine. The use of Hebrew as the language of secular instruction—which for a time just before the First World War was seriously challenged by German—is now an accepted fact. Hebrew literature, apt to languish in the Diaspora, has found a fruitful field in the congenial atmosphere of Palestine, where it acts as a bond between the polyglot Jewish population and is thus welding them into a cultural entity. It is indeed significant that the foundation of the Hebrew University on Mount Scopus in Jerusalem was laid by Chaim Weizmann in the presence of Lord Allenby on July 24, 1918, when the sound of cannon was still heard in the land, and that Haim Nahman Bialik, who may justly be recognized as in the apostolic succession to the classical and the great Hispano-Hebrew poets, was regarded as the foremost citizen of the re-established Jewish National Home.

While it was taken for granted that the Jews would be able to create a spiritual center in Palestine, there were for some time serious misgivings as to whether they would have the capacity for developing on independent economic lines. The enforced divorce of the Jews from the soil in the lands of their Dispersion and their concentration in certain callings have deprived them there of the means of economic self-sufficiency. In these respects, it is the supreme merit of the Jewish National Home that, relatively freed from outside pressure, the Jews have been given the opportunity to return there to a normal economy, and have thereby been able to manifest their productive abilities beyond question. It would seem as if, having lain fallow for many centuries, their physical energies have at last found a fruitful ground and have flowered far beyond expectations. The youth of this nation, repressed by a thousand devices, yearned for the hour of deliverance; and long before the gates of the ancient Promised Land had again been opened, there were innumerable young men and women who were fully equipped ready to enter it. They were the Haluzim (pioneers) whose story is the epic of the rebuilding of the land that had lain waste since their ancestors had been driven out of it.

This soil, barren or infested with malaria, and sand-dunes that were no-man's-land, have become Jewish settlements rich with verdure and fruit, teeming with human activities and aspirations. In less than two decades over 200 Jewish villages, with a population of about 120,000 souls, arose to bear witness to the desire and capacity of a limitless agricultural expansion. The Jordan has been harnessed by Pinhas Rutenberg (1879-1942) to generate electric power and light, and the Palestine Potash Works have brought life to the Dead Sea. Where the camel of the desert still walks with measured gait, the latest machinery of agriculture and industry has been installed. The Jewish town of Tel Aviv, with its 200,000 inhabitants, has grown from a suburb of Jaffa into the most vital city on the shores of the eastern Mediterranean. The new Jewish quarters that have arisen in Jerusalem and Haifa, the orange groves along the coast, the colonies in the Emek, manifest that, in spite of the lack of previous experience and before they had a State, the Jews had, by their own exertions and by resources voluntarily contributed, created rural and urban settlements in Palestine such as are only to be found in the most advanced countries in Europe.

§ 6. *Prelude to a Commonwealth.* When on February 27, 1919 a Zionist delegation was received by the Council of Ten at the Peace Conference in Paris and the United States Secretary Robert Lansing asked the meaning of a "Jewish National Home," Dr. Weizmann replied that the Zionist Organization would build up gradually a Jewish nationality so as to make Palestine as Jewish as America is American and England English. It is on record that the conception of an eventual Jewish Commonwealth not only arose in the discussions on the future of Palestine in the British Cabinet and in the interpretation of the war aims by the principal Allied and Associated Powers but was made the subject of public approval by statesmen responsible for the reshaping of the new world-order after the great struggle. This was particularly endorsed and emphasized by David Lloyd George, who was the British Prime Minister at the time of the Balfour Declaration and the Peace settlement. To be sure, owing to the ensuing war-weariness and gathering opposition, the ideal of a Jewish Commonwealth was reduced in the mandate to a Jewish National Home in Palestine, and the British administration in that country confined Jewish aspirations within the narrowest limits possible. But such has been the dynamic force of Jewish development in that country that it nevertheless acquired certain attributes which went to the making of an autonomous community. The Jewish Settlement in Palestine in fact, even though involuntarily, tended to concentrate in certain parts of the country; and, though politically part of the general population, was socially, culturally, and even economically, self-contained. It was organized on a democratic basis, with a popularly elected National Council, the *Va'ad Leumi*, while Jewish interests generally were represented by the Jewish Agency for Palestine, which, under article 4 of the mandate, was internationally recognized as "a public body for the purpose of advising and co-operating with the Administration of Palestine in such economic, social, and other matters as may affect the establishment of the Jewish national home and the interests of the Jewish population in Palestine and, subject always to the control of the Administration, to assist and take part in the development of the country."

The Jewish population of Palestine, which by the end of 1918 had been reduced to 55,000, rose, largely by immigration, to about 450,000 in 1939, thereby constituting nearly

30 per cent of the total inhabitants and thus representing the largest proportion of Jews in any country of the world. The Jews composed the whole of the population of Tel Aviv, were a majority in Jerusalem and Haifa, and predominated in certain rural parts of the country. They were practically autonomous in the important field of education, and maintained their own extensive health services. The port of Tel Aviv, which had arisen owing to difficulties experienced by Jews in the Jaffa harbor, was a factor even more important politically than economically. The growing participation of the Jews in the British security and defence forces was an especially significant indication of their part in the maintenance of law and order in the country. Even though tardily, it was realized that, in practice as well as in theory, the Zionist policy of co-operation with Great Britain entailed reciprocal relations towards the Jews on the part of the British Administration in Palestine.

An Arab revolt in Palestine, which, owing to the uncertainty of British policy and the anti-Jewish encouragement of Nazi Germany and Fascist Italy, raged throughout the land from 1936 to 1939, put the political future of Palestine into the melting pot. From the time of the British occupation in 1918 and an agreement for an Arab-Jewish understanding made on January 3, 1919, between Dr. Weizmann on behalf of the Zionist Organization, and the Emir (later King) Feisal representing the Arab cause at the Peace Conference, the Jews consistently maintained a policy of friendship with the kindred Arab people in Palestine. This was particularly indicated not only by the repeated recognition of Arab rights by Zionist Congresses but by the remarkable policy of non-retaliation (termed *Havlagah,* i.e. self-restraint) to Arab terrorism on the part of the Jews.

In order to bring out an agreed settlement of the claims of Arabs and Jews in Palestine, the British Government convened representatives of the Jewish Agency for Palestine,

of the Arabs of Palestine and the neighboring Arab States
to a Conference which was held at St. James's Palace in
London in February and March 1939. The British proposals
envisaged the abrogation of the mandate and the consequent
establishment of an independent Palestinian State in treaty
relations with Great Britain. The Jewish delegation, headed
by Dr. Weizmann, declined, however, to accept these proposals since they restricted Jewish immigration for the next
five years to such an extent that the Jews should form not
more than one-third of the population, and subsequently
Jewish immigration would only continue by consent of the
Arabs as well as of the British administration. Since this
would have constituted the Jews in their National Home as
a statutory minority under the permanent domination of a
hostile Arab majority, the Jewish delegation held that, as
the Jews in Palestine would thus be exposed to the same fate
as that of the Assyrians in Arab Iraq, the proposals offered
no basis for a settlement.

The widespread persecution and economic repression to
which the Jews were subjected over a large part of Europe
reinforced the hopes which gave rise to the Balfour Declaration and to which the mandate for Palestine by the League
of Nations gave universal support. The very difficulties in
the way brought to light, if only on the horizon, the project of
an independent, sovereign Jewish State promoted by one
of the Great Powers of the world. Even though the Partition
of Palestine advocated in 1937 by the Royal Commission
under the chairmanship of Lord Peel did not result in the
proposed establishment of a Jewish State, there remained
on record the acknowledgment of the justification of Jewish
national aspirations in Palestine. The ideal which thus
emerged into a concrete form was destined to be realized
ten years later.

CHAPTER IX

A RECORD MARTYRDOM

§ 1. *An Unparalleled Catastrophe.* No period in the annals of the Jewish people presents so tragic a spectacle as that ushered in by the Second World War. It was a period of barbarity and terror, which gradually spread over the greater part of Europe in the wake of the ruthless Nazis, and in which millions of Jews, after enduring indescribable torments, were doomed to death. Not since the overthrow of Judea by the Romans was there an epoch equal to it in magnitude of catastrophe, in the extent of the region afflicted, or in the multitude of victims. Indeed, if one counted up the numbers of Jews who are recorded to have perished in the sequence of calamities and massacres that formed such distressing landmarks in the last nineteen centuries of their history, the total would fall far short of the vast toll claimed by Hitler. For he aimed at the destruction of the whole of the Jewish people, and, although he was unable to accomplish his diabolical purpose, he achieved a formidable part of it.

§ 2. *Pre-War Sufferings in "Greater Reich," Italy, and Hungary.* The sufferings of the Jews on the Continent did not begin with the outbreak of the war : they were intensified and aggravated by it to an unparalleled degree. They began (as mentioned in a previous chapter) with the advent of Hitler to power in 1933. His first victims were the Jews in Germany, whom he degraded and pauperized as a prelude to their flight or expulsion. Even during the ten years before he became Chancellor, his followers had violated and wrecked scores of Jewish cemeteries and defiled over fifty synagogues; and as soon as he secured control over Germany he mobilized all the powers of the State in pursuit of his satanic crusade. Not only were the Jews gradually deprived of the civil rights conferred upon them at the establishment of the German Empire, but they were subjected to disabilities and humiliations that signified a reversion to the barbarism of the Middle Ages and soon outstripped it. The so-called Nuremberg laws for "the protection of German blood and honor," decreed in 1935, constituted the fanatical racial principle as the basis of the German State; and two years later the screw of oppression was tightened by the eviction of all Jews from trade and industry, by their being compelled to wear the yellow badge resurrected from medieval times, the traditional six-pointed "Shield of David," and by their being banned from all public institutions, places of entertainment, parks, and health resorts. The only escape from this persecution was by emigration, and although this entailed the loss of the greater part of their possessions, 300,000 Jews had left after the first five years of Nazi despotism.

As soon as Hitler invaded Austria, in March 1938, the Jews in that country were likewise subjected to violence, plunder, and imprisonment, deprived of civil rights, and robbed of their means of livelihood. In the following November occurred the greatest pogrom in German history, when throughout the "Greater Reich," as though in response to a signal, Jewish shops and their contents were demolished, houses were looted and wrecked, synagogues were set on fire, and 20,000 Jews were carried off to concentration camps. Early in 1939 came the turn of the Jews in Czecho-Slovakia: within a week they experienced all the outrages inflicted upon the Jews in the Reich in the course of six years. The plight to which the Jews were thus reduced prompted President Franklin Roosevelt to convene an International Conference at Evian to organize facilities for emigration, but although it was attended by the delegates of thirty states its discussions proved futile. Palestine, which could have provided a home for tens of thousands, was, at the request of the British Government, strictly barred from consideration. The result was that the Jews were driven to their own devices: they procured whatever visas, legal or faked, that they could, crowded into ships and cargo vessels, many unseaworthy, and sailed to all parts of the world in search of asylum.

Not content with crushing the Jews in the lands over which he tyrannized, Hitler also insisted on their oppression in every land that fell under his influence. The first to succumb was Italy, where Mussolini, who had previously condemned anti-Semitism and derided all Nazi theories, tamely swallowed Hitler's ideology and enacted a series of anti-Jewish decrees, with ruinous consequences to tens of thousands of loyal citizens, many of whom had rendered distinguished services to the State. Hungary, which had a reactionary development of its own, likewise followed in the Führer's footsteps. In May 1938 a law was passed for the limitation of Jewish activities in business undertakings and liberal professions, and, as this did not satisfy the Nazi Government, a more rigorous decree was enacted the following year. This measure, besides increasing restrictions in the economic sphere, deprived all but 1 per cent of the Jewish citizens of the suffrage.

§ 3. *Repression in Poland and Rumania.* In Poland and Rumania, too, hostility to the Jews was on the ascendant. As long as Marshal Pilsudski was alive, any violent manifestation of anti-Semitism was promptly suppressed, as he understood full well that it would harm Poland's prestige abroad; but after his death, first the opponents of the Government, and then the Government itself, embarked upon a course of unbridled oppression. From early in 1935 there was an almost continuous reign of violence throughout the country: not only Jewish lives and property, but synagogues and even cemeteries were attacked. Jewish students were singled out for special ill treatment: in all universities they were compelled by their Polish fellow students to keep to one side of the lecture rooms. It was futile to make any appeal to the League of Nations, as Poland had repudiated her obligations to her racial minorities in 1934. In Rumania Jew-baiting had been a national tradition for several decades and received a fresh impetus from the triumph of National Socialism. Many new anti-Semitic papers sprang up all over the country, and Jews were denied not only justice but elementary security of life. A climax was reached at the end of 1937, when the head of the Christian National Party, Octavian Goga, was entrusted with the Government, but the anti-Jewish decrees that he issued caused panic in the country and nearly ruined the Treasury, so that after six weeks he was dismissed. But although there was a change of Cabinet the ordeal of the Jews continued. Thus, even before the beginning of the war about 5,000,000 Jews on the Continent were subjected to various forms and degrees of persecution. But all this was merely a prelude to the monstrous crimes that were to come.

§ 4. *Persecution in Poland.* As soon as Hitler marched into Poland, his hordes hurled themselves upon defenceless Jews with demoniac fury, driving them from their homes at the point of the bayonet or pistol, and shooting or clubbing to death those who could not flee fast enough. Jews were seized wholesale for forced labor, they had to wear the yellow badge, they were placed under curfew, they were given starvation rations. They were herded into concentration camps, which were established in and near many cities, and where the conditions were so primitive and the treatment so brutal that there was a heavy death-rate from hunger, disease, and shooting. By the summer of 1940 the number of Jews interned was estimated at over 1,600,000. About 30,000 were employed on building new roads leading to the Russian frontier, and another 25,000 on regulating the Rivers Vistula and Bug between Warsaw and Lublin. Besides those toiling and suffering in camps, over 400,000 Jews were compelled to work for the German war industry, and largely in factories hastily built in Warsaw and other cities beyond the range of British bombers. Jewish women, too, were conscripted for slave labor, but their lot was at least preferable to that of hundreds who were seized in the streets to be kept in military brothels.

The Germans also carried out wholesale robbery and arson. Gestapo officials and soldiers broke into Jewish homes and pocketed whatever money and valuables they could find. They plundered Jewish shops, factories, and department stores; they despoiled all Jewish libraries and museums. Hundreds of synagogues were destroyed, including several of architectural importance and antiquity, all the ritual articles of silver and all lamps of brass or bronze being seized beforehand. Jewish books were burned in piles, cemeteries were laid waste, and tombstones were used for the building of roads. Ruinous exactions were levied under various pretexts: £500,000 from the Warsaw community and £375,000 from that of Lodz. The Germans established a "reservation" at Lublin, into which they crowded over 30,000 Jews, but owing to a typhus epidemic and railway disorganization they had to call a halt. They then revived the medieval system of ghettos, but in conditions far more intolerable than any previously known. The largest ghettos were established in Warsaw, where over half a million Jews were packed into an area that had formerly contained only half that number. It was surrounded by an eight-foot concrete wall with twenty-two huge gates, which were all shut at night with seven locks. There was a similar walled ghetto in Lodz, while a dozen other ghettos (in Cracow, Bialystok, Kielce, etc.) were surrounded by electrically charged wire.

§ 5. *Massacres in Russia.* Germany's attack upon Russia

in June 1941 brought an avalanche of horror upon the Jews in that part of Poland previously occupied by the Russians, and then upon those in Russia itself. Tens of thousands of Jews from Lithuania, Latvia, and Estonia fled with the Soviet troops, besides vast numbers from Galicia, the Ukraine, and other parts of Russia. Those who remained were driven into ghettos, drafted into labor battalions, and condemned to starvation. Butcheries of thousands were committed at various places in the newly conquered districts in the autumn of 1941, and larger numbers were massacred in the following years. The savagery of the Huns increased as they advanced into the Baltic countries and White Russia, in all of which large Jewish communities were reduced to desolation and ruin. In Lithuania about 10,000 Jews were imprisoned, thousands were seized for labor gangs, and pogroms were carried out in Kovno, Vilna, Shavli, and other towns. A terrible fate overtook enormous numbers in the Ukraine. Thousands of corpses were flung into the Dniester after massacres committed by German soldiers and Ukrainian Fascist bands. Tens of thousands of Jews were slaughtered in the region of Kamenetz-Podolsk, and in Galicia about 8,000, while praying in synagogues, were murdered by machine-guns. Atrocities on an even larger scale were perpetrated in other cities. In Kiev a total of 52,000 Jews and non-Jews were killed, their corpses littering the main streets; and in Odessa, as a reprisal for the death of some Rumanian soldiers killed by a delayed action bomb left by the Soviet troops, the Rumanians drove about 25,000 Jews into a wooden barracks, mowed them down with machine-guns, and set fire to the building.

By the autumn of 1941 there were still 200,000 Jews in Germany and Austria, which had formerly contained 800,000; and as Hitler had threatened that they would all be cleared out, steps were taken to put the threat into effect. About 20,000 were deported from those countries and

Czecho-Slovakia to Poland and occupied parts of Russia, as a preliminary to their destruction. Many escaped this fate by committing suicide, and many died on the journey, as they were packed to suffocation in goods trains or sealed trucks, without food or drink, with little air, and without sanitary conveniences. From the same three countries about 60,000 Jews, including many leading members of the communities of Berlin, Vienna, and other cities, were interned in a special camp at Theresienstadt (Terezin, in Bohemia), where the conditions were more tolerable than in most camps, although from there too several thousand were afterwards dispatched to their doom in Poland. Hungary and Rumania willingly co-operated in this orgy of barbarism. From Hungary 12,000 Polish and Russian Jews were transported to Poland for forced labor; and in Rumania there were anti-Jewish atrocities in several cities, including Bucharest, Jassy, Botosani and Timisoara. The most extensive outrages were those perpetrated in Bessarabia, where almost a third of the entire population was said to have been exterminated and Jews ceased to exist. After massacring about 100,000 Jews in the autumn of 1941, the Rumanians transported over 130,000 Jews from Moldavia, Bessarabia, and Bukowina, to their new Ukrainian province of "Transdniestria," along the River Dniester. There they were dumped into primitive concentration camps, without shelter, with little food, and very scanty clothing, so that scores of thousands perished.

§ 6. *Fate of Balkan Jewry.* The Jews in the Balkans met with no better fate. In Yugoslavia, at the time of the German invasion, in April 1941, there were 80,000 Jews, besides over 6,000 from neighboring lands. Within two years, as a result of Gestapo operations, over 90 per cent of them were dead. At least a few thousand escaped to Italy, and some to Hungary, while numbers joined the partisan forces of Marshal Tito. In Croatia about 6,000 Jews were transferred to concentration camps, and in the notorious camp of Jasenovac, south of Zagreb, there were 40,000 Jews among 300,000 victims of various nationalities who met their fate there. In Greece 8,000 Jews were transferred in 1942 from Salonika to a concentration camp in the Macedonian mountains, and in the following years 45,000 were deported from that city to the German extermination camps in Poland. By the end of the war only 500 Jews were found in that once famous Jewish center. Of all the Balkan countries Bulgaria had the least revolting record. About 25,000 Jews were deported from Sofia to the provincial towns and sustained material losses, but after Bulgaria went over to the Allies in September 1944, they were allowed to return to the capital. The pro-Nazi Government, however, had handed over 20,000 Jews from Thrace and Macedonia to the Germans for removal to Poland. They were afterwards tried as war criminals, and some were sentenced to death.

§ 7. *Concentration Camps in Western Europe.* In Western Europe the Germans proceeded at first rather cautiously, so as not to arouse the resentment of the non-Jewish populations, but gradually they applied their technique of oppression with increasing rigor. In France, Holland, Belgium, and Norway Jews were subjected to the same degradations and hardships that had been the rule in Germany before the war. The Vichy Government passed anti-Jewish laws, which were extended to all the French colonies and even to the mandated territory of Syria. Tens of thousands of foreign Jews as well as thousands of Jews of other categories were interned in some forty concentration or transit camps. The national shame of the land of "liberty, equality, and fraternity" reached its height in July 1942, when French police wagons raced through the streets of Paris to round up Jews of all ages. There was an epidemic of suicides. Children were separated from their mothers, many were offered to strangers for safety, and women with slashed veins threw themselves out of windows.

Of the 110,000 Jews in Belgium before the war, 25,000 escaped to England and France before the German invasion in July 1940; and of the remainder the overwhelming majority were deported during the next three years to concentration camps in Germany and death camps in Poland. In Holland there were also camps under the command of notorious sadists. Hundreds of Dutch Jews married to Christians had to submit to sterilization, which was carried out by German doctors, as all Dutch doctors bravely refused to carry out this act of barbarity. Fortunately the great majority of Luxembourg's small Jewish community were transported in 1940 to Portugal, to await emigration overseas; about half of Norway's Jewry escaped to Sweden, and of Denmark's Jews about three-fourths found friendly asylum also in Sweden.

§ 8. *Campaign of Extermination*. In addition to the horrors of concentration camps and mass murders many Jews met their death through medical experimentation, as they were given lethal injections and treated as human guinea-pigs. But all these methods were too slow for Hitler, as he had set his mind fanatically upon "the annihilation of the Jewish race in Europe"—the phrase that he used in a speech in the Reichstag before the war. In the summer of 1942, therefore, he and the Chief of the Gestapo, Himmler, began to carry out their diabolical plan to exterminate all the Jews within their grasp by a quicker process. All previous atrocities had seemingly been merely rehearsals for the methodical and organized annihilation that took place in the slaughter camps of Poland, where not only the Jews of that country but also hundreds of thousands from most parts of Europe were murdered in cold blood. Vast gas chambers were constructed in the camps of Oswiecim (Auschwitz) and Birkenau (in southwestern Poland), as well as at Tremblinka, Belzec, Maidanek (near Lublin), Sobibor, and other places. The entry into the gas chambers was from a huge "reception hall," capable of holding 2,000 people, which was outwardly camouflaged as a bathing establishment, and the unsuspecting victims believed that they were going to have a shower-bath. Within a few minutes all who had been packed into the gas chamber were dead, and their bodies were removed to large furnaces to be burned.

Jews were brought to these death camps in trains and cattle-trucks from all parts of Poland and Lithuania, from Holland and Belgium, France and Norway, Germany and Austria, Czecho-Solvakia and Yugoslavia, Italy and Greece. At Oswiecim alone, according to the evidence given at the Nuremberg War Crimes Trials, 3,000,000 Jews were destroyed by poison gas; at Chmelno there were over 1,000,-000, and at Maidanek 750,000. But not all Jews allowed themselves to be led like lambs to the slaughter, as there were several notable instances of desperate resistance in Warsaw, Bialystok, Tarnow, and other cities in Poland. The most imposing demonstration of Jewish heroism was made in the battle of the Warsaw ghetto, which began on April 18, 1943, and lasted six weeks. There were days when 6,000 fully armed Nazis, with all the munitions of war, were engaged, but the defenders fought to such effect that 5,000 Nazis were killed and wounded, after 5,000 of their own number had been killed. When further resistance was useless the Jews burned down the factories in which they had been working; thousands escaped to fight in the ranks of the Polish partisans, but some 20,000 were deported to the death camps. Four months later the Jews of Bialystok fought a desperate battle lasting two weeks, in which the ghetto was set on fire and 40,000 of them fell. There was a revolt even in the death camp at Tremblinka, where many German and Ukrainian guards were killed.

§ 9. *Rescue Measures*. When the news of the mass exterminations first reached the Governments of Great Britain and the United States at the end of 1942, they issued a strong condemnation and declared that those guilty of the crimes would not escape retribution. But their declaration produced not the least effect: the campaign of holocausts continued until the end of the war. Desperate endeavors were made by the Jews to save themselves. Some thousands from Central and Eastern Europe succeeded in reaching the Black Sea ports during the first half of the war, but their efforts to secure entry into the one land where they were most secure of a brotherly welcome, namely, Palestine, were foiled because they did not possess official certificates for admission. Their exclusion was totally unjustified, even on the basis of the White Paper of 1939, which limited the number of admissions during the next five years to 50,000, as it also authorized the entry of 25,000 Jewish refugees. Yielding to appeals for rescue measures, the British and United States Governments held a conference at Bermuda in April 1943, but it was abortive. Early in 1944, therefore, President Roosevelt created a War Refugee Board to carry out "effective measures for the rescue, transportation, maintenance, and relief of the victims of enemy oppression, and the establishment of havens of temporary refuge." Special attachés were immediately dispatched to the American Embassies and Consulates in Spain, Portugal, Sweden, Egypt, and Turkey: they were invested with extraordinary powers and furnished with ample funds. The result of their unconventional methods was that tens of thousands of Jews were rescued. Their efforts were supplemented by the negotiations conducted by the Jewish Agency with Russia and Turkey for transit visas to enable refugees to pass through to Palestine; and as the British Government relaxed its regulations in the latter period of the war over 60,000 Jews succeeded in reaching Palestine. Several thousand also found asylum, not only in Sweden and Portugal (as already mentioned), but also in Switzerland and Spain.

§ 10. *Extent of Losses*. When the war was over it was

found that the total number of Jews who had been exterminated by mass slaughter, starvation, and disease was 6,000,-
000. The Jewish population in Europe in the summer of
1939 was 9,500,000, so that the loss amounted to nearly two-
thirds. In the indictment presented to the Nuremberg War
Crimes Tribunal in October 1945, against twenty-four leading members of the German Government, the persecution
and extermination of the Jews occupied a prominent place.
The extent of the Jewish losses arrived at by deducting the
number of survivors from the pre-war Jewish population
of Europe was confirmed by a Gestapo document submitted
to the Tribunal, which stated that 4,000,000 had been killed
in various camps and 2,000,000 put to death in other ways,
chiefly shooting by operational squads of Security Police
during the campaign against Russia. It was a much greater
loss proportionately than that sustained by any other people
in the war, and it consisted entirely of civilians.

The annihilation of nearly two-thirds of European Jewry
has not only transformed its physical composition, but also
caused the most serious ravages to its social structure, its
economic position, its intellectual wealth, and its spiritual
resources. Its effects have been distributed unevenly over
different countries, for while in Germany and Poland the
Jewish community has shrunk to about a thirtieth of its former size and that of Austria to a twenty-fifth, Hungary and
Rumania were left with nearly half of their pre-war Jewish
population. The casualties comprise not only millions of
Jewish families, who have either been wiped out entirely or
cut down to only one or two members each, but also former
populous communities like those of Berlin, Vienna, and
Warsaw, which have shriveled to mere skeletons, and famous
centers of Jewish learning, like Vilna and Kovno, which
have become mere names. The Jews whose calamity has had
the widest repercussions were those in Poland, for the destruction of their community and of the neighboring one in

Lithuania has proved a disastrous blow not only to European but also to world Jewry, as they provided, for a period of about two centuries, the greater part of the intellectual and spiritual leadership that helped to build up Jewish communities in all corners of the earth.

The hopes that had upborne the Jews throughout the years of oppression, that their liberation would be followed by a period of peace and tolerance, were falsified, for when they returned to the countries from which they had been deported, they, in most cases, met with scant sympathy from their Gentile neighbors. The reason for this unfriendly attitude was twofold: first, the Nazi invaders had in every country inoculated the inhabitants with the virus of enmity for the Jews so thoroughly that its maleficent effects continued long after they departed; and secondly, a feeling of resentment was aroused by the demand of the returning Jews for the restoration of their property, which they found in the possession of strangers. In Poland particularly there was an outburst of criminal violence against them, which lasted for nearly two years after the war, and in which a few hundred of them were killed. The result was that there was a mass exodus into the camps of "displaced persons" in Germany, Austria, and Italy.

§ 11. *Displaced Persons.* The "displaced persons" camps, or D.P. camps, as they came to be called, were a distressing feature of post-war Jewish life on the Continent. They were originally concentration camps, whose survivors refused to return to the countries from which they had been deported, as they feared that they would find there neither safety nor contentment. There were altogether about 30,000 Jewish survivors, who looked like crawling skeletons. Many of them, indeed, at first went back to their homes, only to find that they could no longer live there, and so returned to the camps, which at least provided them with shelter until they could leave Europe for a land overseas. Most of them originated from Poland, but there were also many from Hungary, Rumania, and Slovakia, as well as three states that existed no longer, Lithuania, Latvia, and Estonia. The original inmates of the camps gradually increased in number, as they were joined by Jews who found it impossible to settle down again in their former homelands and decided that their only salvation lay in emigration. By the end of 1945 there were about 100,000 Jews in the D.P. camps in Germany and Austria, besides another 25,000 in Italy, and two years later the total number had risen to about 250,000. The camps were administered by committees elected by the inmates, material support was largely furnished by the American Jewish Joint Distribution Committee and the Central British Fund for German Jewry; while the Jewish Agency established training farms for those who wished to engage in agriculture in Palestine, and also provided teachers for Hebrew and religion. The great majority of the D.P.s wished to settle in Palestine, and were helped to do so; others went to join relatives in England, the United States, and other countries. By the spring of 1950 their number, through continued emigration, had fallen to 30,000, and it was expected to reach vanishing point in the course of the year.

§ 12. *Emigration from Europe.* The position of the 20,000 Jews in Germany and 12,000 in Austria who lived in small communities was anything but satisfactory. They felt themselves surrounded by enmity, and met with insuperable difficulties in their efforts to recover possession of their homes and businesses. Laws for the restitution of confiscated Jewish property had been passed, but unfriendly officials prevented most of the Jews from benefiting by them. The position was much the same in Poland (after the cessation of violence), as well as in Hungary and Rumania. The result was a strong incentive to emigrate, particularly to Palestine, although in the "People's Democracies" the Government put a brake upon this movement. On the other hand, the Jews in Bulgaria and Yugoslavia were relatively free from intolerance, yet the overwhelming majority of them too, without any official hindrance, went to join their fellow Jews in the upbuilding of the State of Israel.

CHAPTER X

WAR SERVICES AND PEACE TREATIES

§ 1. *Services in all Allied Nations.* It would be a mistake to conclude from the preceding chapter that the part played by the Jews in the Second World War was purely passive. On the contrary, it was very active, in accordance with their traditional loyalty and their readiness always to make every sacrifice in defence of their native or adopted country. They fully realized that upon the issue of the great conflict depended the future of civilization, which meant their own future too, and they therefore responded to the call of duty with all their energies and resources. They were egged on by a particular spur, for Hitler had declared war upon the Jewish people long before he began his assault upon other nations, and they were keen to hit back. They served in the fighting forces of all the Allied nations; and on land, in the air, on sea, and under the sea, they displayed a daring, skill, and valor at least equal to those of their comrades in arms. For the first time Jews fought only on one side, for Germany and her vassals, after having deprived them of their civic and even human rights and persecuted them so barbarously, were consistent in excluding them from their armies.

§ 2. *Jews in British Defence Forces.* The number of Jews of the United Kingdom who served in the British armed forces (according to the official records of the Jewish Chaplains) was 60,000 men and women, of whom over 14,000 were in the Royal Air Force and 1,500 in the Royal Navy. As the total Jewish population of the country at the time was estimated at 385,000, they formed over 15 per cent, a higher proportion than among the general population. They fought and fell in every campaign in Europe and in the Middle and Far East in which British troops were engaged. They sanctified their ancestral faith on the battlefields of Libya and Abyssinia, of Greece and Syria, of Italy, France, and Germany, as well as in the garrisons of Gibraltar and Hong Kong, of Singapore and Sierra Leone, of Iceland and Malta, and on troop ships sailing over many seas. They held important positions in all three services, those in the army including four brigadiers. That they acquitted themselves with credit was attested by Sir James Grigg, Secretary of State for War, who, in referring to the liability of Jews of British nationality to serve in the British forces, said that "this was an obligation which they had carried out very fully and faithfully," and that "honor was due to them." Further testimony was provided by the fact that 1,150 British Jews were killed in action, or were killed or died on active service, and 179 were posted as missing, while 568 received awards. Two distinguished officers who died in battle were Brigadier Frederick H. Kisch, C.B., D.S.O., Chief Engineer of the Eighth Army, and Major Wigram, of the Royal Fusiliers, famous as the pioneer of the new system of battle-drill that was accepted as an essential part of British infantry training. The awards included one Victoria Cross, two of Companion of the Bath, five of Commander of the British Empire, three of the George Cross, four of the Air Force Cross, nine each of the Distinguished Service Order and Distinguished Service Cross, and fifty-six of the Distinguished Flying Cross.

Jews also took a very active and prominent part in the Civil Defence Services from the beginning of the war, exhibited great daring and courage, and received many George Medals and British Empire Medals. The Jewish refugees from the Continent contributed 4,000 men to the Auxiliary Military Pioneer Corps, of whom the first five companies went with the British Expeditionary Force to France. They were afterwards represented in all branches of the army, navy, and air force, took part in engagements on all fronts, and shared in the landing on the Normandy coast on D-day. A considerable number became officers, many gained awards, and no small number paid the supreme sacrifice.

§ 3. *In Dominion Defence Forces.* The fighting forces of all the British dominions contained a goodly proportion of Jews. In Canada there were at least 16,560 Jewish men and women on active service, besides Canadian Jews who joined the armies of Great Britain, the United States, or other Allied nations. Their casualties numbered 776, and awards were conferred upon 122. In South Africa, where there was no conscription, the Jewish community of 100,000 contributed approximately 10,000 to the armed forces. There was a total of 1,151 casualties, and of 179 decorations and commendations for war service. Field-Marshal Smuts wrote: "In the years that follow this war it will surely be remembered that, whoever else faltered or failed, the Jews played their part by the side of the Allies." Both Australia and New Zealand furnished relatively large contingents of Jewish fighters. Out of a Jewish population in Australia that was hardly more than 32,000 in 1940, over 10 per cent, namely 3,872, were in the defence forces, while the casualties included at least 117 killed and a large number of wounded. New Zealand Jewry, numbering at the time hardly more than 3,000, was represented in the defence force by at least 350, and the number of casualties was comparatively high.

§ 4. *In American Defence Forces.* The largest Jewish contingent for the Allied armies was, thanks to their numbers, furnished by the Jews of the United States. It consisted of 550,000 men and women, over 10 per cent of the Jewish population, and forming the equivalent of thirty-seven divisions. It included nineteen generals and four admirals or commodores. There were over 38,000 casualties, of whom 11,000 were listed dead; and over 61,000 awards for valor and meritorious services were given to more than 36,000 Jews. A Jewish sergeant who fought as bombardier in Alaska, in the Pacific, and in Europe, received thirty decorations. At Pearl Harbor there were a score of Jewish heroes. The last words describing the brave stand at Corregidor were wirelessed by a young Jew, and another helped to bring General MacArthur out of that scene of danger.

§ 5. *In the Soviet Forces.* The Jews of the Soviet Union provided a contingent that was estimated at 500,000. Among the more than 158 nationalities of the Union they were fourth in the number of Red Army heroes and war workers whose services won special recognition from the Soviet Government. A total of 63,000 military decorations were awarded to them, and many received several each. The Red Army included about 100 Jewish generals, all of whom were noted for their ability and valor and several distinguished for their successful strategy. The best known was Lieutenant-General Jacob Kreiser, who became famous for his skilful defence of Moscow against the German invaders, when his division completely smashed an army corps. Besides the impressive part taken by the Jews in the regular fighting of the Soviet armed forces, they also bravely participated in the struggle of the guerillas and partisans.

§ 6. *Services of Polish, French, and Greek Jews.* In Poland the Jews showed remarkable courage and self-sacrifice during that country's brief struggle against the invader, and many of them continued to fight with the Polish forces in different areas. Only five weeks after the beginning of the war, the Polish General Staff announced that 32,000 Jews had fallen in defence of the country and 61,000 had been taken prisoner. The Polish Army that was afterwards organized in France contained a proportion of Jews that ultimately amounted to 12 per cent; in the Polish Legion formed in Russia 15 per cent were Jews, and in that raised in Great Britain there were over 1,000 Jews. Three Jewish soldiers were awarded the Order Virtuti Militari, equivalent to the Victoria Cross.

France had 80,000 Jews, about half of them refugees, in her defence forces. Many held important commissions, including several generals; hundreds were awarded decorations for gallantry; but the number who were killed, wounded, or taken prisoner are unknown. Of the 40,000 foreign Jewish volunteers in the French Army about 15,000 were refugees from Germany and Austria, who were mostly sent to the Foreign Legion in North Africa and Syria. Many of the latter were the first to cross the Palestinian frontier with the Poles after the collapse of France: they joined the Free French forces under General Catroux and took part in the battles for Syria. The Greek Army contained a relatively high percentage of Jews, several of whom were officers. There were 7,000 Jewish soldiers from Salonika alone who took part in some of the heaviest fighting of the war on the Albanian front.

§ 7. *Services of Palestinian Jewry.* The part played by the Jews of Palestine was of special significance, partly because conscription was out of the question in that mandated country, and partly because, at least in the earlier part of the war, the Government betrayed little interest in Jewish support. Dr. Weizmann, President of the Jewish Agency, made the Government a formal offer to provide a Jewish division for service wherever required, but it was turned down apparently because of the effect that it was feared acceptance would have upon the Arabs.

Nevertheless, there was eventually a total of 25,800 Jewish volunteers (including 4,000 women), as against about 9,000 Arabs, a proportion inverse to their respective ratio of the population. The Jewish combatants were distributed among all branches of the British defences forces and acquitted themselves well on all fronts in the Near and Middle East—in Libya and Tunisia, Abyssinia and Eritrea, Greece and Syria, Sicily and Italy. Among the 10,000 British troops taken prisoner in Greece and Crete, there were 1,000 Jews. After five years of war the repeated request for the formation of a Jewish brigade was granted by the British Government. This brigade, whose members carried the Zionist flag and bore a shoulder-flash with the Shield of David, did active service in the campaign in Italy, and was congratulated on its achievements by Field-Marshal Alexander. Exceptional services were rendered by a group of thirty-two Jewish volunteers (including five girls) who were parachuted into the Balkan countries for the purpose of organizing intelligence work and helping escaping Allied prisoners-of-war. Seven of them were captured, tortured, and shot. The name of one, Hannah Senesh, a Jewish girl born in Hungary, who was fired by the spirit of a Joan of Arc, has become a legend in Israel.

§ 8. *Total Jewish Contribution.* The total number of Jews who took active part in the war amounted to about 1,410,000, as will be seen from the following list:

United States	550,000
U.S.S.R.	500,000
Poland	150,000
British Empire	90,772
France	80,000
Palestine	25,825
Greece (approx.)	8,000
Yugoslavia	5,000
Belgium	500
	1,410,097

§ 9. *The Peace Treaties.* When the Peace Conference was held in Paris, in the summer of 1946, for the purpose of drafting treaties with the satellite allies of Nazi Germany, namely, Rumania, Hungary, Italy, Bulgaria, and Finland, delegates of the leading Jewish representative organizations assembled there in the interests of their people. They were not concerned with Finland, whose Jews were few in number and had been treated justly by their Government as long as it was free from German pressure. But they submitted proposals for the inclusion of articles in the treaties with the other four countries, which were designed to remedy the grievances of their Jewish inhabitants and to ensure their rights, liberties, and status. The total Jewish population that had survived in the ex-enemy countries was 700,000, but as the Conference could not consider the conclusion of treaties with Germany and Austria, the number on whose behalf the proposals were submitted was somewhat less. When the definitive treaties were approved by the Council of Foreign Ministers in Paris, in February 1947, they were found to contain three articles relating to the position of the Jews, although the latter were not specifically mentioned. The first of these secured to all persons, "without distinction as to race, sex, language, or religion, the enjoyment of human rights and of the fundamental freedoms, including freedom of expression, of press and publication, of religious worship, of political opinion and of public meeting." The second provided that there would be no discrimination between persons "on the ground of their race, sex, language, or religion, whether in reference to their persons, property, business, professional or financial interests, status, political or civil rights, or any other matter." And the third provided for the restoration to its rightful owners of property expropriated under the "racial" dispensation, and for communal use of properties belonging to communal institutions or to exterminated families.

All the countries passed laws for the restitution of confiscated property, but only a small percentage of the Jews affected succeeded in recovering part of their former possessions. As for the heirless and unclaimed Jewish property, which was quite considerable, Hungary and Rumania passed laws for its transfer to their Jewish communities. In the British and American Zones in Germany laws were passed for the administration of unclaimed Jewish property by so-called "Successor Organizations," such as the American Jewish Joint Distribution Committee and the Jewish Agency, likewise for the benefit of the local Jewish community.

As for citizenship rights in Rumania, a law was enacted in that country in 1947, to confer such rights upon all those who had lived there in 1920, and upon those who had been or would be repatriated from Russia (provided they were Rumanian citizens before 1940); and also to invalidate the Goga decree of 1938, which had rendered tens of thousands of Rumanian Jews stateless. At last, therefore, the scandal of Jewish "statelessness" was at an end.

§ 10. *Reparations*. There was one further measure taken to redress the wrongs of victims of Nazi persecution who were "non-repatriable." The Paris Reparations Agreement of December 21, 1945 provided that a share of reparations consisting of all the non-monetary gold found by the Allies in Germany and a sum not exceeding twenty-five million dollars should be allocated for their rehabilitation and resettlement. The non-monetary gold referred to the jewelry stolen from Jews and to the teeth-fillings removed from the bodies of victims of extermination, and the twenty-five million dollars came out of the proceeds of German assets in neutral countries. It was agreed that 90 per cent of this gold and money and 95 per cent of the heirless assets in neutral countries of victims of Nazi action should be for the assistance of Jews. The International Refugee Organization was entrusted with the administration of the funds, of which the Jewish portion was handed over to the American Joint Distribution Committee and the Jewish Agency for approved schemes of resettlement. The two main countries from which the funds were obtained were Switzerland and Sweden. But the total that was made available for Jewish purposes was only an insignificant fraction of the enormous value of Jewish property that had been stolen or destroyed by the Nazis and their satellites.

CHAPTER XI

THE JEWISH STATE

§ 1. *The Need for Independence.* The most important outcome of the Second World War for the Jewish people was the establishment of the State of Israel. It was the fulfilment of a two-thousand-year-old dream, which had sustained the Jews throughout their countless vicissitudes, and which the Zionist movement had been created to bring into realization. At the end of the First Zionist Congress, Herzl wrote in his diary: "At Basle I founded the Jewish State. If I were to say this today, I would be met by universal laughter. In five years, perhaps, and certainly in fifty, every one will see it. The State is already founded, in essence, in the will of the people to the State." Owing to political conditions the idea of a Jewish State was for long entertained only as a remote possibility, and it was not until 1937, in the report of the Palestine Royal Commission, that it was first advocated officially. But although the British Government expressed approval of it for a time, they abandoned it under the pressure of the Arab rebellion and, two years later, adopted as their policy the White Paper of 1939, which foreshadowed the end of Jewish immigration into Palestine and the conversion of the country into an Arab State, with the Jews as a permanent minority. Despite the men ce of that document, the Jews of Palestine rendered Britain and her allies the most loyal help throughout the war; but the terrible catastrophe that overwhelmed the Jews of Europe brought home to the Zionist leaders the imperative necessity for a radical change of policy when the war was over. They came to the conclusion that a comprehensive solution of the Jewish problem demanded the transfer of a substantial proportion of European Jewry to Palestine, and that this involved unlimited immigration and a large-scale utilization of the country's resources, which could be achieved only by giving the Jewish National Home the powers of a State.

The need for an independent Jewish State was expressed in a resolution adopted at a conference of all Zionist parties and organizations in the United States in 1942, and confirmed in the same year by the Zionist General Council in Jerusalem. Two years later the Executive of the Jewish Agency submitted a memorandum to the Mandatory Government, to draw the logical conclusion from the Balfour Declaration and decide in favor of constituting Palestine as a Jewish State; and two weeks after the war was over Dr. Weizmann presented a memorandum to the Prime Minister (Mr. Winston Churchill) requesting an immediate decision to that effect. When the Labor Government was elected in July 1945 the Zionist leaders expected that the White Paper would at once be scrapped, as it had been vehemently denounced by spokesmen of the Labor Party, which had a long and consistent record of sympathy with Zionist aspirations. They therefore asked the Government for 100,000 certificates for Palestine for part of the remnant of European Jewry, and President Truman addressed a similar request to the Prime Minister (Mr. Attlee). Neither received a favorable reply.

§ 2. *Labor Government's Changed Policy.* The Labor Government completely reversed their traditional policy of friendship towards Zionism, apparently because they wanted to be sure of the support of the Arab States, and of an uninterrupted supply of oil from the Middle East, in the event of a conflict with Russia. The affairs of Palestine were transferred from the Colonial to the Foreign Office, and the Foreign Secretary, Mr. Ernest Bevin, became the principal exponent of the Government's changed policy. The response to the requests of the Zionist leaders was the appointment by the British and American Governments of a Joint Committee of Inquiry to investigate the problems of Palestine and of European Jewry, and to propose recommendations for a solution. The Joint Committee, after completing its inquiry, published a report in April 1946, in which it unanimously proposed that the 100,000 certificates be given immediately, that the land sale restrictions in Palestine (based on the White Paper) be abolished, and that Palestine continue under the mandate pending the execution of a trusteeship agreement under the United Nations. Although Mr. Bevin had promised that if the report of the committee were unanimous he would do his best to carry it out, the Government insisted upon unacceptable conditions. The result was that the Government continued to admit into Palestine only 1,500 Jews a month, and employed a fleet of destroyers, aeroplanes, an army of 100,000, and thousands of police in intercepting refugee boats coming from the Mediterranean ports and arresting their "illegal" human freight, who were promptly interned. The reaction of the Jews of Palestine, particularly of the militant *Irgun Zvai Leumi* (National Military Organization), was to commit acts of violence against Government and military buildings and personnel—a policy that was condemned by the Executive of the Jewish Agency and other Jewish authorities. The Government responded by seizing the refugee ships, imposing curfew, deporting suspects to Kenya and Eritrea, and carrying out military searches in agricultural settlements. They also made a raid upon the Jewish Agency offices and interned Zionist leaders for some months. These actions evoked further outrages by the *Irgun,* and as the refugee boats continued to arrive the "illegal" immigrants were deported to Cyprus.

Thereupon the British Government, having buried the report of the Anglo-American Committee, attempted a new solution. They proposed a cantonization plan, which consisted in offering the Jews and Arabs limited autonomy in small provinces subject to a Central Government, and made acceptance of this plan a condition for the transfer of 100,000 Jews. It was rejected by both Jews and Arabs. Mr. Bevin next proposed a five-year trusteeship agreement to be approved by the United Nations, under which certain undefined areas with Jewish or Arab majorities would have local self-administration under the control of the High Commissioner, and that Jewish immigration would be 4,000 a month for the first two years, after which the High Commissioner would consult his Advisory Council or refer the matter to the United Nations. This proposal too was rejected by both Jews and Arabs. Consequently Mr. Bevin referred the whole question to the judgment of the United Nations.

§ 3. *United Nations' Historic Decision.* The General Assembly, which met in April 1947, resolved, after a thorough discussion, to appoint a special committee consisting of representatives of eleven neutral states to proceed to Palestine to study the question and draw up a report. This committee (called "U.N.S.C.O.P." for short) published its report four months later: it comprised a majority report recommending the creation of a Jewish State and an Arab State and a minority report favoring an independent Federal State. The majority report proposed that the two States should become independent after two years and that before their independence was recognized they must adopt a democratic constitution and sign a treaty for the economic union of Palestine. During the transition period Britain should carry on the administration of Palestine under the auspices of the United Nations, admit into the proposed Jewish State 150,000 Jews, and abolish the land sale restrictions. The Jewish State should include Eastern Galilee, the Esdraelon plain, most of the coastal plain (from south of Acre to just north of Ashdod), and the whole of the Beersheba sub-district, including the Negev. The Arab State should include Western Galilee, the hill country of Samaria and Judea, except the city of Jerusalem, and the coastal plain from Ashdod to the Egyptian frontier. The city of Jerusalem should be placed under an international trusteeship of the United Nations, and its Governor, who should be neither Jew nor Arab, should be appointed by the Trusteeship Council.

The report of U.N.S.C.O.P. was subjected by the General Assembly to a three months' discussion, in the course of which the Jewish spokesmen agreed in principle to the partition of Palestine, but the Arabs demanded an Arab State in the whole of the country. Finally, on November 29, 1947, the General Assembly adopted the partition plan by 33 votes to 13 (more than the requisite two-thirds majority).

§ 4. *Role of American Jewry.* The historic events culminating in Jewish Statehood were powerfully furthered by concerted efforts on the part of Jewish communities throughout the world. The largest of these, in the United States, assumed unprecedented tasks in the Zionist political and fund-raising spheres, particularly during the crucial years 1943-1948. American Zionist political action grew out of the conviction that the Jewish people could no longer rely on Great Britain in seeking to achieve national rebirth, that the center of the political struggle would be in the United States, and that large-scale organization of public opinion would be imperative to win the support of the American Government.

This policy characterized the work of the American Zionist Emergency Council which, under the leadership of Dr. Abba Hillel Silver, launched a nationwide program of public relations designed to convert official Washington from an attitude of indifference to one of sympathetic support. In the summer of 1943 the inaugural gathering of the American Jewish Conference—the first democratically elected body representing the totality of American Jewry and entitled to speak on its behalf since the First World War—voted overwhelmingly in favor of a Jewish Commonwealth. With the Jewish community thus on record, the Council next sought non-Jewish aid for its program. The activities of the American Christian Palestine Committee, representing large numbers of churchmen and educators, and the coöperation of the American labor movement served to project the question of a Jewish State into U. S. public life as a chief issue of the day.

Nevertheless, the Department of State persisted in supporting the British White Paper policy. Early in 1944 the Wagner-Taft Resolution on Palestine was introduced in Congress. Despite strong endorsements of the Resolution by leading Senators and Representatives of both major parties and by the press, the Administration brought about a postponement of action through the intervention of the War Department, which argued for delay on military grounds. It was nevertheless apparent to the Administration that a large section of American public opinion was deeply concerned with the matter and, on March 16, 1944, President Roosevelt issued the first clear-cut expression of sympathy with Zionist aims to come from a leader of any of the great powers since the beginning of the Second World War.

In the summer of 1944 the Republican and Democratic parties, at their national conventions, included planks in their respective platforms favoring the opening of Palestine to unrestricted Jewish immigration and colonization and the establishment there of a free and democratic Jewish Commonwealth. Subsequently, on October 15th, 1944, President Roosevelt gave his support to the plank in the Democratic platform and stated: "I am convinced that the American people give their support to this aim and, if re-elected, I shall help to bring about its realization." However, this declaration was not followed by corresponding action on the part of the Executive branch of the government.

The Palestine Resolution was re-introduced late in 1945.

Although the opposition of the State Department under President Truman was no less vigorous than it had been under President Roosevelt, Congress was determined to act, and the measure was overwhelmingly adopted on December 19th, 1945.

Following Mr. Bevin's refusal to agree to the admission to Palestine of 100,000 Jewish refugees, whose transfer had been recommended by the Anglo-American Committee of Inquiry, a Cabinet Committee was appointed on June 11th, 1946. The product of the discussions between the deputy members of this Committee and a corresponding British group was the Morrison-Grady Report, which was actually the British Foreign Secretary's plan for the federalization of Palestine. Acting in response to an indignant public opinion, President Truman rejected the plan. On October 4, 1946, Mr. Truman declared that "substantial immigration into Palestine cannot wait a solution to the Palestine problem and . . . should begin at once." On October 28, he released the text of a letter to King Ibn Saud, in which Jewish immigration into Palestine and "the upbuilding of the Jewish national home" were firmly espoused.

When the Palestine question was finally referred to the United Nations, the American Section of the Jewish Agency, under the chairmanship of Dr. Silver, was charged with the task of presenting the Jewish case. American Zionists were again chiefly concerned with convincing their government that it should take the lead in support of the Jewish position, in pursuance of the clearly expressed wishes of the American people. Such leadership on the part of the American delegation was demonstrated on November 29, 1947, when the United States warmly urged other nations to follow it in voting for the partition plan.

§ 5. *End of Palestine Mandate.* It was agreed that the Jewish and Arab States should come into existence on October 1, 1948, and that until then Palestine should be administered by a United Nations Commission, which should arrange with the mandatory power for the evacuation of seaport areas in the future states at an early date. Britain announced that she would leave Palestine on August 1, 1948, and that she would neither co-operate in the execution of the scheme nor allow any other authority there while the mandate lasted. The Assembly thereupon appointed a commission of five to go to Palestine to carry out the scheme. The epoch-making decision of the United Nations caused a thrill of joy throughout the Jewish world, but the jubilation of the Jews in Palestine was short-lived as organized attacks by the Arabs began both there and in the neighboring Arab lands. Bands of armed Arabs crossed the Jordan, and by the spring of 1948 there were 6,000 Arab troops in the vicinity of Nablus, besides the Arab Legion of Transjordan, which had taken up its quarters also on the west of the Jordan. But while the Government allowed these invaders to come into the country, they continued to hunt down the refugee boats and to send the so-called "illegal" immigrants to Cyprus, thus provoking further outrages by the *Irgun.* Moreover, as they barred the entry of the United Nations Commission, the *Haganah,* the Jewish self-defence organization, determined to enforce the United Nations' decision themselves. Beginning with the capture of Haifa, they soon had control over Acre, Tiberias, and Jaffa, and the tactics which they employed, coupled with the flight of the Arab leaders, caused tens of thousands of Arabs to flee in panic. The increasing disorder and violence led to the appointment by the Security Council of a truce commission to effect a cessation of hostilities. It also impelled the Government to bring the mandatory regime to an end many weeks earlier than they had originally intended. On May 14 the Union Jack was hauled down from Government House, and the last High Commissioner and his staff departed.

§ 6. *Birth of Israel.* On that same day the Jewish State

sprang into existence. At a joint session of the Executive of the Jewish Agency and the *Va'ad Leumi* (National Council), Mr. David Ben-Gurion, as Prime Minister of the new State, proclaimed the establishment of the State to be called Israel. He declared that it would be open to the immigration of Jews from all the countries of their dispersion, and would promote the development of the country for the benefit of all its inhabitants; that it would be based on the precepts of liberty, justice, and peace taught by the Hebrew prophets, would uphold the full social and political equality of its citizens without distinction, and guarantee full freedom of conscience, worship, education, and culture. He also affirmed that it would safeguard the sanctity of the shrines and Holy Places of all religions, and dedicate itself to the principles of the Charter of the United Nations. Mr. Ben-Gurion concluded by announcing the names of the members of the Cabinet, in which he was Minister of Defence as well as Prime Minister, and Mr. Moshe Sharett was Foreign Secretary. Dr. Weizmann, the veteran head of the Zionist movement, was declared President of the State.

§ 7. *Arabs' War against Israel.* As soon as the British Administration had withdrawn, the five neighboring Arab States—Egypt, Iraq, Transjordan, Syria, and Lebanon—invaded Palestine for the purpose of destroying the Jewish State. The Arab armies, which were joined by a contingent from Saudi Arabia, directed their attack mainly against Jerusalem and the road from this city to Tel Aviv, but the Jewish troops offered vigorous resistance. The Security Council thereupon appointed Count Folke Bernadotte of Sweden as mediator to effect a truce. After a month's truce Count Bernadotte submitted proposals to the Jews and Arabs for peace, but they were rejected and hostilities broke out again. He succeeded, however, in arranging a second truce without time limit, and then negotiated with representatives of Israel and of the Arab States to ascertain upon what terms he could draw up proposals for a peace settlement. After he had dispatched his Report to the Secretary-General of the United Nations, he and his assistant were unfortunately shot dead, and the Government of Israel denounced this dastardly crime.

§ 8. *Bernadotte Proposals Rejected*. The principal proposals of Count Bernadotte were that the Negev should be defined as Arab territory and Galilee as Jewish territory, that Haifa and Lydda airport should be free ports, and that Jerusalem should be under the control of the United Nations, with a maximum measure of autonomy for its Jewish and Arab communities and safeguards for free access to the Holy Places. These proposals, which were discussed by the General Assembly during the autumn of 1948, were approved by the British Government, who thus showed that they were reconciled to the Jewish State. But they were turned down by the Government of Israel, who were opposed to the transfer of the Negev to the Arabs in exchange for Western Galilee, as it formed two-thirds of Israel's territory; and as they were rejected also by the Arabs, they were dropped altogether. The General Assembly then appointed a conciliation commission to effect a final settlement between Israel and the Arab States. Meanwhile the State of Israel received recognition from a steadily increasing number of states, so that it was admitted as a member of the United Nations on May 11, 1949. Britain accorded it *de facto* recognition on January 28, 1949 and *de jure* recognition on April 27, 1950.

§ 9. *Israel's Victory*. Two years after its establishment, the State of Israel had already made considerable progress towards its consolidation. It had astonished the whole world by its victory over the joint forces of the six Arab States, but its success was due to what the Jews called their secret weapon: *"En Brerah,"* the Hebrew for "No option!" After two thousand years of dispersion and tribulation, and after a calamity of unparalleled magnitude, they at last had the opportunity of regaining their independence and had to win.

They therefore fought with desperate courage and tactical skill, and they won. Of the 10,000 square miles of mandated Palestine, Israel occupied all but 2,000, consisting of a rectangular area south of the Lake of Tiberias, which was annexed by the Kingdom of Jordan, and a small strip of the coast, including Gaza, held by the Egyptians. The Jews also occupied the new city of Jerusalem and had uninterrupted control over the road to the sea as well as over the Negev. They were strongly opposed to the internationalization of Jerusalem, which had been proposed by the United Nations, as such a scheme, even if capable of implementation, would have deprived the State of Zion; but they agreed to an international regime confined only to the protection of the Holy Places. A Government quarter was rapidly developed not far from Tel Aviv, in a district called Hakiryah, which hummed with the feverish activity of a score of ministries. But many of these were gradually removed to Jerusalem, and the legislative chamber, the Knesset, originally set up in Tel Aviv, was also transferred to the Holy City, which was proclaimed the capital.

§ 10. *Progress and Prospect.* Young as the State was, it had quickly acquired all the attributes and appurtenances of a sovereign power. In addition to its rapidly developed army, it also had a competent air force and the nucleus of a navy. It had its own courts of law and police, its own coinage, banknotes, and postage stamps. It was represented in the leading capitals of the world by its legations and consulates, and diplomatic missions of numerous states had taken up residence in its own metropolis. Above all, it had thrown open its shores freely to all Jews, and had welcomed 400,000 within a couple of years. They had come not only from Central and Eastern Europe, which had such bitter memories for them, and to some extent from Western countries, but also in far greater measure from Arab lands—Yemen and Iraq, Egypt and Syria, Morocco and Tripolitania—where

Moslem wrath at the creation of Israel had made life for them unbearable. It was a veritable "ingathering of the exiles," increasing the Jewish population of the Holy Land to over one million, and making it the third largest Jewish community in the world.

Thus had the prayer that had been offered up by Jews throughout the ages, ever since the overthrow of Judea by the Romans, found solid and splendid fulfilment. The State had been ushered into existence by those who had toiled and planned in the ancestral homeland, but their success was also due, in no small degree, to the feeling of kinship that knit them to their fellow Jews throughout the globe and to the material help received from them. That bond of solidarity should continue into the boundless future. Spiritual or cultural attachment to the land of their forbears, now revived and restored for a new era of national creative endeavor, should not in any way lessen the loyalty of Jews to the lands in which they dwell. For the new State cannot and will not claim their political allegiance, but will be to them a source of pride, even as it should be both to them and to humanity at large a fount of hope that, in the words of the prophet, "from Zion shall go forth the Law, and the word of the Lord from Jerusalem."

INDEX

AARON, 25
Abba Arica (Rab), 63
Abraham, 23
Abraham ibn Ezra, 95
Abrahams, Israel, 168
Abravanel, Isaac, 120, 121, 133
Abravanel, Samuel, 133
Abtalion, 48
Abulafia, Abraham, 129
Acre, 242
Adiabene, 54
Adler, Cyrus, 174
Adler, Hermann, 168
Adler, Nathan Marcus, 168
Aelia Capitolina, 61
Agnon, S. J., 155
Agrippa I, 54, 55
Agrippa II, 55, 56
Agudath Israel, 179
Ahad Ha'am, 155, 202
Akiba ben Joseph, 61, 66
Albo, Joseph, 126
Alexander Jannaeus, 12
Alexander, Samuel, 177
Alexandra Salome, 42
Alharizi, Judah, 125
Allgemeine Zeitung d. Judentums, 162
Alliance Israélite Universelle, 178
American Christian Palestine Committee, 240
American Jewish Committee, 174
—— —— Congress, 174
—— —— Historical Society, 175
—— Joint Distribution Committee, 181, 233
American Zionist, 239
Amoraim, 69, 75

Amos, 33
Anan ben David, 85, 86
Anglo American Committee, 241
Anglo-Jewish Association, 179
Antipater, 44
Anti-Semitism, 181, 182
Antokolski, Marc, 170
Apocrypha, 66
Apollos, 54
Aquila, 66
Arab Lands, 245
Arab Legion of Transjordan, 242, 243
Arab State, 235, 236
—— States, 243, 244
—— War, 243
Archelaus, 44, 45
Aristobulus I, 42
Aristobulus II, 43, 44
Artom, Benjamin, 168
Asch, Shalom, 156
Asher ben Jehiel, 126
Ashi, Rab, 75
Ashkenazi, Solomon, 134
Ashkenazi, Zebi Hirsh, 137
Asser, Tobias, 177
Assideans, 46
Australia, 228
Austria, 212

Baal Shem-Tob, 139, 140
Baeck, Leo, 178
Bahya ibn Pakuda, 94
Balfour Declaration, 202, 203, 236
Balkan Jewry, 217
Bar Cochba, 60, 61
Bar Giora, Simon, 59
Barros Basto, A. C. de, 122

Basnage, J. C., 143, 212
Bedersi, Jedaiah, 125
Belgium, 218, 219
Ben-Gurion, D., 243
Benjamin, Judah P., 174
Benjamin of Tudela, 95
Ben Jehudah, Eliezer, 155
Bergson, Henri, 177
Bermuda Conference, 221
Bernadotte, Count F., 243, 244
Bevin, Ernest, 241
Bialik, Haim Nahman, 155, 206
Biro-Bidjan, 192
Blum, Léon, 164
B'nai B'rith, 179
Board of Deputies of British Jews, 167
Börne, Ludwig, 150
Brandeis, Louis D., 174, 201
British Administration, 243
British Government, 244
Britain, political and social conditions, 165, 169
British White Paper, 240
British Forces, Jews in, 226, 228
Buber, Martin, 141
Büchler, Adolph, 168
Bulan, King, 88
Bulgaria, 218, 225
Bush, Solomon, 175

Cabbalah, 126, 127
Cabinet Committee, 241
Cabinet Ministers, 166, 168
Canada, 228
Cardozo, Benjamin N., 174
Caro, Joseph, 132, 160
Central Conference of American Rabbis, 174
Central and Eastern Europe, 245
—— Union of German Citizens, 179
Charter of United Nations, 243
Chazars, 87, 189, 191
Chmielnicki, 187
Christiani, Pablo, 124
Churchill, Winston, 236

Cohen, Hermann, 177
Cohen, John Jacob, 169
Comité des Délégations Juives, 180
Communists, 187
Concentration Camps, 218, 220
Conference (St. James's Palace), 210
Crémieux, Adolphe, 150, 178
Crescas, Hasdai, 126
Cyprus, 242
Czechoslovakia, 212

Daniel, 35
David, 28
Deborah, 27
Denmark, 219
Deportations, 216, 220
Displaced persons, 223, 224
Disraeli, Benjamin, 151
Donin, Nicholas, 123
Dönmeh, the, 131
Dreyfus, Alfred, 182
Dubnow, Simon, 141, 159
Dunash ibn Labrat, 91
Duran, Simon, 126

Ebionites, the, 40
Egypt, 243, 245
Ehrlich, Paul, 176
Einstein, Albert, 176
Eleazar ben Kalir, 92
Elijah, 32
Elijah of Vilna, 137
Emigration, 224
"En Brerah," 244
Epstein, Jacob, 177
Essenes, the, 46
Estherka, 116
Evian Conference, 212
Eybeschütz, Jonathan, 137
Ezekiel, 33
Ezra the Scribe, 37, 38, 39

Feisal, King, 209
Finland, 231
'Fiscus Judaicus,' 60, 72, 74
Flexner, Simon, 177

France, 218, 230
Frank, Jacob, 131, 132
Fränkel, David, 152
Fränkel, Zecharias, 162
Frankfurter, Felix, 174
Franzos, Karl Emil, 172
Freud, Sigmund, 177
Fried, Alfred, 177
Friedländer, David, 158
Friedländer, Michael, 168

Galilie, 244
Gamaliel I, 67
Gamaliel II, 67
Gans, David, 131
Gans, Eduard, 158
Gaster, Moses, 168
Gaza, 245
Geiger, Abraham, 159, 162
Gemara. *See* Talmud
General Assembly, 244
Geonim, the, 83, 84
Germany, 193, 195, 212
Gershom ben Judah, 98, 108
Gestapo, 215, 219
Ghettos, 215
Goga, Octavian, 214, 233
Goldfaden, Abraham, 156
Goodman, Paul, 122
Gordon, Leon, 155
Government House, 242
Government of Israel, 244
Grätz, H., 159
Greece, 218, 227
Guide of the Perplexed, 96, 97
Gulkowitsch, Lazar, 141

Haber, Fritz, 176
Haffkine, Waldemar, 177
Haganah, 242
Haggadah, 48, 72
Haggai, 48
Hai, Gaon, 34
Haifa, 244
Hakiryah, 245
Halachah, 42, 72
Ha-Measseph, 154

Hanucah, 42
Hasdai, Abu al-Fadhl ibn, 92
Hasdai ibn Shaprut, 91
Haskalah, the, 154
Hasmoneans, the, 42
Hassidim, 139, 141
Hebrew Literature, 155
Hebrew University, Jerusalem, 206
Heine, Heinrich, 150, 158
Hellenism, 40
Hellenistic Judaism, 49, 52
Heller, Yom-Tob Lipman, 136
Herod, 43, 44
Hertz, Heinrich, 176
Hertz, Joseph H., 168
Herz, Henriette, 157
Herzl, Theodor, 183, 200
Hess, Moses, 183
Hezekiah, Gaon, 84
High Commissioner, 242
Hildesheimer, Israel, 163
Hilferding, Rudolf, 193
Hilfsverein der Deutschen Juden, 179
Hillel, 48, 49
Himmler, 219
Hirsch, Clara de, 179
Hirsch, Maurice de, 180
Hirsch, Samson Raphael, 162
Hirsch, Samuel, 162
Hitler, 194, 211
Holdheim, Samuel, 162
Holland, 219
Holy City, 245
Holy Land, 246
Holy Places, 244, 245
Hore-Belisha, Leslie, 167
Hoshea, 30
Hovevi Zion, 183
Hungary, 187, 220
Hushiel, 91
Hyrcanus, John, 42, 43, 48
Hyrcanus II, 42, 43

Immanuel, of Rome, 133
International Refugee Organization, 233

Iraq, 243, 245
Irgun Zvai Leumi, 242
Isaac, 23
Isaac ben Sheshet, 126
Isaac Elhanan Weshibah College, 160
Isaac of Troki, 137
Isaacs, Sir Isaac, 167
Isaacs, Rufus Daniel. *See* Reading, Marquess of
Isaiah, 33
Israel, 245
Israel Baalshem. *See* Baal Shem-Tob
Israels, Jozef, 177
Italy, 196, 197

Jacob, 23
Jacob Tam, 99
Jacobs, Joseph, 168
Jacobsohn, Israel, 161
Jaddua, High Priest, 39
Jaffa, 242
Jamma, 66
Jehiel, of Paris, 123
Jehoiachin, 33
Jehoiakim, 31
Jekuthiel ibn Hassan, 93
Jeremiah, 33, 35
Jeroboam, 29, 30
Jerusalem, 245, 246
Jerusalem, proposed internationalization, 245
Jesus of Nazareth, 51, 52
Jewish Agency for Palestine, 221, 233, 236, 243
—— Colonization Association, 180
Jewish Commonwealth, 240
—— Historical Society of England, 168
—— Joint Distribution Committee. *See* American Joint Distribution Committee
—— National Fund, 200
—— Publication Society of America, 175
Jewish State, 243

—— Territorial Organization, 202, 203
Jewish Theological Seminary, New York, 175
Jews' College (London), 160
Joce, of York, 112
Johanan ben Zaccai, 49, 66, 67
John of Gischala, 58, 59
John the Baptist, 47
Jonah Gerondi, 123
Jonah ibn Janah, 91
Jonathan, the Maccabee, 42, 196
Jordan, 242
Joseph, chagan, 89
Joseph Hacohen, 133
Joseph ibn Nagdela, 92
Josephus, 58
Joshua, 26
Joshua, High Priest, 36
Josiah, 81
Jost, I. M., 159
Judah ben Meir, 98
Judah Halevi, 93, 94
Judah Hayuj, 91
Judah ibn Ezra, 93
Judah Löw ben Bezalel, 136
Judah the Patriarch, 69
Judas Maccabeus, 42
Judea, 246
'Judeans,' 187
Judges, the, 27
Jung, Guido, 197

Kadoorie, Sir Elly, 122
Kaganovitch, Lazar, 191
Kai-Fung-Foo, 62
Karaites, 86, 87
Kimhi, David, 95
Kingdom of Jordan, 245
King Ibn Saud, 241
Kisch, Brigadier F. H., 228
Klotz, Lucien L., 189
Knesset, 245
Krochmal, Nahman, 159

Lake Tiberias, 245
Lassalle, Ferdinand, 151

Latzki, Jacob Wulf, 189
Lebanon, 243
Leeser, Isaac, 175
Lemmlein, Asher, 129
Leo Hebraeus, 133
Leon of Modena, 133
Levi ben Gerson, 126
Levin, Rahel, 157
Levita, Elias, 133
Levy, Sir Daniel, 169
Levy, Uriah P., 174
Liebermann, Max, 177
Lipman, Yom-Tob, of Mühlhausen, 137
Lippmann, Gabriel, 177
Lippold, 148
Lloyd George, David, 201
Loeb, Jacques, 177
Loewe, Louis, 178
Lopez, Roderigo, 117
Lorqui, Joshua, 118
Lublin, 215
Luria, Isaac, 134
Luzzatti, Luigi, 151
Luzzatto, Moses Haim, 137
Luzzatto, Samuel David, 159
Lydda, 244

Maccabeans, the, 41
Mack, Julian, 180
Maimon, Solomon, 153
Maimonides, Moses, 95, 96, 122, 123
Malachi, 48
Manasseh ben Israel, 144
Mancroft, Lord, 167
Mandate (Palestine), 204, 243
Mapu, Abraham, 155
Mariamne, the Hasmonean, 44
Marranos, 120, 122
Marshall, Louis, 174
Marx, Karl, 151
Maskilim, 154
Massacres, 215, 218
Mattathias, the Hasmonean, 42
May Laws, 171
Medigo, Elias del, 133
Medina, Sir Solomon de, 165

Meir of Rothenburg, 124
Meisel, Mordecai, 104
Melchett, Lord, 167
Meldola, Raphael, 168
Menahem ben Saruk, 91
Mendele Mocher Sepharim, 156
Mendelssohn, Abraham, 157
Mendelssohn, Felix, 159
Mendelssohn, Moses, 151, 157
Mendesia, Gracia, 134
Micah, 33
Michelson, Albert, 177
Midrash, 48
Minister of Defence, 243
Mishnah. See Talmud
Mishneh Torah, 96
Molcho, Solomon, 129
Monash, Sir John, 186
Mond, Alfred. See Melchett, Lord
Mond, Ludwig, 177
Montagu, Edwin, 91, 167
Montefiore, Claude G., 168
Montefiore, Sir Moses, 167, 178, 179, 180
Morais, Sabato, 175
Morocco, 245
Morrison-Grady Report, 241
Mortara, Edgar, 178
Moses, 24, 25
Moses ben Enoch, 90
Moses de Leon, 128
Moses ibn Ezra, 95
Moses, the Torah of, 25
Moslem, 246
Motzkin, Leo, 180
Munk, Salomon, 159, 178
Mussolini, 193, 197
Myers, Sir Arthur M., 169
Myers, Sir Michael, 169

Nahmanides, Moses, 124
Nasi, Joseph, 134
Nathan bar Isaac Hacohen, 91, 94
Nathan ben Jehiel, 133
Nathan der Weise, 152
Nathan, Ernesto, 151
Nathan, Lord, 167

Nathan, the Prophet, 32
Nazarenes, the, 53
Nazis, 193, 195, 219, 220
Negev, 244
Nehemiah, 37
Nehemiah Cohen, 130
New Testament, the, 54, 71
New Zealand, 228
Nieto, David, 137
Noah, Mordecai Manuel, 174
Nordau, Max, 200
Norway, 220
Nuremberg Laws, 212
—— Trials, 220, 222

Obadiah, chagan, 88
Onias, Temple of, 49
Oppenheimer, Joseph Süss, 148
Ort, 181
Ose, 181
Oswiecim, 219
Ottolenghi, Giuseppe, 151, 197
Ovadia, Nissim, 179

Pale of Settlement, 171
Palestine, 245
Palestinian Jewish soldiers, 243
Paul, 52, 54, 78, 197
Payetanim, 91
Peace Treaties, 231
Peel, Lord, 210
Pekah, 30
Perez, I. L., 156
Peter, 197
Petrus Leonis, 133
Pfefferkorn, Johann, 142
Pharisees, the, 45, 46
Philippson, Ludwig, 162
Philo Judaeus, 50, 51
Pilsudski, 213
Pinsker, Leon, 183
Pobiedonostzev, 171
Polak, Jacob, 136
Poland, 135, 188, 189, 213, 214, 222, 231
Portugal, 221
Preuss, Hugo, 143

Prime Minister, 243
Prince of the Captivity, 68, 74, 75, 79, 83
Prophets, the, 32
Proselytism, Jewish, 53
Protocols of the Elders of Zion, 182
Psalms, the, 28
Pseudo-Messiahs, 128

Rabban, Joseph, 88
Rabina II, 75
Rapoport, S. J., 159
Rashi, 99
Rathenau, Walter, 193
Reading, Marquess of, 169
Reform Judaism, 160, 163
Rehoboam, 29, 30
Reparations Agreement, 233
Reubeni, David, 129
Reuter, P. J., 177
Riesser, Gabriel, 151, 164
Romans, 246
Roosevelt, President Franklin, 221, 240
Rosenbaum, Simon, 189
Rosenheim, Jacob, 179
Rossi, Azariah dei, 133
Rothschild, Baron Edmond de, 183, 200
Rothschild, Baron Lionel de, 166
Rothschild, first Lord, 166
Rothschild, second Lord, 203
Royal Commission, 210, 235
Rubinstein, Anton, 170
Rumania, 189, 217, 222, 233
Ruppin, Arthur, 200
Russia, 190, 199, 215, 216
Rutenberg, Pinhas, 207

Saadia, Gaon, 84, 85
Sabbethai Zebi, 130, 131
Saboraim, 75
Sadducees, 45, 46
Salomon, Haym, 172
Salomons, Sir David, 166
Salonika, 218

Samaritans, the, 37, 38
Samson, 27
Samuel, 27
Samuel, Arthur Michael. See Mancroft, Lord
Samuel, Herbert, Viscount, 167
Samuel ibn Nagdela, 92
Sanhedrin, the, 43, 48, 66, 67
Sasportas, Jacob, 130
Sassoon, Sir Philip, 167
Saudi, 243
Saul, 28
Saul of Tarsus. See Paul
Schanzer, Carlo, 197
Schechter, Solomon, 168, 175
Schiff, Jacob H., 174
Schneur, Salman, 155
Schulman, Kalman, 155
Secretary Council, 242, 243
Secretary General, 244
Seixas, Gershom Mendes, 173
Senesh, Hannah, 230
Septuagint, 50, 66
Sforno, Obadiah, 133
Shalom Alechem, 156
Shammai, 48, 49
Sharett, Moshe, 243
Shemaiah, 48
Shemariah ben Elhanan, 91
Sherira, Gaon, 84
Sheshbazzar, 36
Shinwell, Emanuel, 167
Shulhan Aruch, 133
Shylock, 117
Sicarii, 45
Silkin, Lewis, 167
Silver Drabbahillel, 239
Simon bar Giora, 58, 59
Simon ben Johai, 127
Simon Cephas. See Peter
Simon the Maccabee, 42
Smolenskin, Perez, 155
Smuts, Field-Marshal, 228
Sokolow, Nahum, 155, 201
Solomon, 29
Solomon ben Adret, 125
Solomon ibn Gabirol, 93

Solomon of Montpellier, 123
Soloweitschik, Max, 189
Sonnino, Sidney, 197
South Africa, 166, 228
Spain, 221
Speakers, Jewish, 166
Spector, Isaac Elhanan, 160
Spinoza, Benedict, 146, 147
State Department, 241
State of Israel, 244
State of Zion, 245
Steinschneider, Moritz, 159
Straus, Oscar S., 174
Strauss, George, 167
Suasso, Antonio Lopez, 165
Sulzberger, Mayer, 174
Süsskind von Trimberg, 156
Sweden, 219, 221, 233
Switzerland, 221, 233
Synod, the Great, 48, 49
Syria, 243, 245

Talmud, the, 69, 70, 72
Tannaim, 49, 66, 69, 72
Tel Aviv, 243, 245
Tibbon, the family of Ibn, 123
Tiberias, 242
Torah of Moses, 25, 26, 35, 38, 47, 48, 67
Torres, Luis de, 141
Tossaphists, the, 99
Transjordan, 243
Tripolitania, 245
Trotzky, Leon, 241
Truman, President Harry, 241
Tschernichowski, Saul, 155
Tschlenow, Jehiel, 202

Ukraine, 187
Union of American Hebrew Congregations, 175
Union Jack, 242
Union Universelle des Communautés Séphardites, 182
United Nations, 241, 242
United Nations Commission, 244, 245

United States, 172, 174, 228, 236
U.N.S.C.O.P., 238, 239
Ussischkin, Menahem, 202

Va'ad Leumi, 243
Vogel, Sir Julius, 169

Wagner-Taft Resolutions, 240
Warburg, Max M., 193
Warburg, Otto, 200
Warsaw, 215
—— Ghetto, 220
Wecelinus, 108
Weizmann, Chaim, 201, 206, 207, 209, 236, 243
White Paper (of 1939), 235, 236, 243
Willstätter, Richard, 176
Wise, Isaac M., 162
Wise, Stephen S., 174
Wolf, Lucien, 168
Wolf, Simon, 174
Wolffsohn, David, 200
Wollemborg, Leone, 197
World Jewish Congress, 180

—— Union for Progressive Judaism, 179
World War, First, 200, 202, 206
—— Second, 211

Yemen, 245
Yevsectsia, 192
Yiddish, 155, 157, 189
Yivo, 157
Yom Tob, of Joigny, 112
Yugoslavia, 218, 225

Zaddikim, 140
Zamenhof, Ludwig, 177
Zangwill, Israel, 202
Zealots, the, 45
Zechariah, 36
Zedekiah, 32
Zerubbabel, 36
Zion, 246
Zion Mule Corps, 187
Zionism, 182, 199
Zohar, 127
Zunz, Leopold, 158
Zutra II, Mar, 75